A Salute to Scituate's World War II Veterans

PRESERVATION OF SCITUATE'S HERITAGE

Copyright 2006

Digitally produced by   CONVERPAGE
                        23 Acorn Street
                        Scituate, MA 02066

ISBN: 0-9728155-4-6

Printed by: Acme Bookbinding
              100 Cambridge Street
              Charlestown, MA 02129

The stories in this book were compiled over a period of many months. They were solicited through telephone calls, newspaper articles and advertising on local cable television.

We have attempted to tell individual stories of commitment, sacrifice, and true patriotism during World War II – both on the part of servicemen and women and on the part of Scituate, their hometown. We are grateful to all who have talked with us and shared their experiences. It is our fervent hope that the stories between the covers of this book will serve to embody the spirit of all of Scituate as well as of our World War II veterans.

Special thanks must be given first, to the veterans and their families who shared their precious pictures and memories with us. In some cases there was a great deal of information available, in others little could be found. We have tried to include all the stories that came our way in large part reflecting the words of the veterans or their families. In particular, thanks to Joe Clapp, a veteran himself who provided us with numerous contacts, pictures, information, and the best stories we have ever heard. Our gratitude also to The Scituate Historical Society and the Office of the Adjutant General, Military Records Branch for their assistance.

Thanks, also to the Massachusetts Historical Records Advisory Board, who awarded us a Documentary Heritage Grant that made this book possible. Also, thanks to the Scituate Cable Commission whose grant was used to purchase equipment making possible the videotaping of scores of WW II Veterans living in Scituate.

Bernice Brown
Paul Crowley
Nancy Curran
Maureen Dowd
Elizabeth Foster
Virginia Heffernan
Pat Jones
Ed Leary
Bobbie Maffucci
Pam McCallum

This book is dedicated to all men
And women
Who have served their country
In all wars!

God bless them

Christmas
1942

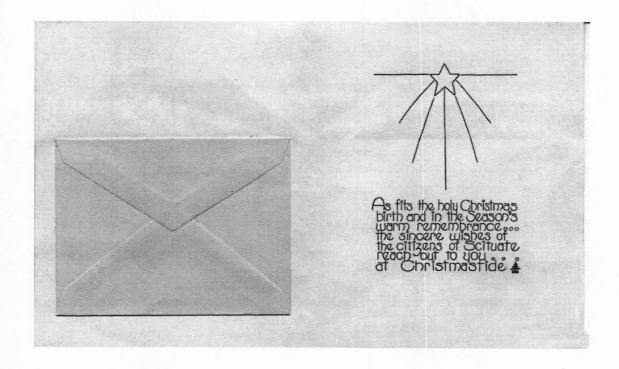

As fits the holy Christmas
birth and in the Season's
warm remembrance...
the sincere wishes of
the citizens of Scituate
reach out to you
at Christmastide

The 1942 Christmas card that was sent to Scituate men and women serving in the military. Each year there was a different original design to brighten the lives of the service personnel and remind them that they had not been forgotten by the folks back home. The small envelope attached to the inner section of the card contained the $5.00 money order that was included.

FRIDAY, SEPTEMBER 25, 1942

CALL MEETING TO AID SCITUATE SOLDIER BOYS

Will Be Held At The Scituate High School Library Next Thursday Evening at 8 o'clock

Following the decision made by the Scituate Board of Selectmen to arrange a plan to send all Scituate boys in the service a present for Christmas, the Selectmen have called a meeting to be held next Wednesday evening at 8 o'clock at which time plans for raising the funds for the purpose and also for the organization of the movement will be discussed.

The plan originated by the Selectmen has met with much favor in the town and many of the residents have already expressed their willingness to assist.

Contact has been made with a number of the lading organizations of the town to assist and a ready response has been secured. All the organizations of the town, patriotic, social, fraternal, civic and religious, will be contacted and will be asked to send representatives to the meeting next Wednesday evening.

Scituate has already 167 boys in the armed forces and more will be in the service before long.

At the meeting of the Board of Selectmen held at the Town office Thursday afternoon, the matter was well considered and it was urged that everybody who might be interested in the plan either write or telephone the Selectmen at once. At any rate the Selectmn want all to attend the meeting. It is important for there is little time now to get organized and get the presents for the boys for Christmas ready.

Scituate intends to stand behind its boys, so be on hand at the meeting and help this movement, truly a worthy one.

The discovery of thank you letters stashed away in a cardboard box at Town Hall marked the beginning of a journey back in time. Writing from all corners of the world, men and women serving in World War II sent these letters in response to a special gift that the town of Scituate had sent to them at Christmas time. In appreciation for the sacrifices made by these sons and daughters of Scituate, the town sent each of them a five-dollar money order enclosed in a Christmas card designed by art teacher Doris Ward. Who were these people, what did life hold for them after the war, and where are they now? And what of the town they so fondly recalled, the town that had thought enough of them to remember them at that special time of the year?

*   *   *   *   *   *   *   *   *   *   *   *

Old editions of The Scituate Herald, annual Town Reports, and copies of the high school yearbook, Chimes, help to bring the 1940's into focus. The Scituate Herald chronicled the activities of the many civic, fraternal and social clubs, town government, and general news relevant to Scituate. Its corps of neighborhood reporters, usually women earning five cents per inch of text, reported the down home news: who had the grippe, who had invited friends in to toast marshmallows, who had been called to jury duty. Nothing was too trivial to report. As one reads <u>The Scituate Herald,</u> a picture forms of a people with a high regard for education, commitment to the welfare of their young people, and a willingness to help out where and when help was needed. Civic pride and the ability to enjoy themselves sustained them during adversity.

THE TOWN   1940-1941

At the beginning of the decade, Scituate (population 4,130) was a semi-rural community with acres of potatoes planted in fields west of Route 3-A, fields of cauliflower growing beside Hatherly Road near Musquashicut Pond, and onion fields located near the Proving Grounds. Throughout the town, fifteen or so farmers cultivated tracts of land, raising a variety of crops to be trucked to the Boston markets or sold at local vegetable stands. Poultry farms, a dairy, and a commercial apple orchard were part of the agrarian economy. Scituate had a reputation for fine produce, and a local newspaper singled out the rhubarb grown by the Youngs and Wilson Brown as having "a twang and a taste you couldn't get anywhere else."

The lobster and fishing industries flourished, and mossing was a thriving business. The "Summer People" provided work for the town's carpenters, gardeners, and other service groups. Visiting yachtsmen were attracted to Scituate Harbor's safe anchorage and the opportunity to go ashore to enjoy its restaurants and shops.

The old-time Country-Store with the New-Fangled Ideas ...

The Welch Co.

Commercial centers at either end of town served their cluster of neighborhoods: the Harbor with its movie theater, bowling alley, renowned Welch's Gift Shop, an A & P, the First National Market, and the 5&10 fulfilled most of the shopping and entertainment needs for people from the Cliffs, Greenbush and the Center. Known as "The Corners," North Scituate took care of the everyday needs for the Minot, Egypt, and West End people, who shopped at the A&P, Bresnahan's Drug, and Seaverns' Store.

There were also small general stores serving individual neighborhoods. A friendly rivalry existed between the two sections, and even today, those who lived in Scituate during the 1940's will say that they never traveled to the other part of town!

Montanari's in Sand Hills, two sons in service.

C.C. Withem store, now site of
Ronnie Shone's, two sons in service.

Hatherly School.

There were two elementary schools, both yellow wooden buildings: Jenkins in the Harbor, sitting square atop a hill, and Hatherly in North

Jenkins School.

Scituate, with maple trees forming an archway down the drive to the front door. A distinctive odor of chalk dust and oiled floors permeated both buildings. Creaking wooden stairs led to the second floor classrooms and a multi-purpose room used by the school nurse, a doctor, and a dentist. The smell of soup and hot chocolate wafted through the halls; students and teachers alike could have a mug on request. No helter-skelter entry to these schools was permitted; students lined up outside the building with boys entering to the left, girls to the right. The same order applied as classes proceeded first to the basement toilets and then out to the playground. Children from the two ends of town met, often for the first time, in the 7th grade at the junior/senior high school.

In 1940 the superintendent was justifiably proud that the state had awarded an A-Rating to the high school, which made it very likely that its graduates, with the proper grades, could attend any college they selected. 20% of Scituate High School graduates went on to higher education, compared to 13% Statewide.

Town Meeting annually voted $1,000 for free adult education classes. Taking advantage of this opportunity in 1940, twenty-nine students registered for typing and shorthand classes, while twenty-five enrolled in woodworking. A short-story writing class and choral singing were added that year. Superintendent of Schools Harold Wingate reported, "For the school year ending in June 1940, two classes in adult-alien education were maintained. These classes… had a total enrollment of fifty men and women and were in session forty-six evenings. Forty-seven of those enrolled were of Portuguese ancestry and three of Italian. On April 11th, forty-two of the group were awarded State Certificates."

Scituate High School had outstanding sports programs for boys and girls. Year after

BOYS' BASKETBALL TEAM
First Row: J. Fitts, R. Sylvester, R. Franzen, R. Amsden, R. Willett, A. Fuller, W. Whittaker.
Second Row: Coach Stewart, E. Dorr, J. Brown, L. Bournazos, Manager E. Gilchrist.

FOOTBALL TEAM
First Row: R. Ewell, L. Bournazos, Manager J. Gillis, C. Patterson, Assistant Manager R. Jenkins, J. Arcana, J. Travers.
Second Row: L. Preston, A. Fuller, Captain R. Hendricksson, Coach Stewart, R. Sylvester, F. Hall, R. Zollin.
Third Row: T. Holland, R. Finnie, J. Vaughan, V. Deal, G. Patterson, R. Foniri, G. Curtis

year, the football teams reigned as South Shore Champions of Class D. Each year the Scituate Kiwanis acknowledged their superior performance with a banquet and the awarding of letters and gold footballs. Speeches by the likes of Jack Conway, then sports writer for The Boston American, or Frank Leahy, the esteemed Boston College football coach, rounded out the evening.

GIRLS' HOCKEY TEAM

First Row: J. Cole, J. Cole, M. Mansfield, G. Bonomi, Coach Vinco, A. Basmajian, M. LaVange,
J. Brown, B. Nichols
Second Row: P. Crowley, G. Wilder, F. Williams, A. Moffitt, J. Arnold, Manager I. Jacobson

The girls' hockey and basketball teams reigned as South Shore Champions for several years. Like the boys, members of these teams received letters and charms recognizing their accomplishments.

It was a time when young people were allowed the freedom to explore their environs without concern. They could pick blueberries where the high school now stands, squelch through the mudflats off the Glades, or head to Third Cliff to dig for clams. It was an adventure to whack through cats briar and underbrush on the Indian Trail to Cohasset, explore the forests of the West End, and fish off the rocks in Minot, the Town Pier, or the Harbor jetties. It was a time when mothers could say, "Go outside and don't come in until lunch (or dinner)."

"Organized sports" were neighborhood kids gathering for an impromptu game of baseball or touch football. Hop-scotch and jump rope were mainstay games for girls, and marbles/aggies were serious sport for both boys and girls in the spring. Teen-agers gathered at friends' homes to talk, play cards or Monopoly, and listen to the records of Harry James, Glenn Miller, the Dorsey Brothers, and Benny Goodman. From jitterbugging to waltzing, dancing was popular with all age groups. High schoolers learned the fox-trot and waltz at the PTA sponsored dancing classes, which might close the evening with the jaunty "…Doing the Lambeth Walk." Twenty cents would admit you to the record hop on Tuesday night at Fieldston; older folks were invited

The Cliff Hotel, Minot Beach, No. Scituate, Mass.

to their Thursday night "old fashioned dancing." The Sand Hills Community Center offered dancing to a six piece band; the Bamboo Lounge at the Cliff Hotel provided a small combo, while the young crowd gathered at Broad Cove in Hingham.

When the Satuit Bowlaway opened in the Harbor with its "ten modernistic alleys," numerous leagues formed for men and women, who celebrated the season's end with banquets and awards. Another first on the South Shore was the Weymouth drive-in movie: "New England's first outdoor theatre, continuous showings from dusk to mid-night, admission thirty-five cents per person." And where could something for everyone be found on a summer's day?

Paragon Park.

Paragon Park, of course. Merry-go-round to roller coaster, bumper cars to the Tunnel of Love…everyone has happy memories of the Park.

The Scituate Herald carried a weekly listing of community organizations' upcoming meetings, and usually a story or two about some special club event.

> "The Grange held its annual picnic on Peggotty Beach."
> "The Rod and Gun Club held its fifth annual trials at the Lawson Race Track."
> "Sydney Gates featured merchandise from his store in a fashion show for the Church Carnival."
> "The Dramateurs presented a Gay Nineties Night production, Bertha the Beautiful Typewriter Girl. The audience was invited to wear gay nineties Costumes to the play and to the old-fashioned dance, which would follow." Admission was 50 cents.
> "Saint Mary's Bowling League had a festive bowling awards dinner at Hugo's. Music was provided by Millie Whorf and all were invited to join in a sing-along."

For those interested in exploring current events and political issues, there was the Forum offering its members stimulating monthly programs. Some townspeople expressed concern that the Forum was a little too liberal, even a little "pink," a euphemism for

Communist in those days. The Betterment Club, a civic-minded group of ladies, put their interest in landscaping and horticulture to work maintaining the plantings at several town sites. Their particular concern at this time was to eradicate ragweed, but the project appears to have received more publicity than support from the Town.

Many organizations generously supported programs for Scituate youth, as they would later support the Christmas Card Project. The Girl Scout Committee provided three scholarships to Girl Scout Camp, one girl to be chosen on merit from each of the three troops. An Annual PTA Scholarship Dance provided funds for a worthy graduate and the Betterment Club and the Monday Luncheon Club also donated scholarships to a deserving high school graduate. The Nursing Service bore the expense of sending three children to TB Camp. Girl Scouts, Boy Scouts, and Nautical Patrol Boys were entertained by the Grange at the Curtis Estate with a cookout; all of them gathered around a council campfire for a sing-a-long accompanied by an accordion and two buglers. The Kiwanis sponsored an amateur show for 15 year olds and up at the Grand Army Hall.

Sunday represented a day of rest, and with few exceptions businesses closed for the day. At mid-day, families sat down to Sunday dinner and spent the afternoons visiting with family and friends. On weekend afternoons, the Satuit Playhouse was a popular destination for teen-agers. Typically, the long program opened with a "March of Time" newsreel, followed by a cartoon, a short feature such as a travelogue, a "B" movie as a second feature, and, finally, the main attraction. The newsreels had a visual impact that radio and newspapers couldn't match; they were the "television" of the period. Many recall being at the movies that Sunday afternoon when the film was interrupted for an announcement that Pearl Harbor had been attacked.

Families gathered around their radio, the home entertainment medium of the day, to hear a "Lux Radio Theater" drama, listen to "Major Bowes Amateur Hour," or laugh at the banter between Edgar Bergen and his saucy "Dummy," Charlie McCarthy. Teen-agers tuned in to "Your Hit Parade" and an all-around favorite, "The Shadow," ("Who knows what evil lurks within the heart of man?") Children enjoyed "Jack Armstrong, the all American Boy," and "Little Orphan Annie," with her decoder badge.

The town celebrated Memorial Day, sometimes called Decoration Day, with a parade of Scouts, veterans groups and their ladies auxiliaries, and town officials, all marching smartly to the music of the high school band. Roadside viewers applauded, and men respectfully removed their hats as the flags passed by. Scouts later placed a red geranium on every veteran's grave. The South Shore Light described "Memorial Day as a season of veneration and decoration of family burial plots, especially the places where veterans of America's wars are laid to rest."

Town of Scituate Memorial Day Parade.

The Fourth of July was a noisy, exciting day as fireworks stands sprang up all around town, and homes and stores proudly displayed their bunting and flags. Young children could have sparklers and perhaps a cap pistol with a roll of caps; the older ones liked "torpedoes," those little paper packets of some gritty explosive to be slammed on the ground for a big bang. A wide range of fireworks from bundles of "baby fingers" to rockets delighted the bigger boys, and at night, bonfires might be set on the beaches. The highlight of the evening was the grand fireworks display at the Hatherly Country Club, which welcomed all. In addition to the colorful bursts of rockets were set piece illuminations of the flag, perhaps Abraham Lincoln, or some other patriotic symbol, lighting up the night sky. A highlight of the summer was the Firemen's Ball, held in July, also at the Hatherly Country Club. Young and old alike enjoyed the music and entertainment, which might feature a high-wire act, a comedian, or a tap dancer. In 1941,

14

the program ran from 9 to 10 p.m., followed by dancing to the Ken Reeves Orchestra from 10 p.m. to 1 a.m. That was the last time the event was ever held.

At the end of the summer, everyone enjoyed the Marshfield Fair. Horse racing drew big crowds, but the competition among the farmers displaying their best produce also attracted large numbers of people. At the 1941 Fair, John Brown won the prize for heaviest squash; Tilden Farms earned a "first" for cauliflower and another award for their sweet peppers.

As significant to the holiday as the turkey dinner was the annual Thanksgiving Day football game. The sports editor for the 1940 Chimes reported, "In a perfect Fall setting…2000 fans lined up along the sidelines…" At stake was the Championship of the South Shore. Scituate won the hard-fought game!

Bitter cold had ushered in the new decade, and the icemen were delighted. At Old Oaken Bucket Pond, the Clapp icehouse was filled in just a few days with good, solid twelve-inch thick ice. At that time, iceboxes were common enough that ice cutting was a lucrative business, as was the delivery of wood and kerosene, which were widely used for heating and cooking.

Rough seas and rollers at the ledge made the Minot's Lightkeeper's exchange a bumpy affair in January 1941. A hamper of supplies was finally hauled up to the door near the lantern deck, about 80 feet above the water. The keeper being relieved was then lowered by bosun's chair to the Coast Guard boat waiting below.

There was an average of one telephone for every nineteen people. Instead of dialing a number, a person had to be connected via telephone operators. Because local women filled these jobs, they might even inform you that the person you were trying to reach was away. (That apparently was against rules, but it was helpful). "Party lines" meant that several families might share the same line, with each family assigned a distinct ring, so they would know when the call was for them. It was against the rules to "listen in" on someone else's call on the party line, but, of course, it was not unheard of to do so.

Red fire alarm boxes mounted on utility poles provided instant communication with the fire department. Most people knew the location and number of the box nearest their house, and when the fire horn blew, many would pause to count the blasts to determine the fire's location, or at least to be assured that it wasn't in their neighborhood. Two blasts signaled the welcome "all out."

The on-going Depression and war in Europe concerned many Americans. To bolster the economy and to pay the town's share of federally-funded relief projects, the 1940 Town Meeting appropriated $20,000. Of the 114 persons on local payrolls, 18 Scituate men worked at the Hingham Naval Ammunition Dump. The town also received $56,564.70, including monies for distribution of surplus commodities and clothing. Federal funds paid for such varied jobs as indexing and classifying old town records, preparing a record of veterans buried in Scituate, constructing water mains on Jericho Road, and building the fieldstone clubhouse and tennis courts at North Scituate. Scituate Club House also benefited from the National Youth Administration, which provided work for youth of both sexes from age 17-21. Employment was found for "young ladies" at the Allen and Peirce libraries, the high school cafeteria, and Town Hall. Some men found work during the depression as door-to-door salesmen selling vacuum cleaners, Fuller Brush products, encyclopedias, and magazines. During the summer months itinerant peddlers walked the neighborhoods selling all manner of goods. One enterprising man who sharpened scissors and knives got attention with his little monkey dressed in a jacket and hat, sitting atop the grinding box.

The ice-houses are gone; recorded messages have replaced friendly telephone operators; Minot's Light is automated; the fire alarm boxes and certainly the monkey have disappeared, but football rivalries, the fishing fleet, Fourth of July bonfires, the Harbor bowling alley, and many of the other aspects of life in a small town remain.

RUMBLE OF WAR

Although proclaiming neutrality, the United States government was clearly preparing for the inevitability of war when, in July of 1940, Congress passed a bill to build a "two ocean Navy," and in September created the Selective and Training Service Act, which called men between the ages of 21 and 36 to register for the draft in October; in June, 1941 the conscription age was lowered to 18. Service was to be for one year with no assignment to foreign soil. One of the first fifteen men from the 95th District to have his number drawn, Joseph Donovan of Scituate reported to the Induction Center in November, 1940.

Thomas Lawson & Colonel Schuyler in front of GAR Hall

Two Army Colonels living in Scituate represented the town's opposing views on entering the war. Colonel C. W. Furlong had been an intelligence officer during World War I. At a Boston University Forum he spoke forcibly against America going to war: "We have two allies," he said, "the Atlantic and the Pacific." On the other hand, Colonel Philip Schuyler, also a World War I veteran, contended that the country must give more than moral support to the Allies. In June 1940, Governor Saltonstall appointed him chair of Scituate's Committee on Public Safety, part of a statewide organization. He organized a committee comprising the Fire, Police, Water, and School Departments, as well as representatives from the two Veterans' Associations. Lines of command and communication were established to meet anticipated conditions should the country go to war. Early in 1941, a call went out to all ex-servicemen of Scituate to register with the Committee on Public Safety in order to identify skills and aptitudes that could be beneficial in time of emergency. The Committee announced that it would register public-spirited men and women for non-military service in emergencies. When the United States entered the war, these recruits were invaluable as auxiliary fire fighters and policemen, air raid wardens, ambulance drivers, canteen workers, and aircraft warning observers. Some also acted as auxiliary Coast Guardsmen patrolling the waters off Scituate in pleasure craft on loan to the government for the duration.

The 1940 presidential election race between incumbent Franklin D. Roosevelt, seeking an unprecedented third term, and Wendell L. Wilkie was hotly contested, and feelings ran high. Wilkie Workers Clubs formed on the South Shore, and the Scituate Chapter organized an attention-getting auto parade from Scituate Center to the Harbor. A Scituate Herald article declared, "Never before in the history of this country has an election been considered to be so important. With war in Europe and many disturbing influences in our own country, the people are determined to vote their choice at the polls next Tuesday. 2,484 of the 3,015 registered voters, approximately 80%, cast votes in the election. The Scituate Herald carried the results, with the comment, "As usual the Republicans carried the town hands down." Wilkie received 1726 votes to 692 for Roosevelt, yet Roosevelt won the national election.

Months before war was declared, businesses cautioned the public about potential shortages. The Ford Motor Company ran an ad in early 1941 announcing a cutback in production so as to meet defense needs. Another small company revealed that it could not repair obsolete refrigeration equipment because of the "inability to purchase necessary metal parts…" The local Irish moss industry was affected because moss was used in the manufacture of nitroglycerin for explosives. Children picked the moss off the rocks; men filled dories using long-handled rakes, and they all delivered it to mosser George Dwyer, who reported up to "fifty kids weighing [the moss] sometimes." Even the women gathered moss that summer to be dried at the Proving Grounds on Hatherly Road.

WAR DECLARED

On December 7, 1941, the Japanese attacked Pearl Harbor. On December 8th classroom radios enabled students to listen as President Roosevelt asked Congress to declare "that a state of war existed between the United States and the Japanese Empire." Germany and Italy declared war on the United States on December 11th.

The Scituate observation post in the Army Aircraft Warning Service and the local Air Raid Report Center were immediately put on twenty-four hour alert. On December 9th the Air Raid Report Center received notice of an impending German attack. Repeated short blasts of the air raid horn signaled the schools to dismiss all students to their homes. Some recall their mothers dressing them warmly and sending them to the cellar for safety; others recall filling pails with sand and placing them in the attic to put out potential fires. Most just wondered and waited. It was a false alarm, but apprehension lingered for some time afterward. School administrators met to discuss protective measures for students in the event of an actual enemy raid. School basements would serve as air raid shelters; sandbags placed outside each basement window would offer protection against shell fragments and flying glass. Battery-type lanterns were placed in all schools. Teachers who had not taken first aid courses were requested to do so. In order to discourage them from hasty action, the high school principal met with boys who wanted to enlist, assuring them that they would be of more value to their country with at least a high school diploma.

When a call went out for more Civil Defense workers, the Red Cross announced that new classes in first aid for men and women would begin January 7th, and its Motor Corps prepared a course on auto mechanics. Areas of the Town were declared off-limits, as Army, Navy, and Coast Guard units took up posts from the Glades to Fourth Cliff. The New England Telephone Company advised the public that long-distance telephoning would be restricted, "…we ask people in New England not to make calls on Christmas Day to points south of New York, west of Chicago or the Maritime Provinces. Such calls, in this time of emergency, may interfere with other calls vital to the nation's safety."

Maryann Mahoney Vinal

The Army imposed a number of wartime regulations. Fearing that bright lights might aid enemy ships or planes at night, a dim-out of automobile lights was imposed, requiring that the top half of headlights be painted black. Dim-out regulations allowed vehicles the use of parking and tail-lights only when driving in restricted areas, primarily streets near the ocean: the entire length of Hatherly and Jericho Roads, Oceanside Drive, and all of North Scituate Beach, Minot, Humarock, the Harbor, and the Cliffs. Homeowners were ordered to install blackout curtains in all windows to ensure that no light escaped. Families were advised to have one room heavily blacked so that some light could be used in the event of illness or children's needs.

Air raid response instructions were distributed to all households. In the event of an alert, all streetlights would be extinguished, and at the same time three short blasts would sound on the fire horns throughout town.

Until a fire horn could be mounted on Ray's Garage on Clapp Road, police motorcycles traveling at high speed with the siren blowing constantly would alert West End residents.

Ray's Garage.

Two regular blasts on the fire horn, repeated, signaled the "all clear," and streetlights would be turned back on. The Committee for Public Safety reported, "The great majority of people have shown a willingness to cooperate fully in observing the dim-out regulations ordered by the Army. The few who still refuse to accept restrictions in good grace are manifesting little regard for the safety of others, and will be dealt with accordingly." The Scituate Herald ran a story in August 1942 about a "prominent resident of North Scituate Beach who refused to comply with the request of an Air Raid Warden to extinguish his house lights. He was taken to Court where the judge made it very clear that all wartime regulations must be

FRED "TICKEY" STANLEY   FRANCIS MURPHY

absolutely observed, even if they may seem unnecessary to the individuals concerned. He was fined $25.00."

Rumors circulated that summer residents would not be allowed to open their homes, but authorities assured them that this was not true. There would, however, be some restrictions on summer activities: boating and swimming at night would be prohibited, and all boats must tie up during fog. The Coast Guard required that all boaters obtain identification cards, and that fowl hunters carry identification passes, restrict their hunting to inland waters, and not use motors on their boats.

MILITARY PRESENCE ON THE HOME FRONT

Massachusetts Home Guard camped out on the Dunphy Family tennis courts.

Every effort was made by the townspeople to make the servicemen stationed in town comfortable. Financed by the USO, the Servicemen's Recreation Committee set up a recreation center for all servicemen at the Colonial Inn on Meetinghouse Lane and held weekly dances with junior hostesses "under the supervision of senior hostesses." The Inn also offered sleeping accommodations for the servicemen, forty in the summer and twenty in the winter. A group of ladies from the Congregational Church Mayflower Guild met weekly to mend the soldiers' clothing, and a local artist painted watercolor portraits of the men to send home.

Various organizations arranged entertainments for the servicemen. The Scituate PTO invited all servicemen to a Military Ball at the high school auditorium, where the Red Cross provided refreshments. Seventy-five servicemen attended a Christmas party held at the Women's Club; the evening festivities included an elimination dance and prizes for the best waltzers. A USO-sponsored dance took place at the Odd Ladies Hall, opposite the former Peirce Library. The USO also transported girls by bus to dances at USO centers in Norwell and to Camp Edwards on the Cape. The Red Cross entertained some fifty men, all stationed along the waterfront, with a Christmas dinner served at various billets. The Scituate Garden Club gave books and magazines to the Harbor Coast Guard Station. Every two weeks, a local man sent a film to the Station, and the First Cliff Association provided refreshments. Local groups also gave money to the Red Cross for the purchase of wool to knit sweaters for the Coast Guard.

A family at North Scituate Beach, like many other families, welcomed servicemen to their homes. Young ladies were invited to socialize with the boys in the rumpus room, where they played ping-pong or shuffle-board, tried their skill/luck at the pinball machine, or danced to music from the record player. Quite a few servicemen met the girls of their dreams at these gatherings, got married, and settled down in Scituate after the war.

First Cliff Coast Guard Station.

Shortly after the declaration of war, Army and Navy units were dispatched to the Glades, stationed at WRUL in the Proving Grounds, and assigned to the Coast Guard Stations at North Scituate Beach and the Harbor. The men at WRUL billeted in the Club House at Sand Hills and ate their meals at the guest-

"Smokey."

house on Otis Place, whose owner, Winnie McIntyre, had obtained the government contract to feed the soldiers. According to historian Gerald W. Butler, "In 1940 the former Radio Compass Site at Fourth Cliff had been authorized by the U.S. Army as one of four sites around Boston Harbor to receive modern coastal defense batteries in anticipation of U.S. involvement in World War II." Work began very soon thereafter. Barracks and ancillary buildings were made to look like cottages and painted bright colors to give the appearance of ordinary vacation houses. The gun implacements and fire control towers were camouflaged as well. The installation included two six-inch guns, machine gun nests, and anti-aircraft weapons.

These men were billeted at The Humarock Lodge and at the rear of Clark's Store building.

On November 1, 1942, the Office of War Information took over WRUL, the international short wave radio at the Proving Grounds on Hatherly Road. Subsequently, two additional transmitters were placed there in May 1943. The WRUL site broadcast the Voice of America throughout the world. Interestingly, Andrew Thurson, a naval gunner in the Norwegian navy from Flekkefjord, Norway, heard these broadcasts on both the Atlantic and Pacific Oceans. He remembers,

Andrew Thurson

"WRUL was the strongest short wave radio station in the USA at that time, coming in loud and clear just about anywhere in the world. It was often used by the Norwegian government in exile in London, to contact the 40,000 seamen manning the world's fourth largest merchant fleet, serving the Allied cause. Often the King of Norway, Haakon VII listened and sent taped messages to WRUL to be sent to the sailors in exile. This helped to keep up the morale of the Norwegians united in the war effort…Because of this valuable service, the station and its staff collectively were awarded the Saint Olaf Medal by his Majesty, the King. This is one of the highest awards the King can bestow for outstanding public service. Little did I know that I would be married and living in Scituate a quarter century later."

The transmitter was last used in 1979.

ORGANIZING FOR WAR

1942 became a year of intense organizational activity. Clocks were set ahead one hour to "War Time" on February 8th. The Committee on Safety supervised and enforced all dim-out regulations set forth by the Army, maintained a twenty-four hour attack warning center, and established a medical center under the direction of the Red Cross.

In February, previously unregistered men between the ages of 20 and 44 were placed in a draft category. By April those between the ages of 45-65 were ordered to register as potential draftees to work in essential industries. On January 6, 1942, forty-nine South

Shore boys left for the Boston Induction Center. There would be many more goodbyes as families saw their sons off at the Greenbush station, the most ironic departure being November 11, 1942, Armistice Day, which commemorated the end of World War I, "The War to End All Wars."

The Office of Civilian Defense recruited for its "Women's Defense Corp" classes, an eight week course covering modern chemical warfare, the identification of four war gases, precautions and treatment of gas casualties, general emergency first-aid, and military drill. Women could select either the Motor Corps or Canteen as their primary unit. The Office of Civil Defense also conducted recruitment and training for air raid wardens, auxiliary firemen and policemen, emergency first aid workers. and aircraft warning personnel.

The Japanese rampaged across the Pacific, taking over lands whose names were unfamiliar to most Americans. Their loss to the enemy would have far-reaching effects on the American consumer: most of the world's rubber, tin, and quinine came from Malaya and the Dutch East Indies, while French Indonesia had a rich supply of oil and a silky fiber called kapok, used in life jackets and sleeping bags. Recognizing that there would be shortages of essentially every commodity, the Office of Price Administration established rationing boards nationwide. Scituate Ration Board No. 271 started operation in January, 1942; members served on one of four panels: Food; Tires and Gasoline; Fuel Oil; and Price Control.

All production of automobiles, radios, mechanical refrigeration, vacuum cleaners, washing machines and most electrical appliances stopped early in 1942. Restrictions on the purchase of new tires and tubes went into effect on January 5, and a 35 MPH speed limit was adopted as a means of conserving rubber. Gasoline rationing began in May, with three categories of eligibility: The average, "nonessential" citizen received the "A" book and sticker; they would have to get by on three gallons a

Scarsilloni's Garage.

week! War workers and those who needed their cars for business received the "B" classification, which entitled them to eight gallons per week. Doctors and other "essential" persons received a "C" classification, which had no limitations on gas use. In December the Governor issued a proclamation asking drivers to make every Sunday a gasless day. A month later Sunday driving was banned, and anyone found driving without good cause was subject to a fine and even the loss of a gas ration card.

Rationing gradually expanded to include canned goods, sugar, meat, butter, shoes, coffee, and fuel oil. The first ration book was issued in March 1942, each family member being entitled to a book and the appropriate stamps. Stern warnings appeared on the cover:

> "A person who finds a lost War Ration Book must return it
> to the War Price and Rationing Board which issued it."

> "Persons who violate rationing regulations are subject to a
> $10,000.00 fine or imprisonment or both."

A bewildering collection of stamps had to be used for specific items.

MEATS, BUTTER- Book 3 brown stamps G, H, and J valid through Dec. 4; stamp K valid Nov. 14-Dec.4th.
SUGAR- Book 4 stamp valid for five pounds through Jan. 15th.
SHOES-Coupon No.18, Ration Book 1 is valid for one pair for an indefinite period, Stamp 1 on "airplane" sheet of Book 3 good Nov. 1 and valid indefinitely. Loose coupons not accepted, except with mail orders.

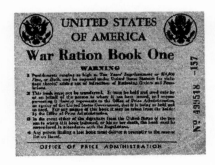

YOUNG PEOPLE AND THE WAR

Essays, stories, poems, and cartoons appearing in the high school yearbook, The Chimes, reveal much about young people's concerns during the volatile decade of the 1940's. Reflecting the uncertain times, the ongoing Depression, and the war in Europe, with its implications for the United States, the stories and essays in the 1940 issue were of a serious nature: "Terror of Russia" (Nazi occupied Soviet Union) and "Military Objective" (Russian attack on Finland) were poignant stories of innocent people meeting death at enemy hands. Two essays try to fathom why wars seem to be inevitable. In the 1941 Chimes, essays and editorials spoke of America in lofty terms: "We must believe in our country, stand up for our ideals, and build a morale that cannot be broken down by dictators, depression, or propaganda," declared Eudora Bartlett, Class of '41. "Of all the graduating classes that have issued forth from high schools through the years, none have had to face the times that quite compare with those of today," wrote Orin Gould, Class of '41.

Before the year ended, America was at war. Edward Gilchrist, class of '42 noted, "When Japan unleashed her treacherous attack on Pearl Harbor on December 7 the whole United States awoke from its lethargy with a start, realizing for the first time that war was actually upon us." For the next four years patriotism reigned, and war was the theme for almost everything printed in the yearbook.

Students quickly joined in the frenzy of organizing for war. Members of the senior class at the high school supported Civilian Defense in numerous capacities: one boy assumed responsibility for mobilizing the boys used as runners, couriers, and members of the first aid squad. Some served as air raid wardens; five became auxiliary firemen, and two were stretcher bearers at the Medical Center. One girl joined the Motor Corps; another joined the Canteen. As the war continued, many more students served as air raid wardens, participated as volunteer "victims" during Emergency Relief practice sessions, helped to roll bandages at Red Cross Headquarters, and assisted with other chores as needed. Some older Girl Scouts volunteered as nurses' aides at the Cohasset hospital.

High school students also participated in special drives; they entered a campaign to "buy a Jeep" and succeeded in reaching their goal of raising $900 in just three weeks. School schedules were arranged to limit time lost from regular classwork for several students who were fully employed by local farmers during the planting and harvesting seasons. Some high school students took summer jobs working on local farms and dairies; it was hard work with long hours, starting many times at 6 a.m. Several high school boys and one girl took their dories out at low tide to harvest Irish Moss, an important ingredient in explosives. In the fall, high school students picked apples at Bulrush Farm and tomatoes at Tilden's farm. Junior high students did their part by planting Victory Gardens; some of the boys raised chickens, and one girl, not to be outdone by the boys, raised pigs.

Scituate School Children Buy First Army Jeep

Pupils of Hatherly School of North Scituate Pledge Money Enough In War Bonds and Stamps To Secure New Car.

The following 2 articles from the Scituate High School 1944 Chimes illustrate the young people's concern and involvement in the war effort:

SERVICE HONOR ROLL

One of the most notable and appropriate gifts ever presented to the Scituate High School by a graduating class was that of the Class of 1943, who left money for the purpose of providing a memorial in honor of the students and members of the faculty of the school who are or have been serving with the armed forces of our country.

The plaque was constructed in the manual training shop under the supervision of Mr. Nels Sandberg. The lettering and design was the work of the art department under the direction of Miss Doris Rowell. Pauline Hardwick of the Junior Class printed all of the names on the roll. The plaque itself is about three feet wide and four feet long, made of pine and having a dark, glossy finish. It contains six rows of names printed with India ink on removable white slides.

JUNIOR RED CROSS

During the Junior Red Cross membership drive, 100% of many of the home rooms contributed, and $30 was collected. This money is kept in the Junior Red Cross account and is used to buy materials for sewing and for contributions to hospitals. Again in April the school contributed in the regular Red Cross drive.

The sewing classes are making and have made layettes and such articles as bed jackets and card table covers for patients in the hospitals. They have also made little girls' dresses and skirts, which were sent to refugee children. The Junior High have made scrap books for children in hospitals.

Ice cream and candy disappeared from the lunch counters, and food shortages necessitated a small increase in prices. Adjustments in the curriculum at the high school put more emphasis on science and math. To promote strength and endurance, physical education programs included more physical exercise; for example, the boys had one hour of physical education each day. For upper classmen, two new additions to the high school curriculum, Pre-Flight Aeronautics and Military Surveying, gave instruction in the fundamentals of aeronautics, meteorology, mapping, navigation, and surveying. A radio kit for teaching the International Morse Code was purchased for use in pre-induction courses.

The schools dropped almost all extra curricular activities, both athletic and social, including festivities to honor championship football, girls' basketball and field hockey teams. Most importantly, students missed many familiar faces as the principal, teachers, and older boys left to enter the armed services or to work in defense plants, where workers were desperately needed. Although urged to finish high school, some students did drop out to join the military or to work in war industries. In 1943, five members of the Class of 1944 left school to work at the Hingham Shipyard, and one joined the Navy.

The younger children contributed to the war effort by assisting in the paper and scrap metal drives. A victory Key for Kollection Kampaign was a great success. The Hatherly School came up with approximately 3,500 keys, which they turned over to the local salvage committee. Not to be outdone, Jenkins School also collected many boxes of keys. Elementary school children also eagerly participated in statewide war bond and stamp drives, hoping to get 90% student participation so they could fly the coveted Minute Man flag over their schools. In response to the government's appeal for milkweed floss to replace kapok used in the manufacture of life jackets and pilots' suits, fifth and sixth graders gathered sixty-five bags!

Old Oaken Bucket Homestead Helps Scituate's Scrap Drive

Indicative of what the individual citizens throughout New England are doing to back up National War effort is shown by the above picture taken at the Old Oaken Bucket Homestead in Scituate.

The present residents, Mr. Woodworth Northey Murray of the ninth generation and his mother, are looking over old items of scrap found in that part of their home, shown, which was the original house built in 1675 and moved about one-hundred yards to its present site in 1835, by four yoke of oxen, and the present home added to it.

The property has been continuously in the possession of and lived in by the Northey and Woodworth families. It was here that Samuel Woodworth lived as a boy, and was inspired to write his famous poem, which he published in 1817 while living in New York City.

These people have always done their full share in every war since the Revolution and are gladly turning in, as a gift, these articles many of which would be prized, at a big price, by collectors.

——BUY DEFENSE BONDS AND STAMPS——

Old Historic Keys Dumped In Scrap Heap

Welch Co. at Scituate Harbor Collected Nearly 70 Pounds of Keys for Scituate Herald—Old State Prison Keys In Lot

Old historic keys, some of them of an historical nature were collected in the "Key for Kollection Kampaign" by the Welch Company at Scituate Harbor in the past fe wweeks.

The keys were collected by the Welch Co. for the Scituate Herald which will turn them over to the wholesale paper industry of Boston which will forward them to government authorities, to be used in the making of guns, shells and other munitions of war.

The Welch Co. installed a small barrel near the main entrance to their store at Scituate Harbor through the courtesy of Russell J. Fish, the manager of the company, and altogether nearly 70 pounds of keys were donated by the residents of Scituate.

Included in the collection were many keys of an historical nature and included among the others, three old keys that were formerly used in the State Prison at Charlestown, Mass. They were identified by proper authorities. One of them was a big key near-

ly seven inches long and was evidently a master key. With it was two other smaller keys, one five inches long and the other 5¾ inches in length. All were very heavy and each one bore a number, which led to their identification as having been used at the state prison. Odd in their design and just filled with the kind of metal which is wanted by the government, these old keys are certainly a curiosity.

Included also in the pile of keys were two big bunches which were contributed by Mrs. Walter C. Brooks of First Parish road. These two bunches weighed eight pounds and there were several hundred of them, of all kinds from the small Yale lock key to the old fashioned latch key so common years ago. They were on a wire ring and were gathered by the late Mr. Brooks, husband of Mrs. Brooks. He was engaged in the real estate business for many years in Scituate.

The large collection incited much curiosity, but will now be turned to good use in backing up our boys in the winning of the war.

We wish to thank the people of Scituate who so generously contributed to the drive for old keys and to the Welch Co., for their co-operation in making the drive a success.

——BUY DEFENSE BONDS AND STAMPS——

WOMEN AT WAR

In its efforts to assist European refugees, the International Red Cross looked to the United States for financial assistance. Scituate had been assessed a $400 quota for the annual 1940 Red Cross appeal, but the town went over the top with $714.10. Some of these funds also underwrote a dental clinic for school children and subsidized summer swimming and life saving classes.

As an expression of their great sympathy for civilians under attack by the Axis powers, Scituate women responded generously in many ways. In answer to the Red Cross appeal for clothing for refugees, the Baptist Church hosted the Red Cross program to knit twenty-one sweaters and sew twelve woolen dresses; those unable to assist with the sewing could donate buckles, buttons, and dress trimmings. Another group made 75 layettes and collected donations of yarn to make baby bonnets, which seemed to be in short supply. The Scituate Woman's Club members also sewed for the Red Cross and participated in a drive to gather warm clothing for the Russian Relief. The Scituate Garden Club joined garden clubs nationwide in providing funds for their British counterparts to purchase a mobile kitchen.

During the war years, over three hundred Scituate women worked at the town's Red Cross Headquarters making surgical dressings, kit bags, and knit garments for service personnel; meetings were held on Tuesdays, Wednesdays, and Thursdays from 10 a.m. to 4 p.m. and in the evening from 7:30 to 9:30 p.m. Methodist Church workers sent tooth paste, writing paper, handkerchiefs, and other useful gifts to distant soldiers and sailors. The Red Cross also sought chairs, tables, small radios, and ashtrays, among other things, to be used in camp and station hospitals, "where our sick and wounded servicemen are being cared for."

Perhaps, the recollection of the devastating influenza epidemic after World War I prompted the near obsession with maintaining good health. Frequently, newspaper and magazine articles dealt with the need for good nutrition and proper hygiene. The Scituate Public Health and Red Cross nurses offered home nursing courses on how to prevent the spread of disease, isolate patients with communicable diseases, and maintain good overall health.

In June 1941, seventeen Scituate women received Motor Corps Certification from the Red Cross after completing a First Aid Course of ten 2-hour sessions and 170 hours in auto mechanics, qualifying them as drivers. After further instruction in ambulance and convoy driving, they drove those needing transportation to the well-baby clinic, pre-school dental clinic, local hospitals, and blood donor centers. They also attended regional meetings to discuss emergency preparedness. The Home Service Division acted as a go-between for people at home and men in the service.

Under the command of local resident Stella McLean, a Scituate company of the Massachusetts Women's Defense Corps formed as a branch of the National Guard. The first group of recruits underwent training in Motor Transport, Canteen Wardens, Household Wardens, and Fire Fighting. They also participated in a statewide mobilization of Women's Defense Corps in Lexington, joining with neighboring towns to proceed in a convoy of 14 cars, a medical car, and a mobile canteen. The Lexington exercises included extinguishing actual fires and combating incendiary bombs. In October, 1942 a M.W.D.C. recruiting drive for women aged 18 - 60 began, declaring that "The Scituate Company must be brought to its full strength immediately as an important function is the evacuation of all civilians in emergency situations." For training purposes, the Massachusetts Public Safety Committee assigned the Company a utility truck, which carried 4 stretchers, blankets, a fully equipped mobile casualty trunk, and canteen equipment: "Each member must undergo a training period in driving. The clutch is operated by hand and works simultaneously with the gears and requires a little practice on the part of drivers before they can drive it smoothly."

Some members had already assisted in clerical and map work for the Guard. When the State Guard went out on maneuvers, corps members would also cover communications and assist in establishing semi-base hospitals outside the area of combat.

The Army was the first to recruit women, running an ad asking, "Can you drive a car? Women with mechanical ability are needed in the Women's Army Auxiliary Corps (WAAC) at once." Some months later The Scituate Herald ran this ad:

"Recruiting of WAVES (Women Accepted for Volunteer Emergency Services): Applicants to be reviewed in Brockton. Parents of prospective applicants are invited to come up and have a talk with the recruiters."

Following suit, the Coast Guard sought recruits for SPAR (Semper parartus: the Coast Guard motto) "In this war the daughters as well as the sons of our Nation are carrying the colors of our armed services."

HELP WANTED 500 WOMEN and MEN

Needed to assemble shells and ammunition. We appeal particularly to young wives whose husbands have gone to war. Also to mothers and to housewives and men not now engaged in essential war work.

JOIN US NOW—TODAY. Unfortunately the war is not over. Much remains to be done and one of the most essential needs is millions of shells for our Armed Forces. The Army and Navy tell us we must increase production.

NATIONAL FIREWORKS, INC., WEST HANOVER PLANT asks you to give your services at good pay now in producing vital 100% war work. Your clearance for work must be secured through your local office of U. S. Employment Service or War Manpower Commission. Apply at Plant Personnel Office, West Hanover, Mass., or at our Brockton Employment Office, 224 Main Street. Guaranteed automatic pay increases. Group incentive plan. Free group health insurance. Good cafeterias. Excellent working conditions.

National Fireworks, Inc.
WEST HANOVER, MASS.

Industries with war contracts also recruited women to work not only as clerks but also as welders, machine operators, and other traditional "man's work." The National Fireworks Company in Hanover sought 55 men and women to assemble shells and ammunitions; their advertisement contained this special note: "We appeal particularly to young wives whose husbands have gone to war."

Women welders, 1943.
L – R. "Hand" Thompson, Claire Williams,
MaryAnn Mahoney Vinal, Mary Ingliss

The war-time housewife had her own challenges: how to prepare sugarless desserts, make soap from fat and lye, prepare countless meatless meals, and use as little gas as possible while running necessary errands. Many of these women also acted as air raid wardens, donated blood, rolled bandages for the Red Cross, and became senior hostesses for USO dances. They collected newspapers and tin cans for salvage drives and saved fat and grease to be used in making ammunition, (dutifully following government instructions to pour it through a kitchen sieve into a can <u>not</u> a bottle).

Everyone was encouraged to have a Victory Garden. Housewives not only grew and produced the crops, but also learned how to preserve them. Plymouth County Extension Service established a "Food Production and Preservation Committee" in every town within its service area. These local committees arranged meetings on gardening procedures and canning, made arrangements for plowing, and conducted Victory Harvest Fairs. The County Agent reported, "Nearly 2,500 Plymouth County women attended 111 canning demonstrations held throughout the summer. These included demonstrations on canning vegetables, fruits, chicken, fish and meat."

On the local level Maud (Mrs. Philip) Bailey recorded her inventory in her daily diary:

8/23/43 Put up 6 quarts blueberries

8/31/43 Put up 9 quarts tomatoes

9/2/43   Put up 12 jars peaches

9/9/43   Put up 12 jars piccalili

9/13/43 Put up 12 jars piccalili

9/17/43 Put up 12 quarts tomatoes

RAISING MONEY FOR THE WAR EFFORT

Jenkins Students.

Even before the declaration of war, the government urged the public to buy defense bonds and stamps. The names changed as conditions changed; defense bonds became war bonds became victory bonds, but they all had the same message: buy, buy, buy. The Kiwanis

Club presented each elementary school child with a Stamp Book and one defense stamp. Local organizations enticed the public to buy bonds with all manner of events. The Scituate Grange held a "Scrap Dance;" admission required a "small sum" and twenty-five pounds of scrap metal. The Grange also received permission to sell bonds and stamps at each meeting, netting $18.20 at their first meeting. South Shore

Hatherly Students.

banks joined banks statewide in a "Back the Attack" effort to go over the top in the sale of war bonds and stamps; all banks stayed open on September 27, 1942, from 5 to 9 p.m. to accommodate those who could not come in during regular banking hours.

An estimated 2,000 people attended Hero's Day, a street fair co-sponsored by the people of Scituate and the Satuit Playhouse. Auctioneer Torrey Little participated in the event by auctioning off a war-trained Siberian Huskie for $1,000. Eugene Buckley had already sent three of his trained huskies to war. Hardcastle Kennel donated dogs trained by the New England Dog Training Club, which had given of their time and skill to train dogs for defense. For further training, the dogs were next sent to Fort Royal, Virginia, to help members of the Army, Navy, and Marines protect storage depots, carry messages, and locate wounded soldiers.

The Red Cross tried to sell a bond for every seat in the Satuit Playhouse. A seating plan of the theater appeared in the lobby, where each bond purchaser could write the name of his war hero on a designated theater seat shown on the plan. The Scituate Rod and Gun Club sold chances on a bicycle displayed in the Welch Co. window. In an era of gas rationing, bicycles had become a favored means of transportation.

SCITUATE HERALD

More South Shore Boys Join Armed Forces

LARGE GROUP LEFT WEDNESDAY MORNING TO BEGIN PRELIMINARY TRAINING FOR SERVICE

Sad News Received From Pacific Area

North Scituate Young Man, Robert Fleming, Makes Supreme Sacrifice

Scituate Officer Dies At Pearl Harbor

Word Is Received of Passing of Lieut Matthew P. Bubin

1943

Lt. Nichols of Scituate Dies In Plane Crash

Well Known South Shore Man Will Be Given Military Tribute on Sunday

Three Scituate Boys Killed In Action

Lieut. Dolan Is Missing

Scituate Boy Held Prisoner By Japanese

THOMAS PARKER EWELL OF U. S. NAVY BEING HELD PRISONER OF WAR IN THE PHILIPPINE ISLANDS

Scituate Soldier Is Missing, Says War Dept.

Mrs. Appleton Notified That Her Son, Wilfred E. Appleton, Has Been Unreported Since February 2

Scituate Soldier's Sacrifice Honored

Lieut. George E. Duane, Who Died In Morocco Awarded Hero's Medal

Hero's Medal to Mother at Ceremonies

More South Shore Boys For Armed Service

Large Group To Leave Greenbush For Camp Devens Next Monday.

1943, THE DARKEST YEAR

As the country entered the second full year of war, civilians learned to cope with shortages and rationing, rules and restrictions, rising prices and increased taxes. They also found that the heaviest price to be paid was the lives of those young men whose names began to appear on the front page of The Scituate Herald as killed or missing in action.

In 1943, the Scituate Committee on Public Safety warned, "The possibility of attack appears to be constantly lessening, but the possibility certainly exists, also the threat of sabotage or ordinary civilian disaster…" Some residents witnessed signs that German submarines had been in the area: oil slicks on the water and sand indicated that a ship had probably been attacked not too far from shore. The continued blackouts and practice air raid drills also reminded them that the country was at war and was vulnerable. Some, however, chafed at the blackout regulations or used the black market to obtain scarce goods. As a result, volunteer members of the Ration Board and the Public Safety Committee undoubtedly had their patience tried. Ration Board #27 issued this statement, "Rationing is necessary and we must expect to have to put up with its inconveniences for some time to come, in order to protect the less well-to-do citizens, by assuring a just division of scarce commodities." In his annual report, the Chairman of the Public Safety Committee said, "Our contribution to the war effort is a very disagreeable and thankless task and we ask your cooperation in backing up our Armed Forces."

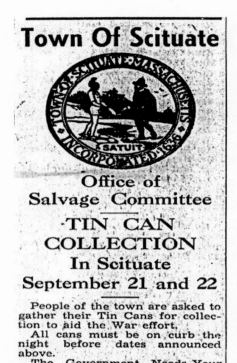

Town Of Scituate

Office of
Salvage Committee

·TIN CAN·
COLLECTION
In Scituate
September 21 and 22

People of the town are asked to
gather their Tin Cans for collection to aid the War effort.
All cans must be on curb the
night before dates announced
above.
The Government Needs Your
Help.
Scituate Salvage Committee

A Town Salvage Committee formed to oversee maintenance of a dump for tin, and they shipped two tons of prepared tin cans in one year. They also conducted a house-to-house pick-up of paper, processing and shipping upward of twenty-five tons during 1943.

The Highway Department experienced difficulty in its efforts to maintain roads due to a scarcity of materials as well as labor. The Public Road Administration rationed tar for almost two years before lifting the ban, which allowed potholes to be filled and roads tarred. During the winter, sand continued to be scarce, its use confined to intersections, hills, and railroad crossings.

Farmers, especially dairy and poultry-men, could not get adequate help. They found feed scarce and expensive, agricultural machinery and replacement parts in short supply, and labor costs soaring. With the assistance of the Plymouth County Extension Service, an individual could receive an agricultural deferment. Through the U. S. Farm Labor Program, the Extension Service placed 614 farm recruits throughout the County, most of them teenagers. Permanent dairy and poultry help proved more difficult to obtain and a shortage continued through 1943.

Early in 1943, one of the most serious civilian concerns focused on the shortage of home heating oil. To determine how much oil they were entitled to, homeowners measured the square footage of their rooms. The Selectmen called a meeting of the Red Cross, Public Safety Committee, Water Commissioners, and the Evacuation Officer of the Division of Defense in order to plan some way to care for people evacuated from their homes because of inadequate heat. "This may become a very real problem for some and it is feared that an emergency may occur at any time." The Welch Co. addressed the problem with an advertisement: "Don't worry about keeping warm – buy a fireplace grate and some fireplace coal." The grate cost $9.30.

In mid-February an amendment to the Stove Rationing Regulation stated that owners of oil-fired heating plants who did not receive enough heat to "safeguard their health and comfort" might be eligible for Stove Certificates available from the Ration Board. The Welch Company then advertised a "Warm-Morning stove for $47.95."

Because of nighttime driving restrictions in 1943, Scituate held its Town Meeting at 1 p.m. rather than in the evening. In addition to budget requests for the Ration Board and the Committee on Public Safety, two war-related items made up the agenda:

1. To sell to the government as many typewriters, in use at the school as the School Committee deemed advisable. Passed.
2. To accept a "Bicycle Law" requiring owners to register their bikes with the Police Department. Passed.

In his annual report, the Chief of Police noted that there had been a noticeable increase in juvenile delinquency, mostly for property damage and theft. He commended the Juvenile Probation Officer of Plymouth County for his untiring efforts to rehabilitate young offenders, trying to protect them from a court record. He also noted that the bicycle registration law had proven very effective and helpful in locating owners of lost bikes, which could then be returned.

Despite all the tensions and hardships encountered throughout the year, people still experienced some light moments in their lives. Such were the Kiwanians, who were taken to their annual mid-winter meeting in an old time wooden bus called a barge pulled by three horses. The barge "Lady Oxford" was once used to meet Daniel Webster and other passengers at the railroad station. Wilson Brown of the Fitts' Farm supplied the barge. Music was provided by a banjo and piano accordion.

HOME TOWN WAR STORIES

Those living along the immediate coast were frequently reminded of the reality of war. Coast Guardsmen and soldiers patrolled the beaches in fair weather and foul. A jeep would be seen parked at the Minot Post Office, waiting to pick up mail for the Army and Navy men stationed in the Glades. Gliding low over the beach in summer, the crews of a Navy blimp dropped Dixie cups inviting the waving girls below to get in touch. In a more warlike situation, pilots in training zoomed in to "attack" the large rocks off North Scituate Beach, the empty shell casings bouncing off the street and beach. Beachgoers witnessed the "bombing" of these same rocks with sacks of a white flour-like substance. It has been said that even Minot's Light was not safe from this "bombing."

Some residents claimed that they could hear the boom of guns or depth charges at night. Others claimed that cracks began to appear in the plastered walls of houses near the beach. The existence of Nazi submarines lurking off Scituate has been corroborated by one of these U-Boat captains, who became acquainted with a Glades resident after the war. According to him, he was ever on the alert for the destroyers coming out of Boston Harbor, ostensibly to get him. What he did not know was that these destroyers were only on training maneuvers.

Two mysteries relate to enemy activities on our shore. One involved the discovery by some teen-age girls of a German Navy hat and blouse buried in the sand at North Scituate Beach. A slight mound in the otherwise flat sand caught their attention. A little digging in the mound revealed the clothes, much to their dismay and excitement. The father of one of the girls turned the clothes over to the police, and nothing was ever seen or heard of the clothes again. Equally mysterious was the experience of Lois Murray, who was permitted access to the Glades to deliver the uniforms pressed by her father, a tailor in Minot. One day, as she and a friend were walking near the Glades first gate, Lois noticed what appeared to be a hole dug in the hillside then covered with brush. Upon investigation, they discovered some oil barrels marked in a foreign language. Lois reported immediately to the Army guard on duty at the second gate. He and a fellow soldier investigated the site, then turned to her and said in no uncertain terms, "You have never seen this and you will never mention it to anybody." And she didn't, until some sixty years later, when she spoke of the incident in a videotaped interview with an Eagle Scout.

Edward Rowe Snow, the "Flying Santa," didn't allow the war to interfere with his annual Christmas flight to drop gift parcels to lighthouse keepers and their families. Finally receiving permission from the Army, he informed the lighthouse keepers of his planned flights. Unfortunately, the soldiers stationed at the Old Scituate Lighthouse on Cedar Point had not been informed. Consequently, when his small plane began to circle the Lighthouse, the possibility of an enemy attack arose in their minds, and they kept a close watch as the small plane circled overhead. Soldiers in a truck with a mounted machine gun stood on alert, with the gun pointed directly at the plane as Mr. and Mrs. Corbett, the keepers, came dashing out to explain to the soldiers the purpose of the plane's visit. It is not known whether "Santa" had gifts for the soldiers as well.

When a Navy blimp crashed in the West End of Town, the Navy called upon the Chairman of the Scituate Public Safety Committee to give assistance. The call came to the Chairman around midnight, and he rounded up a group of men who stayed on duty at the site for 18 hours. The Red Cross Motor Corps arrived on the scene at 1:30 a.m. to serve coffee, sandwiches and doughnuts to Civilian Defense and Navy workers. They stayed on duty until 6:45 p.m. Navy personnel relieved them and rewarded the ladies by serving them dinner.

P.S. Heres a little souvenir. I got a small piece of the blimp last night so thought I would cut off a piece & send it to you. —
mom.

Part of a letter from Mrs. Clapp to her son Joe, relating the story of the blimp crash and containing a "souvenir" of the blimp itself.

WINDING DOWN

Some of the fiercest fighting and most famous WWII battles were still to be fought but there were signs of a slight shift toward normalcy in the civilian world. Town Meeting resumed its customary night-time schedule; Ration Board expenses were approved, but funds for the Committee on Public Safety were indefinitely postponed.

The Committee on Public Safety closed the servicemen's club on Meetinghouse Lane due to the reduction of military personnel stationed in Scituate, but it retained its Motor Corps, Report and Medical Centers, ready to be activated as needed in an emergency. These services were activated during the four-day search for the missing McGrath girl, later found murdered. The Motor Corps served hot coffee and food to the searchers who at one point numbered more than 250 people. During the September 1944 hurricane, the Committee helped evacuate people from Humarock and other endangered areas, then provided them with food and shelter at the high school.

In reporting their activities for 1943 to the town, the selectmen said:

> "The major problem now facing Scituate is the problem of post-war planning, in order that we may be of assistance to the men and women of the armed services returning in peacetime. Of course we want to naturally do those things that will make this desirable transition function smoothly and to provide employment for the returning men".

To this end, the Selectmen organized a committee to work in conjunction with the Emergency Public Works Commission appointed by Governor Saltonstall. The committee asked the heads of town departments to submit project ideas that would provide worthwhile jobs for those being released from both the military and the war industries. The selectmen made it clear that they wanted jobs of value to the town, not mere "make work" jobs.

An editorial in the 1944 Chimes stated, "We are entering a world of chaos and disruption, but we face the future with courage." Most of the essays, poems, and stories in this issue were much more upbeat than those of 1942 and 1943 editions. Six members of this class were already in the service; three had been inducted into the Army Air Corps, but would remain in school through graduation. Student editors dedicated the issue to seven former students, "Those who have made the supreme sacrifice in the service of our country..." The service honor roll included four faculty members and 306 men and women in all branches of the service.

TO THOSE WHO SERVE
Honor Roll dedicated
and presented to the town
by the Scituate Kiwanis
Club, Nov. 21, 1943.

The Town continued to remember its sons and daughters: the Methodist Church unveiled an Honor Roll Board of its members serving in the armed forces; the choir provided special music at the ceremony. In addition, the Kiwanis Club presented a temporary Honor Roll to the Town, which listed the names of all the men and women who had

enlisted or had been inducted into the service, placing the memorial in Lawson Park in November of 1943. Finally, Father Quinlan Playground at St. Mary's Church was dedicated to the Scituate men who had lost their lives.

Although the sacrifices and deprivations both at home and abroad continued, there was some sense of light at the end of the tunnel. At the March 1945 town meeting, articles under discussion looked toward the peace-time future.

> Voted: to raise the salaries and pay of all Town officials and employees 10% for the year 1945.
> Voted: that a committee be established "regarding a parking space at Egypt Beach"
> Voted: to appropriate $500 to enable the newly appointed Airport Committee to make studies "regarding the possibility of an airport in Town."
> Voted: "to appropriate $600 for preliminary working drawings and specifications for a new elementary school building."

In the elections held in November of 1944, Scituate once again strongly supported the Republican ticket, with 1,781 voting for Dewey and Bricker, and 695 voting for Roosevelt and Truman. The nation, again, voted the Democratic Party back into office.

On April 12, 1945, the country was stunned at the radio news flash from Warm Springs, Georgia: President Roosevelt had died of a massive stroke at the age of 63. A few hours later Vice-President Harry Truman was sworn in as the 33rd President and asked his countrymen for their prayers as he assumed that heavy responsibility.

Gen. Douglas MacArthur signs the formal surrender. Behind him are U.S. General Jonathan Wainwirght and British Lt. Gen. Arthur Percival, both were Japanese POW's.
(From scrap book of Joseph Driscoll.)

Germany surrendered on May 7, 1945. V-E Day was declared on May 8th and was marked by celebrations all over the world. The end of the war was announced at 7:30 on August 14th and the celebration began! People filled the streets laughing, hugging, and shouting, while church bells chimed and the Lawson Tower bells rang. V-J Day

was officially confirmed on August 15, 1945, the day was proclaimed a holiday and the celebrations continued. In her diary, Mrs. Maud Bailey described the impromptu parade formed by her family as one led with a drum and another in the group played the tuba. The

Foreign Minister Mamoru Shigemitsu and Gen. Yoshijiro Umezu aboard the USS Missouri moored in Tokyo Bay.
(From scrap book of Joseph Driscoll.)

official surrender took place on board the USS Missouri on September 2, 1945. Our men and women were coming home!

Relieved of further authority, on September 30, 1945; the Rationing Board was asked to transfer their unexpended balance back to the Town. The Selectmen appointed a committee of Veterans Affairs, chaired by Mrs. Mark Murrill; she attended a nine-week course offered by the Commission of Veterans Affairs to become familiar with the regulations concerning the rights and benefits for returning G.I.s. Available one day a week, she assisted veterans and their families with bonus applications, educational programs under the G. I. Bill, disability applications, burial allowances, and numerous other needs.

By the end of 1946, the Director of Veterans Services reported that "of the 443 persons enlisted or inducted from the Town of Scituate, over 75% had been discharged."

In January in 1949, the Selectmen asked Colonel Philip Schuyler to establish liaison with the families of returning overseas war dead. The veterans posts would be in charge of funerals. In each case, the body was met upon arrival back in town, and full military burial honors were rendered at each of the ten graves. Frank Hall, himself a returning veteran, played the bugle at the ceremonies.

LIAISON OFFICER'S REPORT

**REPORT OF THE
LIAISON OFFICER**

Egypt, Massachusetts,
January 11, 1949.

Board of Selectmen,
Scituate, Massachusetts.

Gentlemen:

In October, 1947, you asked me to establish liaison between the families of our returning Overseas War Dead and our Veteran Posts, and to take charge of their funerals. This I have done, and as the last of our boys to be returned has arrived, I beg to make the following report of those so served:

Joseph B. Pina, Jr.	Oct. 27, 1947	Catholic Cemetery
Matthew P. Bubin	Nov. 2, 1947	Fairview Cemetery
Edwin A. Spear	Dec. 14, 1947	Cudworth Cemetery
Edward R. Hooper	Dec. 21, 1947	Catholic Cemetery
Robert W. Fleming	Mar. 21, 1948	Groveland Cemetery
Lionel O. Bush	June 13, 1948	Groveland Cemetery
Bernard J. Kulisich	Aug. 1, 1948	Catholic Cemetery
Eldon H. Johnson	Aug. 22, 1948	Union Cemetery

Congressional Medal of Honor

Herbert Loring	Sept. 12, 1948	Groveland Cemetery
Robert Augustus Cole}	Jan. 9, 1949	Union Cemetery
Robert Allan Cole }		

In every case the body has been met upon arrival in town, and after ascertaining the families' wishes, they have been carried out.

Through the cordial cooperation of Scituate Post American Legion and Satuit Post V. F. W., full Military Burial Honors have been rendered at each grave.

I appreciate the honor accorded me and feel that my mission has been accomplished. I respectfully request relief from further responsibility in this assignment.

PHILIP L. SCHUYLER, Col. Inf. Retd.,
Liaison Officer.

This group of Scituate service men left their mark on a neighbor's shed, and recorded the outcome.

In honor of those who served

In memory of those who fell

WALTER S. ALLEN, JR.

Walter Allen, Jr., was born March 21, 1926, in Scituate. He was graduated from Scituate High School in 1944. His yearbook quote states:

"A mechanic for Uncle Sam he would be. He'll make it, too with his personality."

Walter did, in fact, serve Uncle Sam. He was a Combat Infantry Veteran of World War II. He became a 1st Sergeant with the 47th Infantry Division seeing service in France and Germany. While in Germany, Walter was assigned to Dachau, the infamous Nazi concentration camp, after its liberation.

After World War II, Walter married Margaret Walls. They had four children, there are now seven grandchildren. He continued his service in the Army Reserves for twenty-three years, retiring in 1969.

Walter worked as a plumber. He was also Superintendent of the Scituate Water Department, where he worked for thirty-five years. The square in front of the present water department in Greenbush is dedicated to Walter's memory. In addition, he served as a Special Police Officer for the Town of Scituate and a Security Officer at South Shore Hospital in Weymouth, MA.

Walter S. Allen died on December 22, 1994.

Brainerd Ames.

BRAINERD CUSHING AMES

Brainerd Ames, whose great grandfather fought in the Civil War, was born in Rockland in September of 1921. Despite the fact that his mother was a school teacher, Brainerd quit high school and came to live in Scituate at Lighthouse Point, where his family had a summer home. During the Great Depression, he enlisted in the CCC (Civilian Conservation Corps) and worked in New Hampshire. The CCC was a program proposed by the newly-elected President Franklin Roosevelt. Its purpose was twofold. One was to put thousands of unemployed men to work, and the other was to fight soil erosion and declining timber resources across the country. As a measure of its success, more than three million young men were employed and thousands of acres of wooded areas were preserved.

Along with his friends, John Salvador and the Patterson Brothers, Brainerd enlisted in the United States Navy on September 11, 1942. He received training in California and served in the South Pacific. While part of a convoy, his boat was torpedoed. Due to its severe damage, the boat had to leave the convoy and be towed to a nearby island for repairs. When Brainerd reported to the FPO (Fleet Post Office) to pick up the mail he hadn't received for months, he was told that his boat had been sunk and all hands lost. As living proof that this was not, in fact, true, he was given the letters that had been held up due to his being "lost at sea".

Brainerd married the former Lorraine Ellis while on leave in 1944. After his discharge in October of 1945, they settled in a house on Norwell Avenue in Scituate. There they raised a daughter and three sons. There are now seven grandchildren and five great grandchildren. Brainerd was employed by the Scituate Department of Public Works and pursued a life-long lobstering career, first with a small dory, and eventually, with his 24-foot boat "Tiny". His son, Brainerd Ames, Jr. carries on the tradition, fishing out of Scituate to this day.

Brainerd Ames passed away on January 20, 1985.

The original Anderson Fuel Co. building.

Anderson Fuel Co. today.

ARTHUR W. ANDERSON

Arthur W. Anderson, son of James A. and Doris Wilson Anderson was born in 1927. He was graduated from Scituate High School in 1944.

Arthur joined the United States Navy on May 5, 1945 and gained the rank of Petty Officer 3rd Class. He was stationed in Saipan.

Saipan is an island of about 14 miles in length, surrounded by a coral reef, and part of the Marianas Island Group that was important as the key to the Central Pacific. When held by the Japanese, the islands dominated communications with the Japanese Inner South Seas Empire and when taken by US forces the Marianas provided bases from which attacks were launched on the Japanese Home Islands.

After its capture in 1944, Saipan became the first base for the Army Air Corps' new long-range bomber, the B-29 and an important naval base for US submarines.

Arthur returned to Scituate June 24, 1946 and married Gail George. They have two sons and a daughter. Together with his brother, James, he founded the Anderson Fuel Company, supplying heating oil to generations of Scituate residents.

Arthur Anderson in Saipan.

U. S. NAVAL AIR STATION
PENSACOLA. FLORIDA

Dec. 26, 1943

Dear Sir,

Please allow me to take this opportunity to express my thanks and appreciation to the people of Scituate for their nice gift on Christmas. I wish I were there to express my feelings personally. It does mean a lot to a fellow to know that the folks back home are thinking of us even as we are thinking of them.

Sincerely
James W. Anderson

ENSIGN JAMES W. ANDERSON, U.S.N.R., of 331 Gannett Road, North Scituate, is flying a Grumman Hellcat fighter plane from one of the Navy's Essex-class carriers.

Home Town Boys
FLYING FROM AIRCRAFT CARRIERS IN THE PACIFIC

James W. Anderson

JAMES W. ANDERSON

James W. Anderson was born in 1921. He graduated from Scituate High School in 1939 where he was Class President After graduation he attended Northeastern University.

James entered the US Navy in early 1942 and became a pilot aboard the USS Ticonderoga, an aircraft carrier assigned to Task Force 58 in the South Pacific. James flew Grumman Hellcat fighter planes that had been specifically designed to counter the Japanese Zero fighter planes.

The pilots of the Ticonderoga joined with those of other carriers to sink the Japanese heavy carrier, Nachi and shot down at least six Japanese aircraft and damaged 23 others during the month of November 1944 while providing air cover for forces capturing Leyte. Leyte is one of the largest islands in the Philippine archipelago.

The Ticonderoga pilots helped to thoroughly destroy Japanese installations where forces were being marshaled for suicide raids on the B-29 bases in the Marianas. They also conducted raids on Tokyo itself. The aircraft carrier and her crew weathered two major typhoons in less than six months and several kamikaze attacks during their time in the South Pacific.

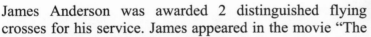

James Anderson was awarded 2 distinguished flying crosses for his service. James appeared in the movie "The Fighting Lady" which chronicled the history of the aircraft carrier, USS Yorktown from its commissioning in 1943 through its role in the Pacific Theatre of Operations. The film was awarded an Oscar for Best Documentary Feature of 1944.

James helped his brother, Arthur, to found the Anderson Fuel Oil Company in North Scituate before moving to California.

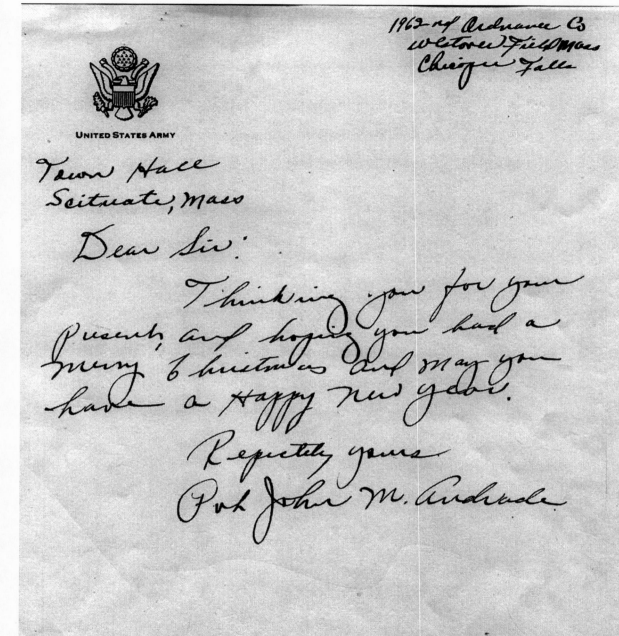

UNITED STATES ARMY

1963 nf Ardnance Co
Wetover Field Mass
Chicopee Falls

Town Hall
Scituate, Mass

Dear Sir:

Thinking you for your
presents, and hoping you had a
merry Christmas and may you
have a Happy New Year.

Respectfully yours

Pvt John M. Andrade

JOHN M. ANDRADE

 John Andrade was born on November 13, 1902, in the Cape Verde Islands. He immigrated to the United States in 1917. John attended night classes taught by Anne Cunneen in Scituate during the 1940's to complete his education. Miss Cunneen taught English at Scituate High School and assisted new immigrants with their reading and writing skills. The Scituate Chapter of the National Honor Society was named in her honor.

On October 14, 1942, John reported to Westover Field in Chicopee Falls, MA, for service in the US Army. He was assigned to the 1962nd Ordnance Depot Company (Aviation). It was from Westover that John wrote his thank you letter to the Town of Scituate after receiving his Christmas card and gift. An article that appeared in the *Scituate Herald* detailing the servicemen's gift program notes that one of the first donations to Scituate's Servicemen's Fund was made by the Cape Verde Association. According to John's daughter, Isabel, "He was very proud to be an American and to have served his country."

After his discharge from the Army, John married Mary Pires of Wareham on December 4, 1943. They had a son and a daughter. There are now three grandchildren. John worked for many years as a gardener and maintained a popular farmstand on Stockbridge Road that was famous for its delicious strawberries.

John Mendes Andrade passed away on March 30, 1988.

Cpl. Ernest J. Barbuto
APO 11067610
47th Air Service Sqd
8th Air Service Grp
APO 713-?
c/o Postmaster San Francisco

May 18, 1945
New Guinea

Dear Sir:

This, I know will be a surprise to you, to hear from me at such a late date.

I want through this letter, to express my sincerest thanks to you and the people of Scituate, who made possible once again the gifts to us in the armed forces.

I wish, also, to express my sincerest apologies for not acknowledging this gift sooner. It would be nice to have an substantial excuse for not writing before, but I'm afraid I haven't.

Since joining the army I have done quite a little traveling. In no case have I seen any other town, or city, who remembered the boys in such a fine way.

As you know I'm still in New Guinea where I have been now for over a year. If you like the tropics and lack of civilization it is ok. As for me I wouldn't trade the smallest part of Scituate for all these tropical isles.

In closing may I thank you all once again.

Sincerely,
Ernest J. Barbuto

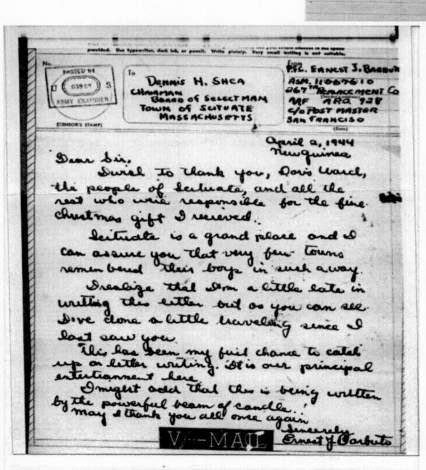

To: Dennis H. Shea, Chairman, Board of Selectman, Town of Scituate, Massachusetts

From: Pfc. Ernest J. Barbuto, ASN 11667610, 267th Replacement Co, MF APO 928, c/o Post Master San Francisco

April 2, 1944
New Guinea

Dear Sir,

I wish to thank you, Doris Ward, the people of Scituate, and all the rest who were responsible for the fine Christmas gift I received.

Scituate is a grand place and I can assure you that very few towns remembered their boys in such a way.

I realize that I'm a little late in writing this letter but as you can see I've done a little traveling since I last saw you.

This has been my first chance to catch up on letter writing. It is our principal entertainment here.

I might add that this is being written by the powerful beam of candle.

May I thank you all once again.

Sincerely,
Ernest J. Barbuto

V---MAIL

ERNEST JOSEPH BARBUTO

On December 26, 1920 Ernest Joseph Barbuto was born to Pasquale and Julia (O'Leary) Barbuto of the Minot section of Scituate. He was graduated from Scituate High School in 1938 and became active in the Army Air Corps in 1943. Ernie served as a Sergeant in the 371st Bomb Squadron in New Guinea and the Bismarck Archipelago. It was vital to regain control of this group of islands from the Japanese in order for General MacArthur to continue his campaign to liberate the Philippines.

Ernie was an Aviation Machinist and he trained at Tufts College in Medford, Massachusetts, and Sheppard Field in Texas before his deployment to the Pacific Theater.

His thank you letter was written in April of 1944, and in it he apologized for his tardiness, explaining that he had been doing "a little travelling." After stating that "Scituate is a grand place and I can assure you that very few towns remembered their boys in such a way," he explained that he was writing his letter by "the powerful beam of a candle!"

Ernie was awarded the Philippine Liberation Ribbon, Asiatic-Pacific Theater Campaign Ribbon, Victory Medal, American Theater Campaign Ribbon and Good Conduct Medal. He was honorably discharged on January 26, 1946, and attended Boston University earning a degree in Business Administration. He was well known in the Insurance business.

Ernest died on February 1, 2003, while a resident at Summit Avenue in North Scituate, that "grand place" mentioned in his letter.

Anne Barnes, third row, second from left.

GEORGIANNE (ANNE) BARNES

Georgianne Barnes, the daughter of William and Vernetta Jones Barnes, was born on April 16, 1924, in Scituate. She attended Scituate schools and was graduated from Scituate High School in 1942, where she sang in the Glee Club.

After graduating from high school, "Anne," as she was known, went to work as an order clerk for the S.S. Pierce Company in Boston.

In June of 1944, Georgianne enlisted in the United States Navy, where she became a member of a group officially known as WAVES (Women Accepted for Voluntary Emergency Service). Numbering over 100,000 by war's end, the WAVES enabled men to be freed up for combat duty. These women performed communications and logistics duties and staffed aircraft control towers. Georgianne received her basic training over six weeks at the US Naval Training School, Bronx, NY. This was conducted at Hunter College, affectionately known as the "USS Hunter." She went on to yeoman training for twelve weeks at Milledgeville, Georgia. Georgianne served in the Field Branch, Bureau of Supplies and Accounts in Cleveland, Ohio, rising to the rank of Seaman First Class, Storekeeper. According to her husband, Eben, she only became seasick once, while on the Great Lakes. She was discharged on November 10, 1945.

On December 22, 1945, Georgianne married Eben Blake Page, III. She became president of one her husband's companies, Blakey Industries, and treasurer of another, Blakey Trucking Corp. The couple had five children, thirteen grandchildren, and fourteen great-grandchildren. Georgianne Barnes Page passed away on November 13, 1994.

Georgianne's twin sister Abbie also served in the WAVES, following her sister, "Anne". She was trained at Hunter College and served at the Naval Air Station in Atlanta Georgia as an Aerologist (weatherperson). She now resides in British Columbia, Canada with her husband Ken Thompson. They have 6 children, 14 grandchildren and 1 great grandson.

Twin Sister, Abbie.

Their brother, William H. Barnes served in the US Navy in the North Atlantic, Italy and in the Pacific. He was a damage control officer aboard the USS Achernar, an Attack Cargo Ship. After the war he returned to Scituate and worked as a school bus driver and custodian. He married Louise Graham. William died on February 9, 1992.

Brother, William Barnes.

Joseph Barry, 1st on right.

Mass being celebrated in New Guinea.

Papua, New Guinea.

JOSEPH WILLIAM BARRY

Joseph Barry, one of seven children of James and Kathryn Donovan Barry, was born in Scituate on May 16, 1912. He attended Scituate schools and was graduated from Scituate High School in 1932. Joe worked as a mosser after high school, gathering the valuable growth from the sea off the Scituate coast, as his father had done.

Along with his friends, George Flaherty, Red Studley, Bill Curran, and his cousin Ray Gillis, Joe enlisted in the Army Air Corps on September 18, 1940. He served with the 356th Army Air Corps Base Unit in Papua, New Guinea, and the Dutch East Indies as an aviation mechanic. Joe was awarded the Good Conduct Medal, American Defense Service Medal and the Asiatic-Pacific Theater Campaign Ribbon with 3 Service Stars. Each Service Star was awarded for individual campaigns in which he participated.

Discharged in May of 1945, Joe returned to Scituate and married Helen White. They had three children: Edward, Kevin, and Kathryn. Joe worked for the Scituate Highway Department for forty years.

Joseph Barry died November 15, 1981.

Scituate Boy Awarded Bronze Star Medal.

Sergeant Herbert E. Bearce Honored for Heroic Achievement in Italy

Sergeant Herbert E. Bearce, son of Henry and Mary Bearce of 19 Tilden road, Scituate Harbor, has been highly honored by being awarded a Bronze Star Medal for heroic achievement in Italy.

Sgt. Bearce is one of the best known young men in Scituate. His father is a World War 1 veteran and commander of the Scituate Post, of the American Legion.

His parents received a number of souvenirs of the war in Europe which are displayed in the window of his father's store at Scituate Harbor. Included is a large banner with the swastika, a German helmet, German lights and byonets as well as a number of other valuable relics taken from the Germans.

Sergt. Bearce is a member of Company H, 141st Infantry Regiment and his citation is as follows:

CITATION:

Herbert E. Bearce, Sergeant, 31356009, Company H, 141st Infantry Regiment, for heroic achievement in combat on 1 June 1944 in Italy. Sergeant Bearce was a member of a machine gun squad in position on a ridge at the extreme left flank of the battalion. The squad was to protect the battalion's exposed flank as it renewed its assault against a ridge 300 yards away. As the attack progressed the battalion became wedged between two ridges and pinned down by fire from numerous small arms on the ridge to its front. Small arms fire on the machine gun squad made its position almost untenable, but he and his comrades held their ground and inflicted many casualties on the enemy machine gunners, snipers, and riflemen atop the forward ridge. A counter attack of company strength struck the battalion's left flank where only his squad opposed the enemy. While the machine gunner continued to support the attack to the front, the squad leader and ammunition bearers repelled the counter attack on the left. Now the squad was engaged frontally and on the flank, with small arms in their midst by the counterattackers. When the riflemen moved forward in their attack, he and his companions fought on alone to repel the counterattack and support the frontal drive. Entered the Service from Scituate, Mass.

JOHN E. DAHLQUIST,
Major General, U. S. Army
Commanding

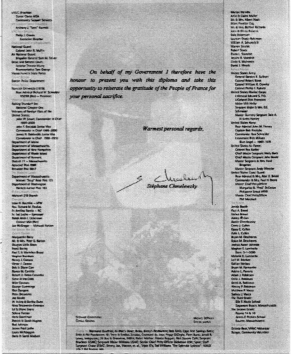

HERBERT E. BEARCE

 Herbert Bearce, the son of Henry (Spats) and Mary Finnie Bearce, was born in Scituate on February 2, 1925. He attended the Jenkins School and was graduated from Scituate High School in 1942. After his graduation he worked for his father at the Moderne Market in Scituate Harbor until his induction into the US Army Infantry on May 12, 1943.

Herb was serving in Italy with Company H, 141st Infantry Regiment when he was awarded the Bronze Star "for heroic achievement in combat on 1 June 1944," according to his citation.

Eight days after D-Day, from August 24 until the 30th in 1944, Herb fought in the Battle of Montelimar in France. The battle took place in a town that straddled the main North-South Highway to the Rhone River Valley in the path of the retreating German Army's 19th Panzer Division. It was here that Herb received the wound that earned him the Purple Heart.

In 1944 the 141st Infantry Battalion earned a Presidential Unit Citation for "extraordinary heroism, gallantry and esprit de corps from 7 December to 19 December in France."

After his discharge as a Technical Sergeant in November 1945, Herb returned to Scituate and his job at the Moderne Market before becoming Superintendent of Maintenance and Transportation for the Scituate Schools. Herb married the former Lelia Hunt of Marshfield on September 7, 1947 and they had three children. There are now six grandchildren and two great grandchildren. Herb is now retired after thirty-three years with the School Department. He does part time maintenance work and enjoys woodworking.

As recently as August of 2000, Herb received a "Special Diploma" from the government and people of France thanking him for his "contribution in the fight to liberate France from the Axis Powers in World War II."

Herbert Bearce on right.

France - H. Bearce,
Nurse, Everett Dorr.

Dec. 20, 1943.

Town of Scituate
Christmas Committee,

The gift I received is
duply appreciated. It makes a
fellar feel good inside to know
the folks back home are thinking of him. Especially at this time
of year.

In the past few months I have
done a lot of traveling and seen
a lot of the country. But this
is no place that means so much
to me in every respect, as my own
home town. I am looking forward
to the day I can return. Also wishing you as much happiness as
you have gave me.

Sincerely yours,

Sgt. Fred M. Bergman

FRED M. BERGMAN

Fred Bergman was born in Scituate on October 21, 1920. He was a life-long resident, living in the same house for seventy-five years.

Fred served in the United States Army from October 13, 1942, until January 13, 1946. He was assigned to the Third Engineer Special Brigade, operating a landing craft and supervising five others in New Guinea and Borneo. Fred was awarded the Purple Heart.

Located in Indonesia, New Guinea and Borneo are the second and third largest islands in the world after Greenland. They lie south east of Viet Nam and Cambodia and were the sites of large rubber plantations. These sources of rubber, vital to the war effort, were highly coveted by both Japanese and American forces and the sites of intense battles.

In his 1943 letter, Fred related, "In the past few months I have done a lot of traveling and seen a lot of the country. But there's no place that means so much to me in every respect, as my own home town. I am looking forward to the day I can return."

After his service, Fred did return to Scituate and worked at commercial lobstering for thirty-four years. He also worked for The Anderson Fuel Company in North Scituate, where he was the dispatcher for twenty-two years. Fred was the assistant Harbormaster and then Harbormaster in the 1950's. He was a former member of the Knights of Columbus and the Scituate Historical Society.

Fred Bergman married the former Clare Stefani and was the father of five children. He had eight grandchildren and two great grand children. Fred retired at the age of seventy-two.

Sadly, Fred passed away on August 8, 2004 shortly after giving this information.

SS Edmond Mallett

UNITED STATES
MARITIME TRAINING STATION
SHEEPSHEAD BAY, BROOKLYN, N. Y.

December 2, 1942

To the Saturate Service Committee,

I wish to thank the committee for the very generous gift that sent to me. I hope it will please you to know that it arrived at a very opportune time and that I appreciate it more than I can express in words.

It really is nice to know that there are persons back home who have an interest in my welfare. At times when I'm feeling low in spirits I'm sure it will brace me up when I think of people such as you who are in back of me and urging me onward to greater heights and ultimate victory in the end.

Thankfully Yours
Lawrence Bonomi

SS Dexter W Fellows

LAWRENCE BONOMI

 Larry Bonomi was born in Sopino, Italy, on October 5, 1922, while his parents, Joseph P. and Gentilina, were vacationing there. He was a life-long Scituate resident graduating from Scituate High School in 1941.

Larry entered the Merchant Marines in 1942. Merchant shipping was vital to the war effort, even before actual US involvement in the war. Many tons of supplies were sent to embattled Britain, enabling them to carry on their defense against German invasion. These merchant ships sailed alone, braving the Atlantic crossing and the threat of being sunk until they reached British escort ships more than halfway across the ocean. The United States' entrance into the war brought German U-boats (submarines) close in to the American East Coast. They torpedoed merchant ships and laid underwater mines to further disrupt the flow of goods, supplies and troops to our allies. Ships sailing from South America up the entire coast carrying oil and raw materials to ports from Florida to Maine were targeted by the U-boats as well. The Battle of the Atlantic raged from September 1939 until May of 1945, causing Winston Churchill to state in his book, The Second World War, "The only thing that really frightened me during the war was the U-boat peril."

Larry sailed on merchant ships from April of 1943 until March of 1946. Traveling between Maine, Boston, and New York, he served on the SS Bruce, SS Harry Garfield, SS Joseph Stanton, SS Samuel de Champlain, SS Dexter W. Fellows, SS Edmund Mallet, SS Joseph H. Hollister, and the SS Sea Robin.

Larry married Ruth Cook and they had three children. After his service, he earned his living as a union laborer, employed by the Quincy Laborers Union, Local 133. He worked on the construction of Scituate High School, Hatherly and Cushing Elementary Schools, and Gates Intermediate School. He was also involved in the construction of the Plymouth Nuclear Power Plant.

Larry loved the outdoors, enjoying gardening, hunting, and archeology. He was a member of the Scituate Beautification Committee's Adopt-A-Lot Program, wherein he was responsible for planting and maintaining the traffic island at Hollett Street and Gannet Road in North Scituate.

Larry Bonomi passed away on November 13, 1992.

Joan Breen with her parents and brother Robert, (in uniform).

Richard and Joan Breen Klein

JOAN BREEN

Joan Breen was born February 24, 1921, in Hanover, Massachusetts. She later moved to Scituate and was graduated from Scituate High School in 1938 and from Simmons College in Boston. She also received a Master's degree in Education from Antioch College in Ohio.

On September 13, 1941, Joan married Richard Klein, an officer in the Air Force Intelligence Service. In July of 1943, Joan enlisted in the WAAC (Women's Army Auxiliary Corps) at Fort Oglethorpe, Georgia, where she received her basic training and went on to attend Officers' Candidate School. Joan and Richard's daughter, Patricia, was born in 1944. Joan eventually served as a 2nd Lt. Commissary Officer and was awarded the WAAC Service Medal.

In 1951 Joan married Sidney Lipshires. She worked as a teacher at Gorham and Lebanon High Schools in New Hampshire. Joan and Sidney had a daughter, Lisa. The family moved to New Jersey where Joan was a Labor Union Activist and worked for the New Jersey Education Association. After her retirement in 1984 she returned to New Hampshire where she opened a bed and breakfast in her home called "The Cottage". She performed in summer stock productions in New Hampshire and Connecticut and was a published poet.

Joan Breen Klein Lipshires passed away on May 18, 2004.

Revisiting Watson Lake in 1997

U. S. ARMY AIR FORCES
SEYMOUR JOHNSON FIELD
GOLDSBORO, NORTH CAROLINA

Jan 6, 1943

Dear Reggie;

It is a little out of my line writing to Town Officials, so you will have to excuse any unimportant mistakes.

I want to express my thanks to the Townspeople of Scituate for my Christmas gift. It was appreciated very much, and also came in very handy. Receiving a letter with the seal of the town on the back, makes you feel very proud. I know I felt that way, but as I read the Christmas verse, I felt a lump in my throat.

I am in the best of health, and enjoying my work. The Army life is not as hard as most people think.

I will close now, by once again thanking the people of Scituate for my gift.

Yours truly
P.T John R. Brown
Seymour Johnson Field
North Carolina

Sign-post Forest at Watson Lake

JOHN RICHARD BROWN

John and his twin sister, Julia, were born on June 4, 1924, to Wilson and Marian (Fitts) Brown. John was graduated from Scituate High School in 1942 and entered the United States Army Air Corps in November of that year.

John's basic training took place at Fort Devens in Ayer, Massachusetts. He also trained at Atlantic City, NJ, and Seymore Johnson Field in Goldsboro, NC, where he attended Aircraft Mechanic School. Engine Specialist School at Chanute Field, Rantoul, IL, came next. This was followed by Small Arms School at Camp Luna, Las Vegas, New Mexico and Arctic Training School at Buckley Field, Denver, Colorado.

In Colorado, the unit received instructions on operating equipment in freezing temperatures, the effects of severe cold on lubricants, and survival in sub-zero conditions following plane crashes. They spent eight days in the mountains building shelters, clearing trails, cooking outdoors and sleeping on pine boughs.

John was deployed to Watson Lake in the Yukon Territory ten miles north of British Columbia. He was stationed there for sixteen months and his unit was responsible for

servicing and maintaining all of the aircraft being sent to Russia under the Lend/Lease Program, in which approximately 150,000 US built aircraft were given to the Soviet Union to aid in their fight against our common enemies, Germany and Japan. Eight thousand planes were delivered via the ALSIB (Alaska-Siberian) Route.

John remembers "The snow was about four feet thick. The temperature was 50-58 degrees below zero for a period of 36 hours. Gas masks froze before you could walk 100 feet."

After being rotated back to Newcastle Air Base in Wilmington, Delaware, in April of 1945, John married the former Ethel Perley Hollis in September. He was assigned to a crew servicing C54 aircraft that were flying wounded soldiers home from Europe. He was promoted to Sergeant in October and discharged November 28, 1945.

After his return to Scituate, John "Bub" Brown served as Scituate Water Commissioner and Highway Supervisor. He also coached Little League and served as Plymouth County Highway Association President. He was President of the Massachusetts Highway Association and Master of the Satuit Masonic Lodge. He and Ethel have three children.

John and Ethel returned to Watson Lake during an Alaskan vacation in 1997. They were amazed by the growth of a "sign-post forest". Twenty-five thousand signs have been added to the single one erected by homesick GI's during World War II.

Tom Brown, 4th from Left, Back Row.

A big catch at Scituate Harbor less than one month before his death.

THOMAS E. BROWN

 Thomas Brown was born in Weymouth, Massachusetts, on July 16, 1924. He moved to Scituate and was graduated from Scituate High School in 1942.

According to "My Life Story,"written for his family prior to his death Tom relates: "Alfred and Jimmie Franzen and I were in the Playhouse (movie theater in Scituate Harbor) on Sunday, December 7th. The lights suddenly came up and the manager got on stage and made an announcement that the Japanese had attacked Pearl Harbor . . . We were graduating in the summer of 1942 and we were all talking of what we were going to do. I said that I was going to join the Marines and Alfred said he was going to join the Paratroops . . we were working at the Hingham shipyard . . .we got our draft notices . . . Alfred went into the Marines. I was told I could get a deferment because I worked in the shipyard, but I told my boss I wanted to go into the service."

Tom became the paratrooper reversing the roles he and Alfred had envisioned for themselves back at the Playhouse when the war had just begun. After training in the United States, Tom was shipped to England to prepare for the D-Day invasion of Europe with the 101st Airborne Division.

On June 6, 1944, Tom was flown across the English Channel, and he parachuted behind the German troops who were manning the Normandy beach defenses. His unit's mission was to take and secure the bridgehead over the River Oise near Carenton, France, directly behind Utah Beach. During their approach to the town, Tom was shot and wounded; he was evacuated to England. After recuperating, he returned to duty and made one more jump, this time into Holland. He participated in the Battle of Bastogne, Belgium. The 101st Airborne Division was completely surrounded by German panzer (tank), infantry and paratroop divisions. When offered the ultimatum by German officers "Surrender or be annihilated in two hours", the Commander of the 101st replied "N-U-T-S". The German receiving the reply couldn't understand the term, the American Colonel answered, "It means to go to hell!" The Americans prevailed, and the Germans were the ones defeated.

Tom was mustered out of the service on December 5, 1945. He received the Purple Heart, Victory Medal, European African Middle Eastern Campaign Ribbon with Bronze Service Arrowhead, Belgian Fourragere and the Distinguished Unit Badge. This last was the first ever to be awarded to an entire division. After working for a time as a pinsetter at the Satuit Bowlaway in Scituate Harbor, Tom married the former Jeanne L. Eisenhauer. They had 2 sons and 3 daughters. Tom eventually became a supervisor for Bay State Gas Company. He was also Scituate's Gas Inspector and the Sealer of Weights and Measures for the town as well as a starter at the Scituate Country Club.

Tom Brown passed away at his Scituate home on November 21, 1995, still carrying the German bullet that had lodged in his body during the war. Besides his children, he is survived by fifteen grandchildren.

Jan., 25, 1943,

Mr. Dennis Shea,
Chairman Of Board of Selectmen,

Dear Sir.,

I wish to extend thru you my sincere appreciation to the citizens of Scituate for their kindness to me.

The card and gift reached me shortly after Christmas. It was good to know that the folks at home were thinking of me.

Thanking you again, I remain

Sincerely

Matthew P. Bubin U.S.N.

January 10, 1945

Dear Mr. Shea:

I wish to thank, thru you, the citizens of Scituate for the lovely flowers sent to me both for last year and for this year.

Last year I could not seem to write a very satisfactory note, but this year I was more able to really appreciate the flowers. Time really does heal and now things are not quite so difficult.

Accept the sincere thanks of myself and the children.

Very truly yours,

Harriet E. Bubin

MATTHEW PETER BUBIN

Matthew Bubin, known to his family and friends as "Metchee," was born in "The Village" section of Brockton in 1909. He was the son of Ludwig and Emilija (Slivinskaite) Bubinas, who were immigrants from Lithuania and had come to Brockton to work in the shoe factories.

Matthew left home when he was 14 or 15 years old and joined the Merchant Marine. He was able to do this by using his older brother's birth certificate and by being able to pass for 18. He started in the lowliest position in the bowels of the ship as a wiper in the engine room. However, by the time of his entry into the United States Navy, he was preparing to take an exam for chief engineer.

Working for American Export Lines, Moore and McCormack and other steamship companies, he traveled all around the world, getting to know people in every country. He was very distressed by the advent of war as he had friends everywhere.

Matthew's sister, Victoria, had moved to Scituate and it was at her house that he met his future wife, Harriet Pepper. Harriet was the daughter of Arthur Pepper, an immigrant from London's West End who became the first chimist of the Lawson Tower bells and Elizabeth Spencer, a descendant of some of Scituate's earliest settlers. They married in 1939 while Matthew was on a three-day pass and had a whirlwind honeymoon at the New York World's Fair.

The young couple spent the first years of their marriage mostly apart as Matthew was still in the Merchant Marine. He was at sea in the Mediterranean when his first child was born. Shortly afterwards he took a job closer to home at the Fore River Shipyard in Quincy enabling him to spend more time with his family. After the birth of twin daughters in 1942, he was called to service in the Navy. In August of 1943, he was stationed in Hawaii where he had the tragic accident that took his life. After leaving a meeting during a blackout, he fell and suffered a compound fracture of his leg. Despite having been appropriately inoculated, he developed tetanus and died in Honolulu, where he was buried for the duration of the war. His body was returned to Scituate in 1947 along with so many others. He is now buried in Fairview Cemetery.

Along with Matthew Bubin's thank you letter, another letter from Harriet was found. This led to the discovery that the Veterans' Committee had sent flowers to surviving family members in the event of a serviceperson's death. Harriet Bubin expressed her sincere thanks on behalf of herself and her children for the flowers she received in 1944 and 1945.

Dec. 14, 1943

Scituate Servicemans Committee,

    I recieved your most welcome gift yesterday and I was very pleased to get it. Such a gift as that allways comes in handy at this time of year. It makes me feel proud to be a citizen of a town which does so much for its boys in the service. I am stationed here in a desert, in Nevada, and it is easy to see the difference between the people here and back home. There is nothing like that New England hospitality.

    I expect to be home New Years, and that money order will serve the purpose of paying part of the expenses.

Thank you again for the gift from home.

              Yours truly,

                Howard F. Burleigh

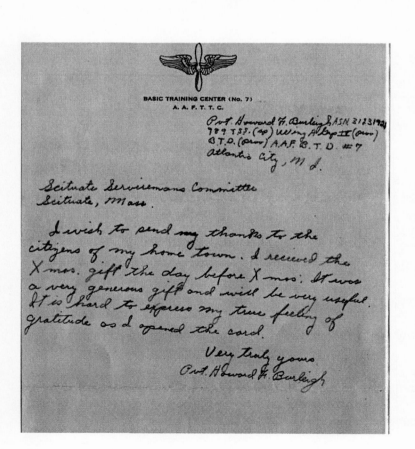

BASIC TRAINING CENTER (No. 7)
A. A. F. T. T. C.

Pvt. Howard H. Burleigh, ASN 31231921
789 TSS. (sp) Wing A Grp II (prov)
BTD. (prov) A.A.F. B.T.D. #7
Atlantic City, N.J.

Scituate Servicemans Committee
Scituate, Mass.

    I wish to send my thanks to the citizens of my home town. I recieved the Xmas. gift the day before Xmas. It was a very generous gift and will be very useful. It is hard to express my true feeling of gratitude as I opened the card.

          Very truly yours
          Pvt. Howard H. Burleigh

HOWARD F. BURLEIGH

Howard Burleigh was born in Scituate on May 31, 1922. He attended Hatherly Elementary School, and was graduated from Scituate High School in 1941. He attended The Franklin Institute, taking courses in automotive maintenance and electricity and worked in the produce department of First National Stores until he entered the service on November 11, 1941.

After basic training in Atlantic City, New Jersey, Howard was sent to Santa Ana Air Base in California and assigned to a Chemical Warfare Section. He went to Las Vegas, Nevada, to attend Aerial Gunnery School, advanced to Corporal and was transferred to Edgewood Arsenal, Maryland, as a Chemical Warfare Instructor.

In his letter, written in December of 1943, Howard says, "There is nothing like that New England hospitality" and at that time, he expected to use his gift to pay part of his expenses to return home at war's end, by the New Year.

Howard received advanced training in Paris, Texas, and then moved to Fort Meade, Maryland, in preparation for overseas duty.

Arriving in the Philippines, he was assigned to the Headquarters of the 38th Infantry Division, Chemical Warfare Section.

Howard was transferred to the 86th Infantry Division until he was sent home in 1946. He was awarded Good Conduct Medal, Asiatic-Pacific Theater Campaign Ribbon, American Theater Ribbon, Philippine Liberation Ribbon with Bronze Service Star, and the Victory Medal.

Howard married Evelyn Bates of Norwell in 1945, and they had five children, including a little girl they adopted from the New England Home for Little Wanderers. They also took care of fifteen babies prior to their adoptions. Evelyn passed away in 1982.

Remarried in 1986, Howard now lives in Middleboro on his ten acre horse farm, where he is retired and cares for his own horses and horses for others. He now has fifteen grandchildren and fifteen great-grandchildren.

FACULTY

FIRST ROW: Mrs. Dolan, Miss Rowell, Mr. Benson, Mr. Calkin, Mr. Wilcox, Miss Hawkes, Miss Harrington.

SECOND ROW: Mrs. Williams, Miss Moulton, Mr. Rogers, Mr. Hawes, Mr. Stewart, Miss Cunneen, Miss Dudley.

THIRD ROW: Miss Giles, Miss Gile, Miss Vollmer, Miss Kingsbury, Mrs. Wilder.

FREDERICK A. CALKIN

Frederick Calkin, son of Andrew and Amelia MacFarlane Calkin, was born on July 17, 1894, in Somerville, MA. He was graduated from the Massachusetts School of Art, studied for one year at George Washington University in Washington, DC, and did graduate work at Harvard and Boston University. He worked in education for ten years at the Springfield Technical High School and for five years at Winthrop High School. He married the former Dorothy Bailey of Scituate on October 8, 1921. They had one son, Thomas. In 1935 Frederick was appointed Principal of Scituate High School.

Frederick witnessed many of his students going off to join the service as WWII began. As principal, he would recommend that they stay and finish High School, maintaining that this would make them more valuable to their country. Many ignored his advice and interrupted their educations to enter the service. On June 15, 1942, at the age of forty-seven, Frederick himself took a leave of absence from his position at the high school, left his home and family on Curtis Street in the Egypt section of Scituate, and enlisted in the United States Army. He was made a Lt. Colonel after his training at Camp Edwards, now Otis Air Force Base on Cape Cod. He served as an Administrative Officer, attaining the rank of Major, and was awarded the American Service Medal and the World War II Victory Medal.

After his discharge in January of 1946, Frederick returned to Scituate and resumed his duties as High School Principal. Shortly thereafter, in 1947, he was named Superintendent of Schools, a position he held until he retired to Hillsboro, NH, in 1951.

Frederick Calkin passed away in 1973.

Frederick's son, Tom, served in the United States Navy. He was graduated from Scituate High School in 1942. Aboard the LST (Landing Ship Tank) 741, he saw action in New Guinea and the Philippines. He was awarded the World War II Victory Medal, American Area Ribbon and the Asiatic-Pacific Theatre Medal. He married Marjorie Smith. Tom passed away on September 20, 1996.

Tom Calkin

George and Betty Carchia

GEORGE CARCHIA

George Carchia, the son of Michael and Esther (Wheeler) Carchia, was born in 1924. He was educated in Scituate schools and lived, for a time, in Brockton. According to his childhood friend, Joe Clapp, George took tap dancing lessons as a child and performed in movie houses in and around Brockton.

George joined the Marine Air Force on December 5, 1942. He received training as a radioman and turret gunner with VMB (Marine Bombing Squadron) 413. He flew aboard PBJ's and B-25 aircraft and attained the rank of Sergeant. PBJ's typically carried fourteen 100-lb. bombs, magnesium flares and anti-personnel bombs. Joe Clapp remembers his friend telling him that when they ran out of bombs on a mission, they would throw out beer and Coca-Cola bottles to harass the enemy because the whistling of the bottles sounded exactly like falling bombs. George served in the Bismarck Archipelago and the Northern Solomon Islands due West of the island of New Guinea. VMB-413 flew raids and submarine searches at night under extremely unfavorable weather conditions.

George was awarded the Distinguished Flying Cross and five Air Medals. These medals are awarded to recognize single acts of heroism or extraordinary achievement while participating in aerial flight, above and beyond the call of duty.

In 1945 George married the former Betty Mariani. They had four children. After the war George worked in carpentry and eventually owned his own business, Carchia Carpentry in Scituate.

George Carchia passed away in 2001.

Carl Chessia.

CARL CLIFFORD CHESSIA

Carl Chessia, known as "Chub", the son of Carl Clifford and Charlotte Young Chessia was born on August 8, 1922 in Scituate. He was graduated from Scituate High School in 1940 where he was Junior Class President. In his yearbook he listed his ambition as "engineer".

After high school "Chub" worked as a moss gatherer and in December of 1942 he was inducted into the United States Army. He served with the 3815th Quartermaster Gas Supply Company driving a 2 1/2-ton truck. He participated in the landings at Normandy driving one of only three trucks that made it ashore. He was awarded the Good Conduct Medal, European African Middle Eastern Theater Campaign Ribbon and the Victory Medal. He was also awarded 5 Battle Stars for supplying the front lines from Normandy to Czechoslovakia.

Chub became a lobsterman when he returned to Scituate after the war. And in 1946 he married Helen Jane Whittaker. They had four sons: Robert Wendell, Thomas Sears, John Carl and Richard Howard. He also worked as an oil truck driver and later for the Town of Scituate from 1969 until 1984 where he was supervisor of Public Grounds. He served on the Housing Authority and as Tree Warden. After he retired he went to work for Webster Cranberry Company in Norwell, MA.

Some of his hobbies included gardening, photography, winemaking and town history. Chub and Jane collected photos and memorabilia related to the Lawson Estate, which they shared at Historical Society dinners and other events.

Carl Clifford Chessia passed away on January 29, 1991.

Somewhere in Belguim   Jan 21, 1945

Dear Committee Members,

I wish to thank you for your Christmas gift.

It gives you a great feeling to know all the people of Scituate are with the "home town" boys in spirit.

When a fellow is so far away from home, he really appreciates his home town. When I was at home I just took it with a grain of salt that I live in Scituate but how I miss it now.

I close for now again thanking the people of Scituate for their remembers + gift.

Sincerely
Howard W. Clapp

Dec 20, 1945.

Dear Selectmen + People of Scituate,

I wish to express my thanks for your very considerate gift.

It gives you a nice feeling to know that the people of your town are thinking of you. It sure gives a soldier a lift in his Army life.

The boys in my barracks said "Boy you come from a nice town" + I said "No" "I come from the best town" Scituate, Massachusetts

Respectfully Yours
Howard Clapp.

HOWARD CLAPP

Howard Clapp, son of Clarence and Annie Haslam Clapp, was born in Scituate on January 26, 1923. He was graduated from Scituate High School in 1940.

Howard enlisted in the service and served with a P 47 Fighter Group. In his 1943 thank you letter, Howard wrote, "The boys in my barracks said, 'Boy you come from a nice town,' and I said, 'No, I come from the best town, Scituate, Massachusetts.'"

In 1945 from somewhere in Belgium, Howard wrote, "When a fellow is so far away from home, he really appreciates his home town. When I was at home I just took it with a grain of salt that I lived in Scituate but how I miss it now."

After the war, Howard returned to Scituate, where he worked as a foreman with the Highway Department and married the former Helen Westerhoff.

Howard Clapp passed away on February 17, 1994 from complications of burns he suffered when his car caught on fire on First Parish Road.

Howard Clapp and his father, Clarence Clapp

U.S. ARMY AIR FORCE

IDENTIFICATION CARD
УДОСТОВЕРЕНИЕ ЛИЧНОСТИ
DOWOD OSOBISTY
LEGITIMACE
LEGITIMACIJA
SZEMÉLYAZONOSSÁGI IGAZOLVÁNY
LEGITIMATION

SIGNATURE

I AM AN AMERICAN AIRMAN.
PLEASE TAKE ME TO YOUR COMMANDING OFFICER AND NOTIFY NEAREST
AMERICAN OR BRITISH MILITARY MISSION IN BELGRADE, BUCHAREST,
POLTAVA OR OTHER NEARBY PLACE. ALSO, PLEASE ARRANGE FOR TRANS-
PORTATION.
THANK YOU

SHOW THIS TO RUSSIANS:
Я АМЕРИКАНСКИЙ ЛЕТЧИК
ПОЖАЛУЙСТА ПРЕДСТАВЬТЕ МЕНЯ ВАШЕМУ КОМАНДИРУ
И УВЕДОМИТЕ БЛИЖАЙШУЮ АМЕРИКАНСКУЮ ИЛИ
БРИТАНСКУЮ ВОЕННУЮ МИССИЮ В БЕЛГРАДЕ,
БУХАРЕСТЕ, ПОЛТАВЕ ИЛИ В ДРУГОМ БЛИЖАЙШЕМ
МЕСТЕ. ТАКЖЕ РАСПОРЯДИТЕСЬ О ПЕРЕДВИЖЕНИИ.
БОЛЬШОЕ СПАСИБО !

Card folded and carried by American Airmen
to be used in the event of a crash or bailout
over Russian held territory.

Noreen, front row middle.

JOSEPH E. CLAPP

Born June 24, 1921, Joe Clapp can trace his family and its land holdings back to a King's Grant in the seventeenth century. He graduated from Scituate High School in 1938 and wants to be remembered as "the Scituate graduate who always wanted to be a pilot." At the time one had to have a college degree to enter pilot training, so Joe busied himself working as a pipe layer for the WPA (Works Progress Administration - a New Deal Program created to provide economic relief for Depression Era citizens).

When Joe heard of an offer of pilot training to those who could pass a college level examination, he took the test, passed with flying colors, was sworn in and returned home to Scituate to find his draft notice awaiting him. He reported for basic training on May 12, 1943 at Fort Devens, Massachusetts, until the miscommunication could be straightened out. From there he was sent to Michigan State College in Lansing, Michigan, where he completed 2 years of college studies in 3 months and was sent to San Antonio, Texas, to train as a pilot, bombardier, and navigator. Selected as a pilot, Joe then went to Basic Flight training and later trained on twin engine planes and received his wings in August 1944 at Ellington Field, Houston, Texas.

On his way to further training in Bangor, Maine, Joe's route took him directly over Scituate. He flew at 500 feet over the town to say goodbye to his family and friends. He eventually arrived in Cerignola, Italy, which was to become his permanent base with the 15th Air Force, 746th Bomb Squadron, 456th Bomb Group. Joe flew B-24 Liberator aircraft and bombed targets in southern and central Europe. The group flew over 185 bombing missions.

After two final bombing runs over the Senio River in Italy, Joe returned from the war on July 13, 1945, flying one of one hundred and nineteen planes arriving at Bradley Field in Connecticut. He married the former Noreen M. Keefe, a 2nd Lt. Army Nurse stationed at Fort Devens, Massachusetts on July 31, 1945. They lived at Fort Devens until Noreen was discharged in September. After living for a time in South Boston, the Clapp family returned to Scituate to the house Joe had built using materials from a dismantled Army barracks building in Savin Hill, Massachusetts. They had four children: 3 girls

Noreen Keefe Clapp

and a boy, and Joe went to work for Alan Wheeler in construction. Joe eventually went out on his own, building homes and doing remodeling throughout the South Shore, Quincy, and Boston. Noreen passed away in 1995. Joe subsequently married the former Patricia McGinnis. She passed away in 1999.

Joe is now retired at age eighty-three. He helped his son, Thomas in the construction business until a heart attack forced him to retire completely in 2003. Joe now lives in Norwell with his daughter on Clapp family land that was once part of the town of Scituate.

Harry J. Cook

HARRY J. COOK

Harry Cook was born in Boston, Massachusetts on July 7, 1921. He attended Scituate schools and entered the service in March 1942. He was stationed first at the Naval Training Station in Boston, MA. He served for a time at Camp Peary, Virginia on the James River near Williamsburg, and the Naval Construction Training Center at Davisville, RI.

While home on leave in 1944, Harry married the former Jean Wagner. When Harry returned to his naval duties, Jean worked as a forklift operator at the Hingham, MA Ammunition Depot, now Wompatuck State Park.

The SeaBees, specialized naval battalions, were created to fulfill the growing need for base construction, primarily in the Pacific Theater, although SeaBee units performed their duties in all theaters of the war.

Harry served with his Combat Construction Maintenance Unit in the Marianna Islands in the South Pacific on the islands of Saipan, Tinian, and Guam. After Guam was captured from the Japanese, the SeaBee units reconstructed the bombed out airstrip. Harry often worked during the night, in the dark, while being subjected to sniper fire from hidden enemy troops. Thanks to the hard work of the construction battalions, Guam eventually became the Advanced Headquarters of the United States Pacific Fleet, a base for B29 aircraft bound for Japan and a huge war supply center.

After his discharge in January of 1946, Harry returned to Scituate and worked for Allan Wheeler Construction as a heavy equipment operator. He retired in 1983.

Harry J. Cook passed away at age seventy-five in 1996.

Jerome Francis Patrick Crowley

Christmas
Dec 25, 1944

Citizens of Scituate,

I want to express my thanks for my home town remembering me on Christmas.

I wasn't sure how to head this letter as I wanted to thank the town as a whole and the wonderful spirit it has.

I am now able to get to Scituate now and then and after not be able to see the town for sometime it really is something. Before I went away I never appreciated it but now I find there is no place like it.

Well I never was much at writing letters so I will close.

thank you again

"Pat" Crowley

JEROME FRANCIS PATRICK CROWLEY

Born March 17, 1924, St. Patrick's Day, Jerome Francis Patrick Crowley was graduated from Scituate High School in 1941. He volunteered for the Navy on December 8, the day after the Japanese attacks on Pearl Harbor. He entered active service in Newport, RI at the Naval Training Station on January 17, 1942. After spending six months in Jacksonville, Florida, at Aviation Machinist Mate School, he was assigned to Patrol Boat (PT) Training in Melville, RI. Located just north of the main United States Naval Base in Newport, RI, Melville was set up in 1941 by the Navy to meet the increasing demand for trained personnel.

PT boats had crews of fourteen men. They were eighty feet long and constructed of mahogany, spruce and oak woods. Capable of travelling at sixty miles per hour, they were armed with twin 50-caliber guns in the rear as well as four torpedo launchers.

"Pat" was eventually sent to the Pacific Theater of Operations and served aboard the PT 156 in the Solomon Islands Campaign. This operation denied the Japanese a series of airbases that had the potential to cut off Australia and New Zealand from their life lines on America's West Coast. Once under American control, these bases provided the support for the retaking of the Philippines.

In June of 1944, Pat returned to the United States and was sent to Florida, where he participated in the filming of the John Wayne movie, "They Were Expendable," based on the W. L. White book depicting a PT Boat Squadron's actions in the war in the Pacific.

At the end of the war, Pat was sent to a base in Iceland, where he met his future wife, Bonnie. In 1947 they returned to the United States, where Pat was discharged. He was awarded the World War II Victory Medal, American Area Medal, Good Conduct Medal, and Asiatic-Pacific Area Medal (with three stars).

At home, Pat has worked in construction. He has been involved in the building of Otis Air Base on Cape Cod; Bedford Air Base; The Callahan Tunnel, connecting East Boston to the City of Boston; The Massachusetts Turnpike Extension, connecting the MASS Pike to downtown Boston; Logan International Airport; and Routes 24, 195 and 140.

He now works as an instructor in a heavy equipment apprentice program. He continues to live in Scituate. He and Bonnie have five children and many grandchildren.

Barbara Curran, Row 4, Second from Left.

BARBARA CURRAN

Barbara Curran was born on July 7, 1921, in Scituate. She was graduated from Scituate High School in 1940. She married Eddie Pelletier before entering the WAC (Women's Army Corps) in May of 1944. Eddie was also in the service and was killed in the war.

After training at Fort Oglethorpe, Georgia, Barbara was assigned as a Supply Clerk and stationed at Goose Bay, Labrador. A large air base had been established in this Canadian Province as part of the "Lend-Lease" agreement executed between President Franklin Roosevelt and Winston Churchill, whereby the United States supplied materiel to aid Great Britain before our official involvement in World War II. Goose Bay was chosen because of its location on a level sandy plain along the polar route to Europe. It served as a refueling stop for aircraft being ferried to our allies. During WWII 24,000 airplanes passed through what became the busiest airport in the world at this time. There were more than 16,000 American Service Personnel stationed in Goose Bay.

After her service ended, Barbara was graduated from the Massachusetts General Hospital School of Practical Nursing. She married Paul Shaw in 1947. After moving to Maine, Barbara worked in hospital settings and did private duty nursing. She and Paul had one daughter, Marie.

Barbara was a lifetime member of the Veterans of Foreign Wars (VFW) and the American Legion. She also served as Post Commander of the American Legion Auxiliary.

Barbara Curran Pelletier Shaw passed away on May 1, 1997.

Benjamin Curran 1947, before Memorial Day parade.

BENJAMIN H. CURRAN

Benjamin Curran, the son of Bartholomew and Delia Freeman Curran, was born in Scituate on August 11, 1906. After being graduated from Scituate High School, he worked as a plumber for J. Edward Harvey.

In August of 1942, Benjamin enlisted in the United States Navy. He was sent to Wentworth Institute in Boston to attend their Diesel School. He next went to Norfolk, Virginia, for his basic training. After spending time in Tampa, Florida, Benjamin was assigned to the USS Shilkellamy, a gasoline tanker that delivered oil and cargo from Brisbane, Australia, to Port Moresby, New Guinea. He attained the rank of Watertender First Class. He also served aboard the USS Niblack, a destroyer that saw action first in the European Theater and later in the Pacific arriving shortly after the Japanese surrender.

Benjamin was discharged on September 9, 1945; he returned to Scituate and his job as a plumber. He married the former Helen C. Horgan, and they had two sons, Wayne and Kevin.

At the time of his death on July 2, 1963, at the age of fifty-six, Benjamin Curran was employed as a custodian at the Scituate Town Hall.

Charles W. Curran

Nov 17, 1944.
Friday

Dear Reggie:
    I received the five dollar money
order which was sent to me for Christmas
and I want to take this time to thank
you and the people of Scituate for the
thought that you sent with it as for
the money I think every one in the
service will be able to use it. I am
well and getting along fine and hope
you and the people of Scituate have
a merry, merry Christmas.
    Thanking you again I remain

    Charles W Curran.

CHARLES WILLIAM CURRAN

 Charles W. Curran was born February 24, 1910, in Scituate, Massachusetts, the son of Irish immigrants from County Cork, Ireland. He was the fourth child in a family of six sons: John, Benjamin, Bartholomew, George (Charles' twin) and Tom (an adopted cousin). He attended Scituate schools and worked as a truck driver and greenskeeper at the Scituate Country Club. In 1936, at age 26, he became a call firefighter for the Scituate Fire Department, and in 1940 he was made a permanent firefighter.

On July 12, 1943, Charles enlisted in the Navy because he was too old (33 years) to be drafted. Although he was married, he felt the need to join the ranks of enlisted men because "everyone needed to do their part to help their country." Charles' choice of the Navy was natural because he had grown up next to the ocean and, he also thought it "better to sleep in a hammock than a foxhole."

Charles completed "boot camp" (Naval Basic Training), Fire Fighting School and the Teachers Training Course at the Newport Naval Base in Rhode Island. He was then sent to Virginia, where he served at Newport News, Norfolk and Camp Peary near Williamsburg. He was temporarily assigned to the SeaBees, the Naval Construction Battalion before being reassigned as a Specialist F, a Firefighter Instructor. His job was to teach recruits how to fight gasoline, oil, and other types of fires on ships and piers. Shipboard fires were particularly horrendous when one considers the amounts of fuel and explosives that were carried, and the dangers faced from submarine and kamikaze attacks.

Charles remembered one recruit from Alabama he had sent into a ship's hold that had been set on fire. The man backed away from the flaming ship and started running down the street shouting "You can shoot me right here, but I won't go in there because it's like going into hell". It took a couple of MP's (military police) to bring him back!

After the war, in November, 1945, Charles returned to Scituate with his wife, Ebba, who gave birth to their son, Charles, in December. Upon his return to civilian life, Charles was reinstated to the Scituate Fire Department. In 1954, he was promoted to Deputy Fire Chief and became Chief of the Department in 1966.

The disciplines learned in the Navy---hard work, honor, loyalty and your good word were the values he worked and lived by. Charles Curran passed away on May 8, 2003.

Chief John F. Curran and his daughters Jean and Mary Susan.

JOHN FREEMAN CURRAN

John Freeman Curran, the son of Bartholomew and Delia Freeman Curran was born in Scituate on March 6, 1905.

John's twenty-six year career in the US Coast Guard began in 1928. He was involved in patrols designed to stop illegal "rum-runners" using the many Scituate beaches and the banks of the North River to bring their goods ashore during prohibition which lasted from 1920 until 1933.

When World War II began, John and other armed guardsmen patrolled Scituate beaches on the alert for signs of enemy landings. During the fall and winter months, it was bitterly cold and at the end of their patrols the men's pants legs would be frozen to their skin from the combination of wind and salt spray. John related that the pants could actually stand up by themselves after removal because of their frozen condition.

During the war years the cliffs, Minot and Sand Hills were sparsely populated. There were no streetlights and very few house lights during the winter months making clandestine signaling very visible to enemy vessels at sea off our shores. It was said that there was an individual living on Third Cliff who was collaborating with the Germans by flashing lights out to sea as messages or to give directions. It was up to the Coast Guard to detect and put a stop to such activities.

John Curran was stationed at various times at the Coast Guard Station on Surfside Road in Minot; the New Coast Guard Station on First Cliff; the Gurnett Coast Guard Station on Duxbury Beach; Boston Light; Graves Light; Boston Lifeboat Station and Point Judith, RI Coast Guard Station. Although John's service kept him on the North Atlantic shoreline, guardsmen were assigned throughout the theaters of World War II. They piloted landing vessels because of their expertise in maneuvering small boats in the surf and onto beaches, many of their lives were lost along with the soldiers they were transporting. Coast Guard vessels provided escorts for convoys and hunted German UBoats in the North Atlantic. According to the US Coast Guard website, the Coast Guard sank a total of thirteen UBoats during the war. In May of 1942 the crew of the USS Icarus, CG sank the U-352 and then rescued the surviving crewmen off the coast of North Carolina becoming the first US servicemen to take German prisoners in World War II.

John married the former Susan Burns and they had two daughters Jean and Mary Susan. He retired from the Coast Guard as a Chief Boatswain Mate in 1954 and later became a custodian in the Scituate schools.

John Freeman Curran passed away on January 18, 1978 at the age of seventy-two.

William Curran and his dad.

Adak, Alaska 1943.

WILLIAM CHARLES CURRAN

 William Curran, also known as "Shillelagh" was the son of Charles P. and Delia Dorsey Curran. He was born on November 12, 1914 in Scituate, MA. He was graduated from Scituate High School in 1932 where he participated in football, basketball and track.

After high school he worked as an auto mechanic. He joined the Army Air Corps in September of 1940 along with a group of his friends. William was assigned to the 247th Army Air Corps Base Unit as a mechanic working on B-29 aircraft. He served in the Aleutian Islands off the coast of Alaska and attained the rank of Master Sergeant.

William was awarded the Good Conduct Medal, American Defense Service Medal and the Asiatic Pacific Theatre Campaign Ribbon with 1 Battle Star.

After his discharge in October of 1945, "Shillelagh" returned to Scituate and went to work for the Scituate Highway Department.

William C. "Shillelagh" Curran passed away on February 27, 1962.

January 10, 1944

Town of Scituate
Scituate, Mass.

Dear Friends:-

Once again the Christmas
season has come and gone and once
more we in service have been
remembered by you with greetings
and gifts.

We thank you from the bottom
of our hearts.

To me Scituate is home.
There is no other place on earth
that can take its place. And it is
most gratifying to be able to
call each one of you "friend."

Thanking you again,
I am,

Sincerely

William W. Curtis
2nd Lt. A.C.

WILLIAM WHITNEY CURTIS

William Whitney Curtis was born in Quincy, MA on July 4, 1903. He spent summers in Scituate with his Aunt and Uncle after the death of his mother. At one time he was employed in the horse barns of Thomas Lawson's Estate "Dreamwold".

After trying to join the Army in 1919 and being discharged for being underage, he furthered his education and applied to West Point where he was denied admission because of a heart murmur.

When his Aunt passed away, William and his wife, Eloise (Stevens) returned to Scituate where, in 1935, The Curtis Home Bakery was established. It initially operated out of the old family homestead and produced doughnuts, Swedish Bread and pies. Eloise gained nationwide recognition for her homemade "frosted Easter Bonnet cakes" which were displayed in the window of the shop on Front Street. They were written up in the Boston Globe's rotogravure section and put on exhibit in the First National Bank in Boston during the Easter Season. The bakery ceased operation temporarily but reopened in 1943 "as a needed morale booster toward the war effort" according to Mayor Curley of Boston.

In 1942, at age 39, William applied for Officers' Candidate School and, minus the "heart murmur", went on to graduate as a 2nd Lieutenant in the US Army Air Corps in 1943. He was stationed at Gander Airfield in Newfoundland and served as Base Mess Officer, gaining the rank of 1st Lieutenant before being discharged in 1946. Gander Air Station was a so-called steppingstone base. Along with bases in Labrador, Greenland and Iceland, they were used to ferry short-range fighter planes from the United States to Great Britain beginning in early 1941 and continuing throughout the war.

William's 1944 thank you letter to the Town he relates that "There is no other place on earth that can take its place. And it is most gratifying to be able to call each one of you 'friend'".

William died at the Brockton Veterans' Hospital on January 31, 1990 and is buried in his beloved Scituate.

Dec 30,1943.

The Selectmon of the town of Scituate
Scituate,Mass.

Dear Sirs:-
        I would like to express my appreciation through you to
the people of the town for the Christmas gift I received several
days ago.It was a very pleasant surprise and came in very handy,
especially right now.In fact,I was envied by the rest of the fellows
and one remarked,"That must be one swell town even if it does have
a tough name to pronounce."
        Things are going along great out here and it won't be long
now.Please give my best wishes for a happy New Year to the people
of the town.

                                Sincerely,
                                Art Damon,Jr.

        Lieut.A.H.Damon U.S.N.R.
        U.S.S.DASHIELL
        %Flt P.O.
        San Francisco,Calif.

THE BOSTON DAILY GLOBE

Destroyer Laffey Went in Swinging at Battleship

Scituate Officer Tells How It Feels to Be Matched Against Goliath

(Photo by Kitrosser)

SURVIVORS—Lieut. (j. g.) Arthur H. Damon Jr., left, and
Lieut. (j. g.) James Williams of the destroyer Laffey, recuperate at Scituate after their little ship punished the Japs
severely before being sunk by a battlewagon.

ARTHUR H. DAMON, JR.

Arthur H. Damon, son of Arthur Herbert and Margery (Spicer) Damon, was born on April 8, 1920. He grew up on Mann Hill Road and was graduated from Scituate High School in 1938. He attended Bates College in Lewiston, Maine, and entered the United States Navy in 1940. He received his commission in 1941.

Arthur was first assigned to the USS Lamson, a destroyer, and was then transferred as communications officer to the USS Laffey. A **Boston Globe** article reported that, after sinking 2 Japanese destroyers and damaging a Japanese cruiser, the USS Laffey was torpedoed by the Japanese destroyer Teruzuki and sunk when her ammunition magazines exploded. Arthur's group of thirty-seven survivors managed to hold on to a raft, which carried badly wounded men, until the next day when they were picked up by US Navy rescue boats. He returned to Scituate for a brief leave before returning to duty on the USS Dashiell, followed by duty aboard the USS Dortch as Executive Officer, taking part in the capture and occupation of Saipan and the Battle of the Philippine Sea. In September 1945, Arthur was assigned as an aide and flag secretary on the staff of Commander Destroyer Force Six, US Atlantic Fleet, serving until August 1947.

After the war, Arthur continued his Naval career in several capacities, including his roles as commanding officer of the USS Maloy, commanding officer of the USS Fechteler, instructor at the US Naval War College, Newport, RI, and chief of staff of the First Naval District, Boston, MA. He was graduated from Duke University in 1948. He married Mary MacDonald of Portland, Maine, and, later, Joan Hamilton of Rye, NY. They lived in Newport, RI, where Arthur was a real estate broker and worked for the Preservation Society of Newport County, serving as a guide at the Breakers, once the summer home of the Vanderbilt family, after retiring from the Navy.

Arthur Damon was awarded the Purple Heart, Presidential Unit Citation, American Defense Medal, Philippine Liberation Ribbon with two stars, the Asiatic-Pacific Campaign Medal with 12 stars, the Navy Occupation Service Medal, the National Defense Service Medal, the World War II Victory Medal, the American Campaign Medal, and the China Service Medal.

Captain Arthur H. Damon, Jr., USN (Ret.) passed away on May 24, 1995.

Richard Damon

RICHARD DAMON

Richard Damon, brother of Arthur, was born on August 30, 1924. He was graduated from Scituate High School and entered the United States Navy in September of 1942.

After attending training schools in Middletown, CT; Athens, GA; Memphis, TN; Bainbridge, MD; and New London, CT, Richard was assigned to the USS Euryale, a submarine tender.

In 1944 the Euryale sailed from New York to Brisbane, Australia, and from there to Milne Bay, New Guinea. This was a strategically important area because it dominated the sea-lanes to Australia, and its airstrip, constructed by Allied Army engineers in 1942, provided a base for attacks over the Solomon Sea. While there, Richard and his crewmates refitted submarines and repaired surface ships. They also established a forward base and rest camp for submariners by clearing the island and constructing buildings, all while refitting twenty-six submarines. In 1944 they moved on to the island of Guam where they constructed another sub base and rest camp.

After the Japanese surrender in September of 1945, the USS Euryale sailed to Sasebo, Japan, the site of a large Japanese Naval Base. They were among the first occupiers of the defeated country. Here the crew worked with Japanese submarines, preparing them for disposal.

Richard was awarded the World War II Victory Medal, the American Theatre Medal, the Good Conduct Medal, and the Asiatic-Pacific Theatre Medal.

After his 1946 discharge, Richard returned home to Scituate and married Ebba Helen Hellman of Portland, Maine, on May 17, 1947. They had three children: Jennifer, Jonathan, and Erick. There are now two grandchildren.

Richard worked as a Life Guard and Special Police Officer, and for several insurance companies. In addition to owning Ebba Damon Real Estate and Damon Insurance Agency in Scituate Harbor, he also worked for FEMA (the Federal Emergency Management Agency) in Washington, DC.

Richard served three terms as a Scituate Selectman, Chairman of the Advisory Board, Civil Defense Director, and President of the Hatherly PTA. He retired in 2002. Sadly, Richard passed away in 2005.

U.S.S. Altair
Div. 5
Fleet Post Office
New York City
New York, U.S.A.
Dec. 10, 1943

Servicemens Committee,
Town Hall
Scituate, Mass.
Gentlemen,

    May I say thank you for the beautiful christmas card and the money order you so thoughtfully enclosed.

    It seems difficult, under the circumstance, to realize that some day I shall return. When I do I hope that I shall be previledged to give what little I may and to work beside my townfolk and to keep Scituate what she is, the finest town on earth.

    May I take this opportunity to wish everyone, great and small, a joyous Christmas and a successfull New Year.

    Thank you again.

        John E. Daniels Jr.

John E. Daniels Jr.
U.S.S. Altair - Div. 5

World War I

JOHN E. DANIELS, JR.

John E Daniels, 1950.

John E. Daniels, Sr., a native of Glasgow Scotland, immigrated to Nova Scotia, and eventually relocated to Boston where his son, John E. Daniels, Jr. was born on August 24, 1898.

At the outbreak of World War I in 1914, John lied about his age and enlisted in the US Navy. He was assigned to the USS Pennsylvania, a battleship that was deployed in the western Atlantic and the Caribbean. John served aboard until the end of World War I in 1918, at which time he and his father formed "The Scottish Company." They presented the songs and plays of Robert Burns, appearing in Nova Scotia, New York, and throughout New England.

John eventually graduated from Bentley College with a degree in accounting. He also graduated from the New England Conservatory of Music, where he met his future wife, who was also a student.

On December 7, 1941, John's old ship, the USS Pennsylvania was in dry-dock at Pearl Harbor. It was damaged but not sunk, and John was incensed. According to his daughter, his exact words were "They can't do that to my ship." He reenlisted in the Navy and was assigned to the USS Altair, a destroyer tender. The Altair carried out upkeep, repairs and tender duty for the Atlantic Fleet and, for a time operated out of Guantanamo Bay, "Gitmo," Cuba where John acquired a pet monkey.

In his letter, written in December of 1945 from aboard the Altair, John wrote of his wish to return to Scituate and help to keep it "the finest town on earth."

After his discharge in 1945, John worked as a salesman for Watson Chevrolet on Brook Street, sang in local choral groups, church choirs and Joe Barca's Barbershop Quartet. He also drove a taxi and worked for Brockton Gas. He earned the title of Mayor of Scituate for his work in collecting litter along the streets. John was also a Past Commander and Chaplain of the American Legion.

Despite some hard times, John always had a bright outlook and with a smile would say, "Everything will be all right."

John E. Daniels passed away in April of 1975.

EGYPT
MASSACHUSETTS
Jan. 2, 1943

To the Selectmen and the Citizens
of Scituate, Mass.

Many thanks for the
Christmas card and the money
order. It was a kind expression
on the part of the citizens of
Scituate to remember their
servicemen in this manner,
and I am sure one and all
appreciated it.

With this letter goes my
wish for a Happy New Year
to you all.

Sincerely,
Hubert Denker,
Chief Boatswain's Mate
U. S. Coast Guard Reserve

HUBERT DENKER

Olive, James and Hubert Denker

Hubert Denker, the son of William and Eleanora DiFatta Denker was born in Dorchester, Massachusetts, on March 30, 1903. His father passed away when Hubert was three years old and his mother when he was thirteen. Hubert went to live with his sister in Haverhill and became a student at Boston Latin School. This is where he first learned to play the violin and dreamed of someday joining the Boston Symphony Orchestra. This dream never came true. He did, however, practice daily and played his fiddle for many local square dances in the 1950's.

He maintained his love for classical music and, according to his son, "when his fingers grew stiff with age, he joked that "fiddlin' country music was harder than playing real music on the violin."

A 1925 Harvard graduate, Hubert served his country as a Chief Boatswains Mate, Police Officer in the Coast Guard guarding the Hingham Shipyard. It was here that 24,000 Bethlehem Steel employees built 100 destroyer escorts and LST (Tank Landing Ships) for the war effort, toiling 24 hours per day, seven days per week. Great care had to be taken to protect the facility from sabotage both from the land and from submarines off the coast.

Hubert married the former Olive Louise Whitehead from Boston on August 7, 1926. She was the youngest of thirteen children and the only one born in the United States. Her siblings were all born in England. Olive's sister, Bertha, was married to architect Maurice Hosmer. He was responsible for the design and building of many homes in the Egypt section of Scituate. Hubert and Olive bought a house at 14 Ann Vinal Road built by Maurice and were living there when their son, James was born.

After the war, Hubert returned to the real estate and insurance business.

He died at the age of 64 in 1967.

Somewhere in England
Dec. 5 43.

Town Hall
Scituate.

Dear Sirs;

I am sending this letter to
thank you for the gift which I received from the Town of Scituate.

It is good to know — that the
folks of the town never forget any
of the many fellows who leave for
service in our armed forces.

I know that we all wish to
get this job done so as to get
back home.

Wishing you all a very Merry
Christmas.
I remain;

Truly yours
Edwin Dolan;

EDWIN LEWIS DOLAN

Edwin Lewis Dolan was born March 10, 1925. A 1942 Scituate High School graduate, he worked at the Bethlehem Hingham Shipyard from October 1942 to May 1943 helping to produce numerous destroyer escorts and LST (Tank Landing Ships). He also served as an Air Raid Warden during this time, patrolling the town to insure compliance with blackout regulations. Because Scituate is a coastal community, this was of particular importance because night time lights shining out to sea could provide beacons to off-shore enemy submarine patrols as well as signposts to enemy saboteurs being landed to furnish information to the Germans.

Eddie was drafted into the Army on May 12, 1943. He became a Corporal in Company K, 121st Infantry, 8th Division, responsible for operating the BAR or Browning Automatic Rifle. This weapon can fire from 300 to 650 rounds per minute and is considered extremely reliable although quite heavy at 15.5 pounds.

In his letter, written from "somewhere in England" Eddie thanked the town for "never forgetting any of the many fellows who leave for service" and expressed his wish to "get the job done so as to get back home."

Like his older brother, Phillip, Eddie fought in Normandy, arriving on July 4, 1944. He also fought in Dinard, Brest and the Crozon Peninsula in France; Luxembourg, Hurtgen, Rhine and the Ruhr Pocket in Germany. He was discharged on November 6, 1945.

Among his awards were the American Theater Ribbon, European-African-Middle Eastern Theater Ribbon with 1 Bronze Service Star, 3 Overseas Bars, Good Conduct Medal, World War II Victory Medal, 2 Bronze Campaign Stars for the Battle of Normandy and the Battle of Northern France. He also received the Croix de Guerre, an award from the French government for specific acts of bravery.

Eddie married and had five children. His son, James E. Dolan II served and died in Viet Nam in 1970.

Edwin Lewis Dolan died in 1994.

Phillip B. Dolan

PHILLIP B. DOLAN

Born on January 30, 1922, Phillip B. Dolan was graduated from Scituate High School in 1940.

Phillip was drafted into the Army on November 11, 1942. He was assigned to the 30th "Old Hickory" Division, (named for Andrew Jackson, famed Indian fighter and victor in the Battle of New Orleans during the War of 1812) 120th infantry. He trained at Camp Blanding, Florida; Camp Forrest, Tennessee; and in preparation for overseas deployment, at Camp Atterbury, Indiana, where over 275,000 men were trained for participation in World War II.

On February 12, 1944, Phillip sailed aboard the SS Argentina, a former Moore-McCormack cruise ship converted to a US Army Transport (USAT) headed to England.

Phillip and the 30th Division landed in Normandy on June 13, 1944, D-Day plus 8, where 600,000 men and 104,000 vehicles came ashore between June 6th and February 18th. They proceeded through Northern France and into Germany, earning the name "Workhorse of the Western Front" for their participation in the Ardennes Offensive from December 16 to January 25, 1945. The Division linked up with the Soviet Army (our allies) at Magdeburg on the Elbe River in Germany in April 1945. According to his wife, Cody, Phillip never forgot the Normandy hedgerows, which were 6-foot high ridges of root-packed earth overgrown with thickets of oak, beech and chestnut trees, flanked by ditches. He also recalled the blitz through France, the rainy Thanksgiving near the Inde River in Germany and the snow and cold in the Ardennes during the Battle of the Bulge. Phillip received a Bronze Star and many campaign medals.

Returning to Scituate in August 1945, he married the former Cora E. Brown the following February. They had one son, Robert John. Phillip remained proud of his unit and their World War II service. He attended many reunions including one aboard the Queen Mary, the ship that brought him home from Southampton, England, to New York.

After living in Hollywood, Florida, for 41 years, the Dolan family returned to Scituate where Phillip passed away in April of 1995.

UNITED STATES ARMY

Dec. 29, 1942

Dear Sirs;

I want to thank you, at this time, for your kind remembrances of me at Christmas time.

I am a lot more fortunate than my many boy friends, from Scituate, as I am so close to home being stationed here at Edwards. I don't know how long I'll be here but where ever my Uncle Sam sends me I'll all ways be thinking of my many friends in the town.

Wishing you all a Happy and Prosperous New Year, I remain,

Sincerely yours,
Joseph A. Donovan

JOSEPH A. DONOVAN

Joseph Donovan was born November 16, 1912. He summered in Scituate at 423 Tilden Road. He was inducted into the army on November 14,1940, and assigned to Camp Edwards (now Otis Air National Guard Base) on Cape Cod as a Military Policeman.

Writing from Camp Edwards, Joseph mentions in his thank you letter that he considers himself "a lot more fortunate than many of my friends from Scituate, as I am so close to home. . . but wherever my Uncle Sam sends me I'll always be thinking of my many friends in the town."

Joseph was later trained in the use of a flame-thrower. This is a weapon which consists of a tank carried on the back of the soldier, connected to a hand held hose which is capable of shooting a burning stream of liquid fuel at enemy troops or positions. It was especially useful in attacking Japanese fortifications in the Pacific Islands. American soldiers were faced with a unique situation where the enemy had constructed strongholds dug deep into the coral hills in positions overlooking American assault forces. These caves were defended by troops who were trained to fight to the death. Surrender was not an option. In order to drive them out and prevent huge numbers of U. S. casualties flame-throwers as well as explosives were used to seal the caves.

Assigned to the 103rd Infantry, Corporal Joseph Donovan was sent to Luzon in the Philippines during the campaign to retake the islands from the Japanese. On March 12, 1945 he was shot and killed while participating in the Antipolo-Teresa phase of the campaign that eventually liberated southeast Luzon. He was thirty-two years old.

Joseph was initially buried in the United States Armed Forces Cemetery at Balintawak Estates, Luzon. His body was moved to the permanent cemetery at the former Fort William McKinley (now Fort Bonifacio) near Manila, where he rests among the 17,206 Americans killed in the Philippines.

His insurance proceeds were sent by his family to the LaSalette Shrine in Ipswich, Massachusetts, where a chapel is dedicated to his memory.

Reverend George J. Williams S.J blessed Joseph's grave in the Philippines in June of 1950. A photo of the service was sent to his family.

ANZIO BEACHHEAD, ITALY
MARCH 13, 1944

To the People of Scituate:

Having been away from Scituate for over a year now,
I have come to the conclusion that no plade can ever equal
or surpass myhome town, Scituate. A person doesn't realize the value of things until they have been taken away
from him. Boy, I'd give anything to see Scituate this minute.

I just received your Christmas Card with the five-dollar
money order. The letter, which was mailed last November,
went through replacement depots and therefor was delayed.
But it came at the right time for me, for I haven't been paid
in 3 months. I can only say, Thanks a Million, folks!, and
hope that will prove to you that I'm pleased with the gift.
It certainly makes afellow feel real proud to know that people
back home are thinking of him.

I certainly have seen plenty of excitement in my five
months of combat in Italy. I have had some interesting times
being an M.P. I am always wishing that I could meet some other
soldier from Scituate, so we could talk about home, friends, and
good old days- I understand that there are several over in this
sector. I'd liked to have their addresses if possible.

Thanks for the card and gift, I really appreciate it.
Hope to be seeing you all soon.

Sincerely yours,

Ernest B. Dorr

ERNEST B. DORR

Ernest Dorr was born in North Scituate, Massachusetts, on May 8, 1922. His parents were W. Stanley and Edith Mabel (McNutt) Dorr. He was graduated from Scituate High School in 1940 and went on to attend Boston University, when World War II intervened.

Ernest served in the 45th Infantry Division, 14th Armored Tank Battalion of the United States Army in the European Theater during World War II.

In his thank you letter written from the Anzio beachhead in Italy, Ernie wrote in 1943, "Having been away from Scituate for over a year now, I have come to the conclusion that no place can ever equal or surpass my home town, Scituate. A person doesn't realize the value of things until they have been taken away from him . . . It certainly makes a fellow feel proud to know that people back home are thinking of him." His gift was mailed in November of 1943 and took over four months to catch up with him in Italy.

Everett and Ernest Dorr

After the war, Ernie returned to Boston University and was graduated from its School of Education. He married Alice Hayward from Brockton in 1947, and they had three sons and one daughter.

Ernie played semi-professional football with the Quincy Manets from 1946 until 1948. He also played for the Bridgewater Town Team. He held teaching and coaching positions at Ipswich, MA, High School, Tilton School for Boys, in New Hampshire, Sippican Elementary School in Marion, MA, and the New Bedford Public Schools until his retirement in 1981. He was the Charter Member President of the Old Rochester Regional High School Boosters Club for its first four years; Past Patron of the Alcyone Chapter #122, Order of the Eastern Star in Marion, MA; Past Master of the Pythagorean Lodge A.F. & A.M. in Marion, MA; member of the Royal Arch Chapter of Wareham, MA; Member of the Sutton Commandery #16 Knights Templar of New Bedford, MA, and a member of the Reservation Golf Club.

Ernest Dorr passed away on November 8, 1989, while playing golf in Bradenton, Florida.

Dec. 3, 1944
Central Pacific

Dear Sirs;
    I have just received your M.O.
for five dollars. I want to thank
you for all that it stands for. It
shows that you people care about us
and think about us when you do
something like that. Really I am very
grateful and it sure comes in handy
for cigarettes and toilet articles.
    Thanking you again.
                    Sincerely,
                Cpl. Everett W. Dorr

EVERETT DORR

Everett "Evie" Dorr was born on August 4, 1924. He was graduated from Scituate High School in 1942, where he was an eleven-letter athlete. He attended Boston University, where he played freshman football. His college career was interrupted in early 1943 when he entered the United States Marine Corps, first as a paratrooper, then as a machine gunner.

In 1944 Cpl. Everett Dorr wrote from the Central Pacific, "I want to thank you for all that it [the money order from the Town] stands for. It shows that you people care about us and think about us when you do something swell like that. Really I am very grateful and it sure comes in handy for cigarettes and toilet articles."

During the Marine amphibious landings on Iwo Jima in 1945, Evie received a severe shrapnel wound to his left leg on the second day of the invasion. He was evacuated to Honolulu and eventually returned to the mainland for treatment. It was feared that he would never be active in sports again, but he surprised everyone. Evie returned to Boston University, where in 1946, 1947 and 1948 he place kicked for the football team winning the coveted Swede Nelson Award in 1947.

Evie and Ernie

After his college graduation, Evie was hired as the coach of Cohasset High School's football and baseball teams. He eventually headed up the basketball, track and golf squads, as well as serving as Athletic Director for twenty-five years.

In 1949 Evie married the former Frances Skinner, and they had three boys, followed by five grandchildren and one great grandchild. He retired in 1959, played golf and went fishing. He was also able to enjoy sports as a mere spectator.

Everett Dorr passed away on November 11, 1991.

James Driscoll

JAMES EDWARD DRISCOLL

James "Ed" Driscoll was born on January 26, 1909, and was graduated from Scituate High School. On September 16, 1942, he enlisted in the United States Coast Guard and was assigned as an Aerographer's Mate. This is a term used in the military to denote a meteorologist or weatherman. Ed served on ships out of Boston, Provincetown, Truro, and Gloucester, Massachusetts; Southwest Harbor, Maine; and Lakehurst, New Jersey.

The role of the Coast Guard during World War II was vital to protecting merchant ships and military convoys from sinking by German U-boats (submarines), as well as preventing secret landings by foreign saboteurs such as occurred on Long Island, New York, in June of 1942, when six German spies were discovered by a Coast Guard Beach Patrol.

A story related by Ed's daughter, Nina, tells of an afternoon Coast Guard Sea Patrol that was signaled repeatedly by a passing navy plane. The plane finally flew so low that Ed and his shipmates could see the pilots waving frantically. The captain of the ship arrived on deck and was able to translate the Morse Coded message from the plane's crew: "Get the hell out of there so we can bomb the German sub you're sitting on top of!"

After the war, Ed, his wife, the former Marjorie Hill, and their two children moved to Japan, where Ed was employed as a civilian with the occupation forces as an auditor in the post office. Later, he went to Korea in a similar capacity. Ed was fluent in the Japanese, German and French languages. He returned to the United States in 1962, and after working for the Federal Government in Northern Virginia, Ed retired and moved to Florida.

James Edward Driscoll passed away in Largo, Florida, on September 4, 1975.

Jan 1, 1944

Dear Citizens,

I want to thank for your Christmas card and present. It was indeed appreciated. It makes a person feel a little happier to know that the people back at home think enough of the boys in the service to make them all presents. It is not very town that contains people like that.

Respectfully yours,
John F. Driscoll
Ensign U.S.N.

USS Omaha
c/ Fl. P.O.
New York. N.Y.

JOHN F. DRISCOLL

Harry   John   Little   Edward   Joseph
Driscoll   Driscoll   Harry   Driscoll   Driscoll

John F. Driscoll, son of John F. and Kathleen (Gabbett) Driscoll, was born April 11, 1921. After the early deaths of their parents, his aunt and uncle raised him, his younger brother, Joseph, and two cousins.

An honors graduate of Scituate High School, class of 1938, he was awarded a scholarship covering four years' tuition at Tufts College in Medford, Massachusetts. Instead, he met all requirements and was appointed to The United States Naval Academy at Annapolis, Maryland, in September of 1940. John was the first young man from Scituate to be so appointed.

After his 1943 graduation, John saw action as a Naval Aviator in the Normandy Invasion. He remained in the Navy and served in a total of three wars. He was awarded the Legion of Merit, the Meritorious Service Medal, and nine additional service and campaign ribbons.

As a Navy Ensign aboard the USS Omaha in January of 1944, John wrote of his happiness and appreciation at being remembered by the "people at home" and remarking that, "It is not every town that contains people like that."

John married and had three children. He made his home in Alexandria, Virginia and in Florida.

Captain John F. Driscoll passed away on March 28, 2003 and was buried with full military honors at Arlington National Cemetery, Washington, DC.

Dec. 9, 1942
15 Highland Street
Springfield, Mass.

Gentlemen:

This is simply an acknowledgment of appreciation for a very kind gesture. It sure is wonderful to realize that you have not forgotten. I am in a U.S. Army Signal Corps School and as far as I know of the towns where the boys come from that they have sent such a fine remembrance. Thanking you once again and wishing you a Happy Christmas and a Happy New Year.

I remain -
Joseph C. Driscoll

JOSEPH C. DRISCOLL

Joseph Driscoll

Joseph Driscoll was born on July 3, 1922, the son of John F. Driscoll, a World War I Naval Veteran, and Kathleen (Gabbett) Driscoll. His parents died when he was a young child, and he went to live with his father's brother and sister, Harry and Nellie Driscoll. They also raised Joseph's older brother, John and his cousins James and Mildred, whose parents had also passed away. Uncle Harry, a Scituate harbormaster, was very proud of the fact that all three boys served in World War II.

Joe was graduated from Scituate High School in 1939 and attended Massachusetts State College in Amherst, MA. He interrupted his education to join the Army Air Corps at the outset of World War II. He served in the Pacific Theater of Operations and saw action in Guam and Iwo Jima.

Joe was awarded the Asiatic Pacific Theater Campaign Ribbon, Good Conduct Medal, American Theater Campaign Ribbon and the Victory Medal.

Following the war, Joe returned to school and was graduated from Bridgewater State College with a Masters Degree in Education. He had a thirty-year career in the Scituate Public Schools as a teacher, administrator, football coach, and Assistant Superintendent. He retired in 1980. He was the father of four children.

Joseph C. Driscoll passed away on January 1, 1996.

Daniel F. Duffey

William G. Duffey

James J. Duffey

John F. Duffey, Jr.

THE DUFFEY FAMILY

All sons of John F. and Mary Lydon Duffey, John, James, Daniel and William Duffey attended Scituate schools.

John Frederick preferred claming and mossing to finishing high school and he did both until he entered the US Army in December 1942. He served in the 7th Field Artillery Observation Battalion in Normandy, Northern France and the Rhineland where he was attached to Patton's Army. He was awarded the Good Conduct Medal, European-African-Middle Eastern Theatre Campaign Ribbon, American Theatre Campaign Ribbon and the Victory Medal. After the war, John returned to Scituate and mossing until he joined the Scituate Police Department in 1956, the same year that he married the former Mary Manning. They had five children, one of whom is serving with the US Army in Baghdad. John retired from the police force in 1985 and now enjoys gardening.

Daniel Francis served with the Army Air Force in the European Theatre as a welder/electrician beginning in 1943. He attained the rank of Corporal and was awarded the Good Conduct Medal, American Campaign Medal,World War II Victory Medal, European-African-Middle Eastern Campaign Medal with 3 Overseas bars. After his discharge Daniel returned to Scituate and married the former Elizabeth Stark in July of 1946. He worked for Paul Young Motors and was appointed to the Scituate Fire Department. He retired in 1985, and passed away November 18, 1997.

James Joseph served in the US Navy aboard the USS Hancock. He married in Florida and moved there where he enjoyed playing golf.

William G. enlisted in the US Navy in 1939 serving in both the European-African and Pacific Campaigns. According to his obituary he fought in five major battle engagements and was decorated for bravery at Okinawa. He received the Bronze Star for valor for going aboard a landing craft and removing an unexploded shell which jeopardized the lives of his shipmates. After his service, William moved to Burlington, MA where he worked for the Department of Public Works as assistant superintendent. He married the former Doris MacDonald.

Frederick Dwyer

FREDERICK J. DWYER

Fred Dwyer was born in Scituate on September 26, 1913. He attended Scituate schools and was graduated from Scituate High School in 1931. In 1942 Fred enlisted in the United States Army, where he attained the rank of T5 Corporal in the 82nd Airborne Division, 504th Paratroop Infantry Regiment, which was the first division to be sent overseas to participate in the invasion of Sicily.

Sicily is an island in the Mediterranean Sea, located just off the toe of the boot that is Italy. It is about the size of the state of Vermont. Designated "Operation Husky," the invasion predated the Normandy landings by eleven months. Its success provided the first ALLIED (mainly The United States, Great Britain and France) occupation of former AXIS (Germany, Italy and Japan) territory. It also served as a base for the invasion of the Italian mainland. Fred's group parachuted behind German lines, and they were tasked with preventing the reinforcement of German defenses.

The 504th PIR next took part in the landings at Anzio, about thirty miles south of Rome. They eventually proceeded through Italy and Belgium and into Germany, where they fought in the Battle of the Bulge in December of 1944.

Discharged in September of 1945, Fred returned to Scituate, and in July of 1948, he married the former Anne Davis. Fred was an "Irish Mosser" along the coast of Scituate, gathering the red seaweed also known as carrageen. The end product is an excellent gelling agent that is used in the food, pharmaceutical, and cosmetics industries. Fred worked as a mechanic at Paul Young Motors in Scituate.

Fred and Anne had three children and three grandchildren.

Frederick Dwyer passed away on July 25, 2004.

Dec. 28, 8 PM
1942?

FORT RILEY, KANSAS

To Whom it May Concern

I received your card and money order today and I just wanted to let you know that I really appreciate it. It come as a great surprise and there is no need to say what it does to a soldiers morale.

I can rightfully say that it makes a boy feel kinda proud to know that he has friends at home and that they will do that sort of a thing for him. I'm sure that all the boys feel equally as happy as I do to be remembered this way and I want to thank you again, this is one soldier who will never forget it.

Gerard Dwyer
Gerard Dwyer

GERARD T. DWYER

Gerard Dwyer was born on December 5, 1918, the son of Thomas and Carrie Doten Dwyer. Thomas was a well-known Irish Mosser who utilized the property known as the "proving grounds" for drying his moss.

Graduating from Scituate High School in 1936, Gerard joined the United States Army where he earned the rank of Technical Sergeant. He served in the 9th Armored Tank Corps for three years.

Gerard participated in The Battle of the Bulge, the German Army's unexpected, all-out effort to prevent the invasion and conquest of their homeland. He saw service in Switzerland, Belgium, England, France, Germany, and Czechoslovakia. He was awarded American Defense Ribbon, Good Conduct Medal, Victory Medal, European and African Campaign Ribbon with Four Battle stars and the Presidential Unit Citation.

Married to Annette (Drew), Gerard had five daughters, sixteen grandchildren and ten great grandchildren. He lobstered, fished and gathered moss out of Scituate Harbor.

Mossing was a widely practiced occupation in Scituate dating back to 1865. It involved backbreaking work rowing out at low tide and scraping the Irish Moss, or carrageen, from the rocks using a fourteen-foot long rake. The moss was then taken to shore, transferred to handbarrows and wheeled to drying areas where it was spread out to be bleached by the sun. After several of these bleachings, the moss was packed into one hundred pound barrels and stored to await sale. Irish Moss is still used as a stabilizing agent in ice cream, sherbert, chocolate milk, yogurt, and whipped cream. It is also used in cosmetics as a skin softener and as an herbal remedy in digestive disorders.

An avid golfer, Gerard was at one time, a groundskeeper at Green Harbor Golf Club in Marshfield, MA.

Gerard Dwyer died on January 20, 2000 at age 81.

10 December 1944.

Service Men's Committee:

Dear sirs:

Just received for the third year the Christmas card and gift from the people of Scituate. The card is beautiful and the prayer thereon most appropriate.

It is an honor and a privilege to be so remembered by the home folks. If the people at home could realize what a feeling of happiness and pride and what a tug at the heart that this message brings to each and every one of us on the far flung fronts of the earth then they would be more than amply repayed for their thoughtfullness, their time and their generosity.

So again for the third time and and I hope with God's grace, for the last time I say thanks again to all of the Committee and all the people of Scituate and I wish them all the best and happiest of holiday seasons.

Yours Sincerely,
Herbert R. Sluyer.

Lathrop, California.
January 11, 1942.

Scituate Town Committee:

Sirs:

I wish to thank the town committee and the people of Scituate for their very thoughtful and practical gift and Christmas Greeting.

I am now on detached service and have been very busy at my work, which calls for long hours, so that I have been unable to write my appreciation and acknowledgement of your message until now.

The card was mailed to Mississippi but before it had arrived I was transferred to Camp Edwards and then here to California. The card followed along persistently collecting a travelogue of army addresses all of it's own and finally arrived here in time for Christmas. To me its travels were an omen. An omen of proof that the good wishes and hopes of the town of Scituate follows its men and women in the service to all parts and climes at all times. So with all the home folks pulling for us like this is how I see it faith. And so I hopes that before another Christmas season rolls around we will all be home again pulling together in a world at peace.

Sincerely
Pvt Herbert R. Sluyer.

HERBERT R. DWYER

Herbert Dwyer was born to Scituate residents James H. and Mary Doyle Dwyer in Somerville, MA. James was employed by the NY, NH & Hartford Railroad and spent his winters closer to his South Boston job. Herb was one of eight children born in Dorchester, South Boston, Somerville and Scituate. The family moved to Scituate full time and Herb was graduated from Scituate High School in 1930 where he was class president, played football and basketball, and was a member of the CHIMES (the Scituate High School yearbook) staff.

Immediately after the Pearl Harbor attack, Herb attempted to enlist. All three branches of the service rejected him. Imagine his surprise when he received his draft notice in April of 1942. Initially sent to Biloxi, Mississippi, he was transferred after a year to Officers' Candidate School at Fort Belvoir in Virginia. He was subsequently commissioned a Second Lieutenant and sent to the Pacific Theater.

Herb's first thank you letter was written from Lathrop, California in 1942 and is interesting in that he notes that his gift had "followed (me) along persistently collecting a travelogue of Army addresses all of it's own and finally arrived here in time for Christmas."

Herb saw service in the Hawaiian Islands, Okinawa and Ie Shima. This last was the island where Pulitzer Prize winning reporter, Ernie Pyle, was killed. Pyle was noted for his stories written for and about the ordinary soldiers of World War II.

After being discharged in 1946, Herb took advantage of the GI Bill and attended Northeastern University, graduating with a law degree. He married Jeanne Bresnahan of Scituate and they had two daughters. Herb remained in the Army Reserves holding the rank of Captain. He was reactivated in 1951 during the Korean Conflict and served at Fort Leonard Wood in Missouri and in Korea itself where he was awarded the Bronze Star.

When he was discharged on August 7, 1952, he returned to Scituate and became the town's first Veterans' Agent before going to work for Westinghouse. He and Jeanne had two more children. By the time he retired from General Dynamics, Herb counted seventy-two jobs he has held since his time in the Army.

Herb now divides his time between homes in Scituate and Florida.

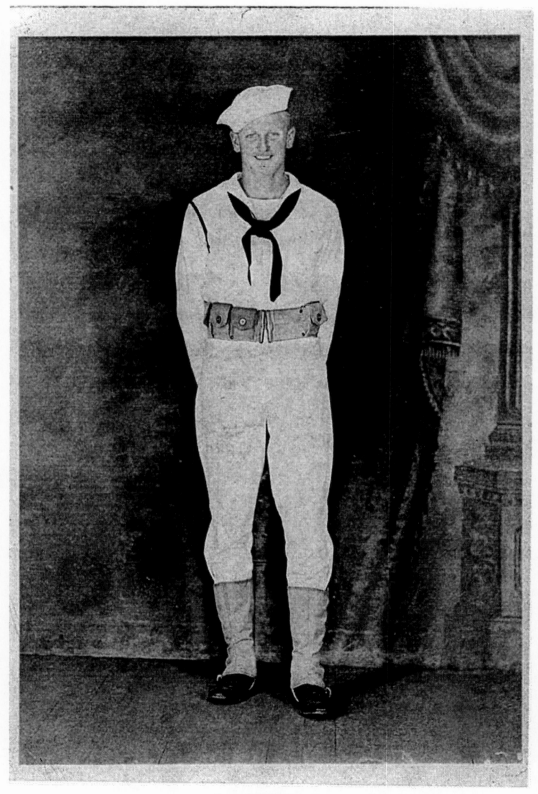

George M. Fallon

GEORGE M. FALLON

George M. Fallon, also known as Marvin, was born on August 6, 1925. He attended Scituate schools

George entered the United States Navy in July, 1943, and served aboard the LST 973, a Tank Landing Ship. Built at the Hingham-Bethlehem Steel Shipyard, this vessel saw service as part of Flotilla 15, Group 43 in and around the Philippine Islands and performed occupation duty in the Far East.

George later related to his wife, Polly, that while in New Guinea the ship acquired a pet monkey which would ride around on George's shoulder.

After his discharge in March of 1946, George worked at Page's Garage in Scituate Harbor and later became a Scituate Police officer. In 1960 he married the former Polly White. They had four children and two grandchildren.

George Fallon passed away on April 13, 1998.

John T. Fallon on Right.

JOHN T. FALLON

John T. Fallon was born in 1924 and was graduated from Scituate High School. When war was declared in December of 1941, John and his friend, Pat Crowley, drove to Boston in Pat's Model A Ford to enlist in the Navy. On January 2, 1942, John left Scituate for boot camp at the Newport, Rhode Island, Navy Base.

After advanced training at Norfolk, Virginia, and Cecil Field, Jacksonville, Florida, "Honk" was assigned to Fleet Air Wing 14, Photographic Squad. He spent time in California and Hawaii before being assigned to the South Pacific, where he remained from 1943 until 1945. He performed many missions there until the war ended.

Fleet Air Photographers proved most valuable during World War II when the service was greatly expanded and modernized. Using still and motion picture cameras, photographs were taken from the air to record maneuvers and battles in every theater of the war. These pictures aided in establishing battle plans and identifying enemy fleet and troop placements as well as evaluating the performance of our own fleet.

When John was discharged in 1946, he received the World War II Victory Medal, Asiatic-Pacific Theater Medal, and the American Theater Medal. With his Navy benefits, he attended Suffolk University and Portia Law (now the New England School of Law) in Boston. On November 24, 1951, John married the former Jane Crowley, and they had seven children. They lived in Florida for eight years, and then returned to Scituate.

Honk died on December 5, 1975.

Australia
Dec 26 43

Citizens of Scituate
    I have just received your Christmas
greetings and present and want to thank you
very much. It is good to know that you folks
back home are fighting to keep our spirits
up, as we work to keep the enemy back.
    It is sort of a strange Christmas here
for us fellows who are used to having
cold and snow to make Christmas more
enjoyable, over here it is as hot as in the
middle of the summer back there. Here they
think of Christmas as a good sunny day, a
couple bowls of beer and a day at the beach.
    You can bet that we are all waiting
for the day we can all come back to
a real old town for our holidays.
    With the best wishes for a Happy New Year
to everyone, will do our best to make it so.
                                    Yours
                                    Aldie Finnie

New Guinea
Dec - 27 - 44

Service Men's Committee

    I received your Christmas greetings
and money on Xmas day - and want
to thank all the folks in Scituate.
I know that if everyone every where had
the fighting spirit that the folks back
there have, this war wouldn't last
long.
    Christmas around these parts isn't much
like -us guys- think of having back
there, while everyone there is sitting
around the fireplace were praying for rain
to cool us off.
    I hope by the next Christmas will
all be back there and celebrate together
            Thanks again folks.
                        Aldie Finnie

ALDEN C. FINNIE

Aldie Finnie was born in Scituate, MA, and was educated at the Jenkins School before graduating from Scituate High School in 1935. After a year of Mechanical Technology study, he went to work for Whittaker Brothers, an auto repair shop in Scituate on First Parish Road.

With the declaration of war, Aldie joined the Air Force and went to Fort Devens in Ayer, MA. He underwent Basic Training at Jefferson Barracks in St. Louis, Missouri, attended the Chicago Aeronautical University to study airplanes, and went on to Springfield, Illinois, as a Sergeant in the 44th Depot Group. While in Illinois, Aldie met his future wife, Olga Pope from Dunn, North Carolina, at a dance.

Aldie eventually was sent to Australia, where he became part of the 81st Air Depot Group and was responsible for the assembly and maintenance of aircraft being used throughout the South Pacific. As a Master Sergeant, Alden C. Finnie and his group of enlisted men were commended for their "initiative and ingenuity in constructing a pre-oiling unit that will in all future operations, reduce by one-half, the time and labor involved in the pre-oiling of aircraft engines." His parents were informed of his accomplishment in a letter from an Air Corps Adjutant that stated, "The example set by your son will serve as an inspiration to all officers and enlisted men of this command."

Aldie wrote two thank you letters, the first from Australia in 1943, commenting that, "It's sort of a strange Christmas here for us fellows who are used to having cold and snow . . . Over here it is hot as the middle of summer back there." In 1944, weather conditions weren't much different in New Guinea when Aldie wrote ". . . while everyone there is sitting around the fireplace, we're praying for rain to cool us off."

Aldie returned to the United States and married Olga. They had three children and four grandchildren. With his brother Jamie, he ran Finnie's Sales and Service, a car dealership, until he retired in 1999.

Dec. 17, 1944

Board of Selectman
Town Hall
Scituate, Mass.

Dear Sirs:
      I want to thank the town
people, by way of you, for the gift that
was sent this Christmas. It was truly
appreciated. I hope that I will be the
last year they will have to send
it. We all hope that it will be possible
to be home in Scituate, Mass. before
very long.
            Again I thank you for the
gift.

                        Yours truly
                        P.F.C. James Finn Jr.
                        Waycross AAF
                        Ga.

JAMES FINNIE, JR.

James (Jamie) Finnie was born April 8, 1923, the third of four sons born to James and Helen (Prouty) Finnie. They all grew up on the family farm on Tilden Road in Scituate, where they raised dairy cows, and Jamie delivered milk by bicycle. He was graduated from Scituate High School after which he joined the Army Air Corps.

While stationed in a radio communications unit in Waycross, Georgia, in 1944, Jamie wrote in his letter, "We all hope that it will be possible to be home in Scituate, Mass before very long."

Jamie didn't get home until the war ended in September of 1945, at which time he returned to Scituate and went to work with his brother Aldie at Finnie's Sales and Service on First Parish Road. He married Dorothy Whitcomb from New Hampshire, and they had four children, nine grandchildren, and five great grandchildren.

A talented craftsman, Jamie built the home he and Dot lived in. He also built a pop-up camper in which he took his family camping each summer. He took up woodcarving and left behind many beautiful carvings for his children and grandchildren. A member of the Tiny Treasures Society, Jamie created miniature furniture pieces, working painstakingly until they were perfect.

James Finnie, Jr. passed away on March 30, 1996, at the age of seventy-two.

James Finnie, Jr.

Retirement Caricature by Bill Sexton

ROBERT W. FINNIE

Born January 1, 1927, Robert Finnie walked to the Old Jenkins School on First Parish Road for the first six years of his education. He went on to graduate from Scituate High School in 1944 and promptly enlisted in the Army Air Corp Reserves. He was called to active duty on April 16, 1945.

Bob was sent to Remote Control Turret School at Lowery Field in Denver, Colorado, and then to Kadena Air Base on the island of Okinawa. Assigned to the 948th Engineering Topographical Company, Bob wrote in his thank you letter in 1946 that "I know that all the men still in the service are just as hopeful of returning to civilian life in Scituate now that the war is over as I, because no other place in the United States or abroad can ever compare to the quiet peaceful home town, of which we have so many fond memories."

Promoted to S/Sgt., Bob returned to the United States in October 1946 and was discharged in December. He worked as a mechanic at Ford's garage on Front Street in Scituate Harbor. He was recalled to service in August of 1950. After serving at Shephard Field in Shreveport, Louisiana, and Lockbourne Air Base near Columbus, Ohio, Bob was once again discharged on September 19, 1951.

Robert Finnie married the former Emily Whittaker in Scituate on January 4, 1951, while on leave. After his discharge from the Armed Forces he joined the Scituate Police Department. He was promoted to Sergeant in 1965. Bob also worked as a locksmith from 1969 until 1996 in the Scituate area, and he owned Bishop's, a Variety Store on Hatherly Road in Scituate for fifteen years. He retired from the Police Department in March 1976.

Bob and Emily have one daughter and two grandchildren.

NAVIGATION SCHOOL
MONROE, LOUISIANA

Dec. 22/42

To Whom it may Concern:

I just a few lines to let you know I received your most welcomed gift. I also a appreciated the gift very much, and I also think that every one else that received this gift thinks the same as I do.

This Army life is not good and I hope the war will over very soon. We are all doing our part, and I know you are doing the same.

Will close now by wishing you all a very Merry Christmas & a Happy New Year.

Thanking you again

Yours very Truly
Pvt Thomas Fitzpatrick

THOMAS FITZPATRICK

Thomas Fitzpatrick, the son of Thomas M. and Katharine (Shannahan) Fitzpatrick, was born in Scituate on April 12, 1922. He attended Scituate schools and entered the service on September 22, 1942.

Thomas' thank you letter was written from Navigation School in Monroe, Louisiana, in December 1942. At that time he spoke of how welcome the gift was and expressed his appreciation to the Town. He also hoped "this war will be over very soon." He subsequently spent two years stationed in Texas. Thomas served in Squadron D of the 138th Army Air Force Base Unit as a Rotary Wing (Helicopter) Mechanic achieving the rank of Sergeant.

Following his discharge on February 10, 1946, Thomas returned to Scituate and worked for Paul Young Motors, where he ran the service department. He married the former Theresa Fitzgerald in 1949, and they had two children.

Thomas Fitzpatrick passed away on Thanksgiving Day, November, 1967.

George Flaherty.

Walter Flaherty.

GEORGE AND WALTER FLAHERTY

George and Walter Flaherty were born in Scituate, the sons of Marcus J., a carpenter, and Hannah Dinnean Flaherty of Stockbridge Road. Walter was born on December 3, 1905, and George was born on April 24, 1915. Both boys attended Scituate schools. Walter was graduated from Scituate High School in 1922. He was manager of the Scituate Town Football Team and worked as a truck driver for the Scituate Highway Department. George was graduated from Scituate High School in 1933, where he played third base for the baseball team, was assistant manager of the basketball team, and acted in the Junior Class play.

George enlisted in the Army Air Force in September of 1940. He joined up along with his friends: Erving Studley, Ray Gillis, Bill Curran, and Joe Barry. George served as an Airplane Armorer with the 22nd AAF Battalion in New Guinea. He was awarded the American Defense Service Medal, Asiatic-Pacific Service Medal, and the Good Conduct Medal. After his discharge in 1945, he returned to Scituate and worked as a self-employed house painter. He passed away in 1971.

Walter was inducted into the United States Army in November of 1942. He served as a First Class Gunner in the Rhineland, Northern France, and Normandy. Walter was wounded on July 12, 1944, in St. Jean de Daye, France. He was awarded the European African Middle Eastern Theatre Ribbon with three bronze stars, Combat Infantryman Badge, Expert Infantryman Badge, and the Purple Heart. After the war he returned to Scituate and worked for the Highway Department. He was registrar of voters until 1956. He retired in 1965 and passed away in 1972.

Feb 3, 1945

To whom it may concern:

I want to take this opportune moment to thank the people of Scituate.

That gift is only a small measure of what the citizens of the town are doing for the war effort. I know that behind that gift lies the hope and the prayers of all the people back home. I know that I was the only fellow aboard my ship that received a personal gift from the home town.

The town is where I went to school and met people who will never be surpassed by anyone in the county.

All of the boys on my ship were wondering where Scituate was. Well my good friends from Scituate I told them. Some of them want to visit. I'll be proud to show them the sights.

I do mean sights. I have been to Italy, Africa, Panama, Guadalcanal, New Guinea, and the Philippines and many other States.

Scituate has the sights. I'm not fooling. That is where I want ever to be. That is why all of the boys and girls in the town are fighting for. Thanks again for the gift. May God watch over you and Bless you one and all.

Sincerely yours
A. Fonini F t c
U.S.S. Fidelle A.P.D 60
F.P.O. San Francisco, Cal.

P.S. I received the money order Feb 5, 1945

ALDIERO FONIRI

Aldiero Foniri was born in a small town outside of Rome, Italy, on November 26, 1918. His father, Armando, came to America first and later sent for his wife and children. They settled in Scituate, MA. After his father died, Aldiero left school to work to support the family.

Al joined the USN in 1944 because he felt it was his duty to support his dearly loved adopted country. He was assigned to the fast transport ship USS Liddle, which had been built at the Charleston, South Carolina Navy Yard and commissioned in 1943. The Liddle was originally a destroyer escort that was reclassified after returning to New York from three round trips across the North Atlantic escorting convoys to Wales, Gibraltar and Tunisia. The Liddle was sent to the Pacific Theater and performed escort duties for supply convoys bound for Leyte Gulf, the Philippine Islands, and the Palau Islands. On December 7, 1944 the Liddle was attacked by Japanese aircraft. Five of the planes were destroyed but a kamikaze (suicide plane) managed to hit the ship's bridge, and the seriously damaged craft was forced to return to San Francisco for repairs.

Just before the Liddle was underway again, Al received his gift from the Town of Scituate and wrote in his thank you letter from San Francisco that "All of the boys on my ship were wondering where Scituate was. Well my good friends from Scituate I told them. Some of them want to visit, I'll be proud to show them the sights. I do mean sights. I have been to Italy, Africa, Panama, Guadalcanal, New Guinea and the Philippines and many other states. Scituate has the sights."

While travelling from New York to Scituate on leave in July, 1944, Al met his future wife aboard a train. She was returning from a vacation in New York with a girlfriend and exchanged addresses with Al. They carried on a correspondence and had several dates. They eventually married in 1948 and moved into the house Al had built for them on Mann Lot Road.

Al worked in construction for Perini Bongarzone after the war. He and Helen adopted two children, Nancy and Joseph. Al Foniri passed away on September 17, 1968.

UNITED STATES MARINE CORPS

Sgt. Angelo Fonisi U.S.M.C.R.
D Battery A.A. Arty. Group
9th Defense Bn. F.M.F.
F.P.O. San Francisco Cal.

Dear Sir,

I want to take this opportunity to thank you very kindly for that fine Christmas gift the Town of Scituate sent me. It certainly is gratifying to the servicemen over-seas to know that the people back home are behind them one hundred percent, especially your home town.

That money order certainly came in handy because pay days are far-in-between down here. Of course we can't go to our favorite store and expect to get anything we want like in the good old days back home, but the little we do get is sufficient to carry us through. But this war won't last forever. All of us that get back are going to make up for lost time, I can assure you.

Thanking the Town of Scituate for that swell gesture—

Yours Sincerely,
Sgt. Angelo Fonisi

ANGELO FONIRI

 Angelo Foniri, the middle of the three Foniri brothers was born on October 19, 1919 in Supino, Italy. In December of 1926 the brothers and their mother joined their father who had preceded them to the United States.

Angelo was a 1939 graduate of Scituate High School. He attended Boston College on a full scholarship. In the spring of 1942, Angelo joined the United States Marines.

After completing boot camp at Parris Island, South Carolina, Angelo was sent to Grove City College in Pennsylvania to study the newly emerging technology of radar. He continued his studies in San Diego before shipping out to the Solomon Islands; a chain of islands spread over seven hundred miles of ocean, twelve hundred miles northeast of Australia.

Utilizing radar with an inadequate range of only fifty miles, Angelo's defense group was to protect the airstrips on Gaudalcanal. Next came Munda on New Georgia Island with its much larger airstrip. By the time Angelo and his comrades reached Guam, they had received their most sophisticated radar equipment, with one hundred and fifty-mile range. This enabled the Marine Corps Corsairs and Army P-38's to gain superiority over the Japanese Air Forces.

Angelo returned home in the spring of 1945. He and Phyllis Mirabella of Boston were married on October 14, 1946. They had a daughter and a son and now have three grandchildren. Angelo has volunteered for seventeen years with the Meals on Wheels program and also works with the Scituate Council on Aging.

UNITED STATES NAVY

Service Men's Committee

Dear Sir;

I don't exactly know how to start this letter. All I really want to say is thanks; a million times - thanks. I just wish I had a chance to thank everyone of the people who contributed to this worthy cause. And I'd to like to thank all the people who helped to gather this huge of some money. And in my opinion they should all be given some type of medal or recommendation for their fine and splendid work they did. Well I know it was only five dollars. But if you was in my place, or in the places

---

of all servicemen who are serving this great and victorious country of United States of America. Well you be surprised how much it helps. I could buy a swell and joyous gift for my family and even by a little thing for friends I have. You see I was in a position where I needed money for some little gift for a Christmas tiding. I've overcome that task, because of the kind and sincere people of the typical American town of Situate. Well I been talking from a large point of view. And the main reason I wrote was to give. Well this may make all the peace loving people of Situate, when I make this statement. Well I've met boys from towns

---

UNITED STATES NAVY

from Fall River, Mass. towns from Iowa, Texas, Cal. and as far North as Montana. And they all say the same thing. They never have any money sent to them from their home town. They also say that I must come from a good and reputable town. And go all out for helping a serviceman. Well I guess that's about all I can say.

I'm afraid I haven't won any medals or citations, or even seen a enemy ship or such. I haven't got the background in the education field to write a half decent letter. I guess I tried my best, like all enlisted men in the armed Forces.

And besides all the medals I want is that discharged pin: To start where I left off. And I know by the past experiences and the meetings with the town folks that I will be accepted and to prove and pay back all you did for me. And I will try to live up to the expectations of being a worthy citizen of the town of Situate.

Yours truly
Rocky

Rocco Zoniri, F 1/c

ROCCO FONIRI

The youngest of the three Foniri brothers, Rocco was born in Supino, Italy, on September 2, 1925. He immigrated to the United States and settled in Scituate with his mother and two brothers.

Rocco enlisted in the Navy when he was seventeen years old in 1942. He wrote an essay that was printed in the Scituate High School Yearbook, *The Chimes,* when he arrived at Basic Training stating: "At last my ambition has come true. I shall be a soldier, - not to fight to destroy the right of the living, but to preserve and protect the democratic ideals of the United States of America."

Serving on a PT (Patrol Torpedo) Boat in the South Pacific, Rocco was in the thick of the fighting. He rescued downed pilots and supported heavily contested beach landings. He was present in Tokyo Bay when the Japanese formally surrendered on September 2, 1945.

Rocco married the former Helen Dellot and eventually moved to Hingham. He worked as a painting contractor for forty years and was a member of the Scituate Chamber of Commerce and the Hingham Sons of Italy. He was also a member of the Knights of Columbus.

Rocco Foniri passed away on June 21, 2003.

Ft. McClellan,
Alabama

December 14, 1943

Dear Sirs:

I want to send this note along
telling you that I certainly appreciated
the Christmas card and also the money
order that you are sending out to
those of us in the services of our
country. I for one am looking
forward to the day when we can
return to our little town on the
south shore and to those that
have been working to do what they
can to not only produce the
articles that we need to win this
war but to help us to remember
our home town.

Sincerely yours
Pvt Edmund Ford

EDMUND FRANCIS FORD

Edmund Ford was graduated from Whitman, Massachusetts High School. A 1938 graduate of Wentworth Institute in Boston, he was living and working as a printer in Scituate when he was inducted into the service on May 29, 1943.

Edmund served as a company clerk at Fort McClellan, Alabama. This was the training site for approximately 500,000 troops, including a company of Japanese-Americans who helped to familiarize American soldiers with Japanese military methods.

In his letter to the Town, Edmund wrote, "I for one am looking forward to the day when we can return to our little town on the South Shore and to those that have been working to do what they can to . . . help us to remember our home town."

Edmund was discharged on January 14, 1946. He returned to Scituate and to his wife, Marie (Wilder) Ford. They eventually had five children, twelve grandchildren and ten great grandchildren. Edmund worked again as a printer until retiring in 1980. He and Marie ran a chair seating business, teaching and repairing caned and rush seats for chairs from 1978 until 2001. They still live on Country Way in Scituate.

Betty Franzen

BETTY FRANZEN

Betty Franzen was born in April of 1921. She was graduated from Scituate High School in 1938 and volunteered for the WAVES in the summer of 1942.

The women's branch of the United States Navy, WAVES (Women Accepted for Voluntary Emergency Service) was established in 1942 to fill clerical positions ashore and eventually expanded to include roles in communications, technology, intelligence, medicine, and science.

After attending boot camp at Iowa State Teachers College, Betty was in the first class graduating from Naval Technical Training School in Norman, Oklahoma. She was given the rating of Aviation Machinists Mate third class and was sent to the Corpus Christie, Texas, Naval Air Station where she remained for the duration of the war, rising to the rank of Machinists Mate first class.

Betty proudly relates that she was in the service for "Two years, eleven months and five days." She also tips her hat "to the Navy Women today who are doing all the things we thought we were going to do."

Betty married an ex Army man, Henry Shortall, in 1947, and they had 2 children. Henry passed away in 1983, and Betty continued to do office work for Wes-Pine Millwork in West Hanover, MA, until her "forced retirement" at age 73 when the company closed. She currently lives in Rockland, MA.

UNITED STATES ARMY
AIR FORCES

Pvt Fred A. Franzen
561st T.S.S.
Scott Field, Illinois
Jan. 22, 1943

Mr Dennis Shea
Chairman, Board of Selectmen
Scituate, Mass.

Dear Sir:

Please accept, for the citizens of Scituate, my sincerest thanks in appreciation of the Christmas card and the generous gift I recieved.

It is a cheering thought to know that Scituate keeps in touch with every one of her sons (and daughters) in the service of our country. To me, that is loyalty and thought-fulness and with both of these virtues we shall get this war over with in very short time.

Thanking you again, I remain

Yours Very Sincerely
Fred A. Franzen

FRED A. FRANZEN

Fred Franzen (left), Richard Franzen (right)

Fred Franzen was born in Scituate, and after graduating from Scituate High School in 1940, he volunteered for the Army Air Corps on December 10, 1942. Fred received his basic training in Miami, Florida. He attended various radio schools in Illinois and Wisconsin. Back in Florida, this time in Boca Raton, Fred learned about the newly emerging field of radar.

From Smyrna, Tennessee, Fred flew to San Francisco and then sailed on a Liberty Ship to Milne Bay, New Guinea, in the Pacific. Liberty Ships were mass-produced during WWII to compensate for the enormous losses being suffered by American Merchant Mariners due to submarine attacks. Over two thousand ships were produced from 1941 until 1945. They were capable of carrying nine thousand tons of cargo in addition to airplanes, tanks and locomotives lashed to the decks.

Fred traveled to numerous Pacific Islands installing radio equipment at American bases. At Clark Field, in the Philippines, he set up search apparatus for the Navy to allow their airplanes to home in on moving aircraft carriers. He also helped install one of the first GCA (ground control approach) systems at Clark Field to facilitate planes landing in the dark or in foul weather.

While overseas, Fred met up with several Scituate boys including Orrin Gould, Bill Bradley and Arthur Montanari, whom he met at Clark Field.

Fred was transferred to Manila just before Thanksgiving to begin his trip home in 1945. He left Manila two days later and flew the polar route - over the North Pole- to Canada and he eventually traveled to Helena, Montana, by train. On Christmas Day all trains halted for the holiday and the returning men were stranded. The Red Cross supplied them all with a traditional Christmas dinner an event Fred says, "I'll never forget."

Officially discharged on December 30, Fred worked for H.H.Arnold, a textile manufacturing company. He married Helen Dunbar, whose family had summered in Scituate, and had 3 sons and a daughter. He retired in 2000 and lives in Rockland, MA.

U. S. ARMY

December 28, 1943
Harvard University
Cambridge, Mass.

Dear Sirs:

I received your card and the money order last week. I want to thank all the people of the town who so generously gave their time and money to show their appreciation of us who are in the serveces. The card was very beatiful and the money was more than appreciated.

I am sure the Town of Scituate is doing more than its share for the war effort.

Very truly yours,
Richard Frazgen

UNITED STATES ARMY

295 Ordnance H.M.Co.
21 December 1944
England

Dear Sirs;

I received your most welcome letter today. The card is beautifully designed and portrays a sincere thought. It shows how proud the citizens of Scituate are of their boys in service. I speak sincerely, too, when I say I'm proud of Scituate as my home town.

Yours Truly,
Richard Frazgen

RICHARD FRANZEN

Richard "Jimmy" Franzen was born in 1925. He was graduated from Scituate High School and was drafted into the United States Army in April of 1943.

After Basic Training at Camp Miles Standish in Taunton, MA, Jim was loading ships at Castle Island in South Boston when he received orders to go to the University of New Hampshire for evaluation. He was then sent to Harvard University for engineering studies.

The Harvard program was disbanded in April of 1944, and Jimmy was sent to Tennessee and then on to Fort Jackson, NC, Camp Gordon, GA, the Aberdeen Proving Grounds in Maryland, Camp Kilmer, NJ, and ultimately he arrived in Liverpool, England.

Jim's unit crossed the English Channel in January of 1945, six months after D-Day, and arrived at LeHavre, France. They traveled to Liege, Belgium, Maastricht in the Netherlands and on into Germany. Jim was on the outskirts of the Battle of the Bulge, headquartered in a coal mine servicing military equipment. He was also sent to the Rhine to install bulldozer blades on tanks. These were used to clear disabled vehicles, oftentimes from bridges where they were blocking the advancement of troops and supplies.

In Detmold, Germany, Jim was appointed mail messenger. He traveled alone by jeep twice a day to get mail from the battalion and return it to the company, forty miles each way. Jim was also close to Dachau at the end of the war with his company and observed what had happened there. This was the site of a German concentration camp where thousands were victims of forced labor, mass murder and horrific medical experiments. There were 67,000 prisoners there at the time of its liberation.

When Jim returned home in 1946, he went to work for the H.H. Arnold Company along with his brother, Fred. He married the former Shirley Trenholm and had four children. Retired since 1999, Jim and Shirley reside in Scituate, MA.

Camp Stoneman
Pittsburg, California
12-14-42

Dear Mr Shea,

The band has just played "The Stars Spangled Banner" and we are lined up for "Retreat".

To a soldier, this means the end of a day's toil, the end of another day of new experiences, and new memories.

I have heard this tune many times, and I have played it many times myself. Today, this grand tune has a more profound effect on me.

I hear in its melodious background, the voices of our energetic and determined citizens of Scituate. I hear them asking of the welfare of their "Sons in the Service". I see in the background, the various hard working organizations who have taken such an active part in the War effort.

Well, Mr. Shea, I had to close my eyes for a moment and reminisce. You people, at home, are the soldiers and your sons and daughters in the Service are proud of you. We have picked up your challenge and will not rest until Victory is ours.

(1)

(2)

Through you, Sir, may I extend my sincere appreciation to those responsible for my card and gift.

May I offer my humble prayer for peace, good health, and happiness to you one and all. May this coming New Year hold a real Armistice in store for us.

Sincerely,
Private Xpistudi Yatro
Camp Stoneman
Pittsburg
California.

LESTER JULIUS GATES

Lester Julius Gates was born in Scituate in October 1916. He was the son of Sidney S. Gates, a merchant born in Russia and the former Ida Cohen. Lester was a 1934 Scituate High School graduate as well as a graduate of Brown University in Providence, RI.

Lester married the former Pearl Baron in May of 1941. He was drafted into the Army in September of that year as part of the first draft registration of World War II. This required all men aged 21 to 36 to register.

Lester wrote his thank you letter to the Town from Camp Stoneman, California in December of 1942. Situated 40 miles northeast of San Francisco, it was used as a staging area and rifle range for troop training by the US Army. For many GIs, it was the their last contact with the United States before being shipped to the Asia-Pacific War Theater. In his letter Lester mentions hearing the band play "The Star Spangled Banner" in camp and having it remind him of Scituate's "hardworking organizations who have taken such an active part in the war effort."

When Lester returned to Scituate, he resumed his stewardship of the well-known Gates Clothing Store, in North Scituate. A second store would later be added in Scituate Harbor. Lester was extremely active in the Scituate community. He was elected State Representative in 1964. He served as Chairman of the Board of Selectmen and Public Works Commissioners. He served on the Planning Board and Advisory Committee, School and Public Building Committees and the Industrial Commission. He was director of the Scituate Federal Savings and Loan Association and a corporator of the Rockland Savings Bank.

Lester J. Gates died in his Scituate home in May 1967 at the age of 50.

CAMP WHEELER, GEORGIA

Feb. 13, 1945

Selectmens Office
Town of Scituate
Massachusetts

To the people of Scituate — I wish to
thank for their very welcome money order
gift of five dollars ($5.).

I wish also to thank the Scituate
Servicemens Committee + Mr. Shea, Chairman
of the Board of Selectmen.

The five dollars ($5.) has been very
useful to me, making it possible to
purchase incidentals very much needed.

Many thanks again

Very sincerely
Pvt. James V. Tilli jr.

JAMES H. GILLIS JR.

James Gillis, son of James H. and Laurette Casey Gillis, was born on August 16, 1926. He was graduated from Scituate High School in June of 1944. In November he joined the United States Army as had his father, James Sr.

In February of 1945, James was at Camp Wheeler, just outside of Macon in Georgia. He had received his Christmas gift from the citizens of Scituate, and he wrote back that it would make it "possible to purchase incidentals very much needed."

James served in Germany as a Military Policeman and in the Motor Pool. He was discharged in 1946. In 1951, James rejoined the Army and served in Japan and Korea. He retired from the Army after twenty-four years of service and went into business in El Paso, Texas.

In 1995, James returned to Scituate. He died in November 2001.

James Gillis, Sr. 1925

December 29, 1942.
Somewhere in North
Africa.

Friends of Scituate;

Just a line to express my thanks to the members of
the Scituate Service Committee. It was really some present to receive
somewhere in "Africa". To realize that no matter where you are in this
world that the people back home still think of us. I will take this
opportunity to thank you for the great number of fellows who thru no
fault of their own will not be able to express their thanks. I will
have to admit that up until now anyway I have been very fortunate or
lucky whatever you wish to call it.

Life here in this section of North Africa is on a rather a half and half
basis. The one thing we have plenty of is "MUD". You people can never
realize what mud is until you have seen some of this African mud it is
really the "McCoy". There is absolutely no soap to be had in town so we
in the army have been real lucky because we have more than enough. For
you people who like wine or champagne why this is the place to come,
plenty of it over here.

The radio has come in very handy, for we listen to the broadcast from the
states when we have the chance. The station that comes in better than any
is none other than WRUL. I can't help think when I hear it how close it is
to my home. Well I will say so-long and thanks again for myself and the
other fellows who are unable to do so, luck to all,

Ray Gillis

RAY GILLIS

Ray Gillis, was born in Scituate to Edward and Margaret Barry Gillis on January 19, 1911. He attended Scituate schools and enlisted in the Army Air Corps in 1940. He received his training in North Carolina and was then sent, as a supply sergeant, to England to prepare for the North African Campaign. It was in North Africa that Ray was wounded. He was sent to Halloran General Hospital on Staten Island in New York. He was discharged from there and returned home.

After the war, Ray returned to Scituate and married the former Norma Emery in 1945. They had two sons and a daughter. Norma ran a well-known ceramic studio in Scituate. Ray worked as a salesman for Firestone Tires and as a Building Supply Representative He retired in 1970.

Norma passed away in 1970. When she knew she was dying, Norma asked her best friend, Barbara McCue, to take care of Ray, which she did for the rest of his life. They were married on August 27, 1972.

Barbara McCue Gillis also served her country as a Yeoman in the Navy, enlisting in November 1942. Stationed at Iowa State Teachers College in Norman Oklahoma, and at Jacksonville, Florida, she was Secretary to the Engine Overhaul Division Officer. Barbara retired from the reserves in 1970.

Barbara McCue Gillis

Ray was an avid Bridge player and played golf at the Scituate Country Club, where he attained two holes-in-one. He was also interested in politics.

Ray Gillis passed away on July 23, 1997.

Vincent and Vilna Gosewisch

Fred and Doris Gosewisch

VINCENT R. GOSEWISCH

Vincent Gosewisch, the son of Frederick and Sophie Sovotzik Gosewisch, was born July 19, 1920, in Belmont, Massachusetts. The family relocated to Scituate in 1927, where Vincent attended Scituate schools and was graduated from Scituate High School in 1938. He then traveled to Germany and attended the Institute of Technology in Berlin. In between semesters, Vincent worked for the United States Embassy in Berlin keeping records of the millions of French and Belgian prisoners of war resulting from Germany's invasions of those countries before the United States became involved in the fighting. He was the last college student to leave Berlin prior to the Japanese attack on Pearl Harbor which triggered our involvement in both the Pacific and European fronts of the war.

After returning to the United States, Vincent joined many other of the town's youth working as a mosser off of Scituate's coast, harvesting the carrageen that is still used in foods and cosmetics.

In August of 1942, Vincent enlisted in the Army Air Corps. He attended Pre-flight School in Monroe, LA and Aerial Gunnery School at Buckingham Army Air Field, FL. When it was time to choose a course for further training, Vincent opted for Navigation rather than the more popular pilot position, much to the confusion of his superiors. He related, in his taped interview recently that he chose this option because he thought it would be of more use to him after the war in navigating his own boat. He did, in fact, sail up and down the California coast after his discharge.

Vincent was an Instructor/pre-flight trainer in Navigational Flying and served stateside. He was awarded the Good Conduct Medal, American Victory Medal and a Citation for saving an airplane in distress.

After the war, Vincent attended Boston University and San Diego State University. He remained there pursuing a career as a college professor. In 1942 he married the former Jane Hill of Scituate. They had a son, Terence. Jane passed away in 1988. Vincent now resides in Costa Rica with his second wife Vilna (Varquero) Gosewisch.

Vincent's brother, Frederick, volunteered for the United States Navy in 1944 at the age of thirty-one. According to his son, Ron, "He skyrocketed to success as a Fireman First Class and was sent to San Francisco where he waited to be shipped out. His ship developed some kind of engine trouble a week or two out of San Francisco and had to return. He used to jest that by the time the war had ended, he'd fought the 'Battle of San Francisco'." Fred married the former Doris Rosenberg in Cohasset on October 15, 1933 and they had two sons, Thomas and Ronald.

Vincent and Frederick were the brothers of Esther Gosewisch Prouty who ran Prouty's Farm on First Parish Road in Scituate for many years. She passed away in 1991.

Scott Field, Illinois
December 16, 1942

To the Scituate Service Committee:

A few days ago I received the money order that the citizen's of Scituate so generously sent me. The most appreciated gift a soldier can receive is money, so perhaps you can realize what a fine gift this money was. The citizin's of Scituate chose the most practical way of sending their Christmas greetings, and I am sure that every fellow in the service feels the same as I do about it.

When I left Scituate to join the Army, little did I realize what I was leaving behind. In the past two and one half months I have been in about twenty different states, and I have yet to find a place that compares with Scituate. I feel sure that if I travel the length and width of the globe, I will never find a place in which I would rather live than Scituate.

As Christmas time draws near, my desire to return to Scituate grows greater, day by day. There is no possibility of me getting home for Christmas, so I must be content with memories of past Christmas's.

Thanks again citizen's of Scituate, and a Happy Christmas to you all.

A grateful soldier,
Pvt. Orrin Gould

ORIN A. GOULD

Orin Gould, the son of Orin A. and Margaret A. McDermott Gould, was born in Watertown on February 18, 1924. He lived in Quincy and Belmont, finally settling with his family in Scituate. He was graduated from Scituate High School in 1941, where he was awarded a medal for highest honors in History.

After high school, Orin was working as a sales clerk and planned to attend Harvard. Those plans were interrupted by his enlistment in the Army Air Force in October of 1942.

Trained as a Control Tower Operator with the 104th AAF Base Unit, he also qualified as a Pistol Aviation Marksman and served in the Mideast Theater of Operations, primarily in North Africa. Orin received the Good Conduct Medal, American Theatre Campaign Ribbon, and the European-African-Middle Eastern Theatre Campaign Ribbon.

December 1945 brought his discharge and an opportunity to pursue his educational plans at Harvard, from which he was graduated in 1948. He married the former Helen Ward on February 7, 1948, and they had a son, Christopher, and a daughter, Janet. There are now three grandchildren. Orin ran the family's rare instrument business for over thirty years. He was involved in making, restoring, appraising, and selling stringed instruments, a business that was begun by Orin's grandfather in 1889. With his historical expertise, Orin expanded the business by documenting and certifying rare violins and cellos, opening branches in Winthrop and Providence, RI. He closed the company in 1998, ninety-nine years after its founding.

After retirement, the Goulds traveled extensively throughout the United States and England, where Orin enjoyed researching the architecture of historic estates. He also practiced organic farming and spent time in the Berkshires.

Orin Gould passed away in July, 2005, at the age of 81.

U.S. NAVAL RESERVE AVIATION BASE
LAMBERT FIELD, MISSOURI

Jan. 10, 1943

Dear Sir,

I wish to express my appreciation and thanks to the people of Scituate for the gift they sent me.

The idea of sending each boy in the service from Scituate some money, was original as no other boys here at this base recieved such a gift.

Thank you again.

Sincerely yours,
Chester R. Gurney Jr.

Reed Jan 17 - 46

Scituate, Mass
January 10. 1946

Dear Mr Shea,

My husband and I wish to thank the Citizens of Scituate sincerely for the flowers sent to us at Christmas. They were lovely and we appreciate the kindness and thoughtfulness shown to us by the towns people.

Sincerely
Ethel Gurney

CHESTER R. GURNEY, JR.

Chester Gurney, Jr., was the son of Chester and Ethel (Kelley) Gurney. He and his sister, Hope, grew up in the family home on Wompatuck Avenue in Scituate. He was graduated from Scituate High School in 1939 and attended Fitchburg State Teachers College in Fitchburg, MA. Chester left school in his sophomore year in 1942 to volunteer for military service.

In the course of one year, Chester advanced from Naval Aviation Cadet to First Lieutenant in the Marine Corps. He was awarded his Navy Wings at Navy Pre-flight School, Chapel Hill, NC, and went on to the Pensacola Naval Air Station. After being assigned to MCAS (Marine Corps Air Station) El Toro in Santa Ana, CA, he became a dive bomb pilot.

While he was stationed at Lambert Field in Missouri, Chester wrote to the Town that "The idea of sending each boy in the service from Scituate some money was original as no other boys here at this base received such a gift."

Chester Gurney lost his life due to mechanical failure of his plane during a flight over the Pacific Ocean on November 25, 1943, Thanksgiving Day.

UNITED STATES
ARMY AIR FORCES

Wednesday
Jan. 24, 1945

Dear Sir:

This letter is a little late, but they say "a little late is better than never."

Just a few lines to thank you and the citizens of Scituate for their wonderful christmas gift.

Five dollars probably doesn't seem like much back there, but in the army it goes a long way.

A lot of the fellows wanted to know where I was from and when I told them they said that Scituate must be a wonderful place and that they wish their town or city would do the same.

Well, thats about all except "thanks a million."

Respectfully yours,

Malcolm F. Hall

MALCOLM FRANK HALL

Frank Hall, the son of Malcolm and Edith Wagner Hall, was born February 10, 1926, on Brook Street in Scituate, Massachusetts. He was graduated from Scituate High School in 1944. Frank served as an Auxiliary Fire Fighter in Scituate from 1942 to 1943. He enlisted in the Aviation Cadet Program of the Army Air Corps in February of 1944.

The Army Air Corps sent Frank from Keesler Field, Biloxi, Mississippi, to Freeman Field, Seymore, Indiana, where he received pilot training. He then went to Lockbourne Field (now Rickenbacker Field) in Ohio and finally to Turner Field in Albany, Georgia.

After Frank was discharged from the service in 1945, he attended and was graduated from Franklin Technical Institute in Boston. He married the former Ruth Wallace Spear on May 14, 1949. Frank remembers playing the bugle as part of the detail that met and escorted the remains of Veterans who were brought back to Scituate for burial after the war.

Frank and Ruth had three children. He went on to become a Call Firefighter in Scituate until 1954 when he became permanent. Frank served the Scituate Fire Department, where he also performed EMT duties, until his retirement in 1982. During this time, Frank also worked first for his father's plumbing business, and later on his own.

Active in the Masons, Frank served as Past Master of Satuit Lodge AF & AM, Past District Deputy Grandmaster, Treasurer of the Satuit Lodge for twenty-five years, and Education Representative for eighteen years. He is also active in The Order of The Eastern Star, where he was Past Patron. In addition, he served on the Scituate Housing Authority for seventeen years and was a Past Chairman. He has been active in the United Methodist Church all of his life.

When he provided his biography, Frank referred to his death as occurring "sometime in the future when I find the time."

Dec. 29, 1942

Dear Folks at Home,
    I thought for a long while trying to think of the right words in which to show my appreciation of your very great thoughtfulness, but all I can say is thank you, knowing full well the inadequacy of whatever I may have to say. With people like those of Scituate in back of all our boys, there can be no doubt as to the outcome of the war. Wherever I may be I'll always look forward to coming back to Scituate and especially the people in it.

    The motto of the Marines is "Semper Fidelis," and I believe it should be awarded to all of you, as individuals, and as a group. I hope I'll be able to serve you as well as you have all of us.

        Respectfully yours,
        Robert C. Hanckel Jr.
        2nd Lt., U. S. M. C. R.

Robert Hanckel

ROBERT CHAMPNEY HANCKEL, JR.

Robert Hanckel was born in Princeton, Massachusetts, at his grandmother's home on August 17, 1920. He attended schools in Scotia, New York, and while in high school there he completed a year in the New York State National Guard. The family moved to Scituate in 1941.

Robert attended Worcester Polytechnic Institute, his father's alma mater, and was named <u>All New England Player of the Week</u> on the varsity football team several times.

In 1941, Robert entered the Naval Air Reserve. He trained at the Squantum, MA, Naval Air Station, where he soloed in open cockpit trainers. After receiving his wings, he underwent advanced flight training at several bases in Florida and was accepted as a Marine fighter pilot.

In December of 1942, Robert wrote in his thank you letter, "Wherever I may be, I'll always look forward to coming back to Scituate and especially the people in it. . . .I hope that I'll be able to serve you as well as you have all of us."

After further flight training in San Diego, Robert bade farewell to his parents and brother and proceeded to Espiritu Santo in the South Pacific, where an airstrip had been literally "carved out" of the jungle. He was assigned to fly a 4FU4, the latest in fighter aircraft.

According to his brother, because of a design flaw in the airplane, a "blind spot" existed, which impeded a full circle line of sight. As a result, Robert had a mid-air collision with another aircraft. There were no survivors. As noted in his flight log: "problem - - - pilot missing." The crash happened on June 9, 1943. Robert Hanckel, Jr., was twenty-two years old.

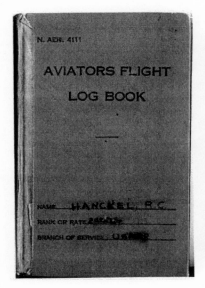

Jan 2
1943?

Gentlemen:

I want to let you know
that I received your very welcome
gift. It could not have come at
a handier time. So at this time I
wish to thank the people of Scituate
for their thoughtfulness and hope they
enjoyed a merry Christmas and will
have a Happy New Year.

Sincerely
Paul Harrigan

Miami Beach   Miami Beach

John Harrigan

Four Scituate Harrigan Brothers in the Service

John J., 20   Paul R., 22   Thomas J., 25   James, 17

SCITUATE, Jan. 21—Harrigan, according to the well-loved song, "is a name that shame never was connected with." Residents of this town know the song and its message well, and why shouldn't they?

They sing the song in tribute to the four sons of Mr. and Mrs. Thomas F. Harrigan, former residents of Dorchester, who make their home here now. All four of the boys, even 17-year-old Jimmy, are wearing the uniform with credit today.

Jimmy, the youngest, is in the Navy, stationed at New York. Tom, 25, oldest of the quartet, is now seeing action with the Army against Axis forces in Africa. Paul, 22, and John, 20, are both in the Army; Paul stationed in California and John training in a New Jersey camp.

HARRIGAN BROTHERS

**James and Paul Harrigan
April 9, 1944 Sicily**

The four Harrigan brothers were the sons of Thomas F. Harrigan and the former Elizabeth Griffith. All served their country in World War II.

Thomas J. was born December 31, 1916. He joined the US Army in the 1930's and served with the 34th Weather Squadron as a meteorologist during World War II. He saw action in North Africa, where he was killed on April 7, 1944. He is buried in the North Africa American Cemetery in Carthage, Tunisia, along with 2,841 Americans killed in that campaign.

Paul R. was born in 1920. He served in the US Army seeing service in Italy. He later married Marie McArdle, and they had 2 children. Paul was a Scituate Police Officer after the war, and he also co-owned South Shore Auto Parts in Scituate. Paul passed away in 2002.

John J. was born July 7, 1922. He moved with his family to Scituate when he was nine years old and was graduated from Scituate High School in 1940. John served in France and England with the 8th Air Force. He married the former Olga Cascia in 1956, and they had three sons. After the war John worked for the Scituate Post Office for thirty-three years, retiring in 1984.

James L. was born on April 5, 1925. He was six years old when the family moved to Scituate. He was graduated from Scituate High School in 1942. James served in the US Navy during World War II aboard a minesweeper. The YMS 3 was constructed of wood to enable it to approach and disable magnetic mines that were made to attach themselves and destroy metal-hulled ships. James saw action in Southern France and Sicily, where he unexpectedly met his older brother, Paul at Easter Sunday Mass in 1944, after which the above picture was taken. James also served in the Pacific Theater, where he participated in several amphibious landings. James worked as a mechanic for a car dealer in Plattsburgh, NY, near the Canadian border, and as an Immigration Inspector until his retirement in 1984. He now plays golf and works around his house. He and wife Brenda have one child and one grandchild.

Thomas Harrigan on right, North Africa.

"There was enough ammunition to keep a division going," said CAPT WILLIAM A. HENDRICKSON of Scituate, Mass., who rode in one of the first tanks to enter the city.

(Capt Hendrickson, 25, is the son of Mr. and Mrs. William A. Hendrickson, First Parish road, Egypt. He is a graduate of Scituate High, 1936, Massachusetts State College, '41, and was commissioned a second lieutenant on his graduation. He went overseas last December.

His wife, the former Miss Jane Witte of Cincinnati, is an expectant mother. Capt Hendrickson has two brothers, one of whom, Robert, 19, is in the Navy, stationed on the West Coast, and three sisters.)

It is all an unbelievable shambles. Our tanks just hosed fire on the buildings from 200 yards, so that though the City Hall building is standing it is in a pretty grim mess.

My first entrance to a conquered city has given me so much else to see that the reaction of the civilians has rather passed me by. According to Nazi officials there are 700,000 people in the town, at least 50,000 of them refugees who "cannot be controlled.

Dec 10, 1942.

Dennis H. Shea, Esq.
Chairman - Board of Selectmen.
Scituate, Mass.

Dear Mr. Shea,

This is to thank the citizens of the Town of Scituate for remembering me at this time. I shall miss Christmas in the old home town, and appreciate her spirit in trying to bring Christmas cheer to those of us in the armed services

Sincerely,
Wm A. Hendrickson Jr.
Lieutenant, 3rd A.R.
10th A.D. A.P.O. 260.
Ft Benning, Ga

Here is what is claimed to ... dairy bull, at ... Farm in Williamstown. He we ... pounds and is 10 years o... is owned by Colonel and Mrs. E. Parmalee Prentice, son-in-law and da... ter of the late John D. Rockefeller.

RECRUITS ROLL BLANKETS

approx 1940

Here are newcomers in the R. O. T. C. unit at Massachusetts State College learning the fundamentals of the science of war by rolling blankets. Left to right, William Hendrickson of Scituate and Ernest Bolt of Windsor.

BAN STRUTTING

WILLIAM A. HENDRICKSON

William A. Hendrickson was born January 18, 1919 in Milton, MA. He moved to Scituate in 1928 and was graduated from Scituate High School in 1936. He attended Massachusetts College (now the University of Massachusetts) graduating in 1940 with a degree in Chemical Engineering. While in college William was a member of the ROTC (Reserve Officers Training Corps) and upon graduation went straight into the Army.

The ROTC was established to provide quality officers to meet the expanding needs of the military. At its outset, the Morrill Land Grant Act of Congress, which created the ROTC program, donated lands and financing to establish colleges which would then provide instruction in agriculture, mechanical and military sciences - the state college systems. During WWII there were 2000 UMASS graduates in uniform, 122 were killed defending their country.

After being assigned to guard the Capitol in Washington, DC, William joined the 777th Tank Battalion and was stationed at Fort Knox, Kentucky. In his thank you letter to the Town from Ft. Benning, Georgia in 1942, William spoke of missing Christmas in "the old home town" and thanked everyone for "trying to bring Christmas to those of us in the armed services". He went overseas to Germany just after the Battle of the Bulge. This was the largest land battle of WWII involving American Forces. It lasted from December 16, 1944 until January 28, 1945. When Germany was clearly losing the war, an attempt had been made to assassinate Hitler and many were of the opinion the German leader had become mentally deranged. This did not, however prevent him from amassing 600,000 troops including eight armored divisions, thirteen infantry divisions and the 5th and 6th Panzer divisions, as well as the German Luftwaffe in an attempt to eliminate Allied air power. Although it was a futile effort on Hitler's part 81,000 Americans were killed or injured, 1400 British killed or injured and 100,000 Germans killed, wounded or captured.

William was attached to Patton's Third Army and with them fought his way through Germany. His Company took Leipzig (the birthplace of the composer, Bach) where they found food and ammunition "enough to keep a whole division going", according to a quote from Captain William Hendrickson which appeared in a Boston Globe article in April of 1945.

After the war in Europe was over, William served as military mayor of several German Towns until his unit was sent home. He arrived seventeen hours after his wife Jane had given birth to his first son. His unit was then sent across the United States in preparation for deployment to Japan. As it happened, they never went.

After the war William worked as a representative for an electrical company and he was president of William A. Hendrickson Co., Inc. in Scituate until he retired.

William passed away on September 14, 1998.

Theodore Holland

THEODORE JAMES HOLLAND

Ted Holland, the son of James and Rena Damon Holland, was born on June 4, 1926. He grew up on Clapp Road in Scituate's West End. After being graduated from Scituate High School in 1944, Ted went to work for Ray Litchfield as a mechanic. He also served the town as an Air Raid Warden, patrolling the West End to insure compliance with blackout regulations.

In April of 1946, Ted entered the United States Army. His basic training took place at Aberdeen Proving Grounds outside of Washington, DC, in Maryland. Established in 1917 as a weapons testing facility, Aberdeen grew to include over 27,000 military personnel at its peak during World War II.

Ted was sent to Walter Reed Army Hospital in Washington, DC, where he worked as a classification/assignment clerk. It was here that Ted met up with Johnny Travers from Scituate and was able to arrange an assignment for him in Japan as part of the occupation forces. This, as Ted relates, "involved no heavy lifting," as Johnny's job was to supervise the Japanese civilians who did all the work.

After his discharge in October of 1947, Ted returned to Scituate and his job at Ray's Garage. In 1951 he married the former Helen McHugh from Norwell. They had two sons and a daughter. Ted later went to work for Anderson Fuel, a job he retired from in 1991.

Ted's older brothers also served in World War II. <u>William</u> saw service with the US Army 345th Infantry in the Rhineland, Ardennes, and Central Europe from October 1944, until July 1945. He served as the Air Raid Warden in the West End ensuring compliance with black out regulations before he entered the service. He married Ann Dement and had six children. William passed away in 1983.

William Holland

Ted's brother <u>Robert</u> was trained as an antiaircraft gunner and served in the field artillery in Europe. He married Claire Burns of Scituate and they had four children. He died in 1997 in Vermont.

Robert Holland

185

Japanese Caves on Okinawa.

SEABEE'S

Hauling Cargo Through the Mud on Okinawa.

WILSON T. HOLLIS

Wilson T. "Bud" Hollis, son of Wilson T. Sr. and Edith (Andrews) Hollis, was born on June 24, 1925, in Scituate, MA. Educated in Scituate Schools, Bud left before graduating from Scituate High to join the United States Navy on November 8, 1944.

He was assigned to the SeaBee Base Camp Endicott, a part of the Naval Training Center at Davisville, RI, where the "Quonset Hut" was invented to fulfill the need for an easily assembled shelter to be shipped to distant bases.

SeaBees are Naval Construction Battalions made up of one thousand enlisted men and thirty-two officers. Trained in military tactics as well as construction techniques, they built over four hundred advanced bases under combat conditions in all theaters of World War II. Their insignia is a large bumblebee, wearing a sailor hat and carrying an automatic weapon. Fifty-five thousand SeaBees were assigned to Okinawa.

According to a poem supplied by Bud, "A SeaBee is a soldier in a sailor's uniform, with a Marine's training----doing Civilian work at WPA wages."

Bud, along with his unit, the 139th US Naval Construction Battalion underwent further training at Camp Rousseau, Port Hueneme, California before being sent to Okinawa, where he served until May of 1946.

As the convoy, in which his unit was traveling arrived in Bruckner Bay, Okinawa, kamikaze (suicide) planes attacked them. Although there were no casualties, Bud's ship was hit. Within thirteen hours of arrival, the unit was unloading, checking, and servicing trucks from cargo ships. The remaining cargo was transported from the beaches to inland supply dumps. The men worked twelve to sixteen hours a day, while being subjected to additional kamikaze attacks. During Bud's service, Okinawa was struck by two typhoons causing tents, equipment, and belongings to be blown away or destroyed.

Bud left Okinawa for the United States aboard the Liberty Ship USS Monrovia in January of 1946 and was discharged with the rank of Machinist Mate 2/c Petty Officer.

In 1948 Bud married Marilyn Uloth. They have three daughters, six grandchildren and, according to Marilyn as of April 2004, five and one-half great grandchildren.

Bud and Marilyn live on land in Scituate that was settled by Bud's great grandparents. Three of Bud's ancestors left their home on this same land to fight in the American Civil War. There now exists the possibility that a seventh Hollis generation will someday occupy this property.

Sadly, Bud Hollis passed away on July 12, 2005 at the age of 80.

George W. Johndrow, Jr.

GEORGE W. JOHNDROW, JR.

George "Bill" Johndrow was born on July 22, 1924, in Arlington, MA. He attended prep school at the New Hampton School in New Hampshire. George moved to Scituate in 1941.

On June 10, 1943, George, like many other Scituate youths, traveled via Greenbush Station to his induction into the United States Navy in Boston. He was assigned to the Navy V-12 Program at Harvard University. This program provided educated officers to the services. The men were considered to be on active duty and were required to take 17 credit hours as well as physical training in a year-round program. George was then sent to Midshipmen's School at Notre Dame University, from which he was graduated as a US Navy Ensign in 1945. After attending Naval Gunnery School at Point Mantara, California, George was assigned to the salvage ship USS Vent serving in the Asiatic-Pacific area. The USS Vent was a two hundred and thirteen foot long ship that carried one hundred and twenty men. The Vent conducted salvage operations and harbor clearance duties in and around the Solomon Islands, Saipan and New Guinea. After the Japanese surrender, the Vent participated in the salvage of several AFD's (Auxilliary Floating Drydocks) that had been grounded on the beaches of Buckner Bay on Okinawa.

George was discharged from the Navy on July 10, 1946. He then attended Northeastern University and was graduated from Boston University with a degree in Economics in 1949. After working in the wool business for ten years, George then became a golf supply manufacturer's representative. He continued his association with golf pros for thirty years.

George married the former Elizabeth M. Cate in 1949. They had four children. Active in all sports, George was the Past President of the Scituate Youth Center.

George W. Johndrow passed away on April 19, 2002.

December 7, 1942

Scituate Service Committee
Scituate, Mass.

Gentlemen,

the other day I received your very nice Christmas card with the enclosed gift. I wish to take this opportunity to thank you for thinking of me at this time of year. I realize the amount of planning that went into a project of this type, and I am sure that everyone appreciates your effort.

I have completed my course out here at Ft. Harrison. It was an interesting course, and I learned a great deal about the Army life and organization. We are now waiting around for shipment, and expect to leave here shortly.

Ft. Harrison is a very nice camp. It is an old Army post located about twelve miles from the city of Indianapolis. It is not very large, and at the present time it is being used for training purposes.

In closing, I wish to thank you all again, and to wish everyone in Scituate a very happy holiday season.

Sincerely,
Nelson Kindlund

Mrs. Eric A. Kindlund
Jericho Beach Road
Scituate, Massachusetts

January 5, 1944.

My dear Mr. Shea —

I presume that you head whatever group was responsible for sending me the flowers and card at Christmas and I wish you would extend to them my most sincere thanks.

War has demanded unusual sacrifice from me. My husband was ill for many years because of service in World War I and now World War II has taken the life of my beloved and only son.

I can only hope that the sum total of all the gallant courage men and women are showing today somehow compensates for the sadness and sorrow and I pray that God will give me the strength to do my part.

Sincerely yours,
Alice M. Kindlund
(Mrs. E. A. K.)

NELSON KINDLUND

Nelson Kindlund, the son of Eric and Olive Roche Kindlund, was born on September 10, 1920. He was graduated from Scituate High School in 1938, where he participated in the Dramatics and Glee Clubs. Nelson attended Duke University and worked summers as a lifeguard at Scituate beaches.

He entered the United States Army in the fall of 1942. He was stationed at Fort Harrison near Indianapolis before being transferred to El Paso, Texas, as an Army Corporal with the Army Antiaircraft Gun Group. It was in Texas, at Fort Bliss, during night maneuvers with an Army convoy, that an accident claimed his life on October 27, 1943. Nelson was twenty-three years old.

Nelson had written a thank you letter from Fort Harrison in 1942 expressing his appreciation for being remembered at Christmastime. The Town also sent flowers to surviving family members in the event of the serviceman's death. Mrs. Kindlund, Nelson's mother, sent three letters. The first, in 1944, thanked the community for the flowers and card and mentioned that her husband had been ill for many years as a result of service in World War I and now, "World War II has taken the life of my beloved and only son." In 1945 she wrote expressing gratitude to the town for not forgetting, and again in 1946 she wrote of her continuing loneliness.

Nelson Kindlund is buried in his family's plot in Forest Hills Cemetery, Jamaica Plain, MA.

Outgoing American Legion Commander Daniel Marini, Auxilary President Dolly Bearce, Incoming American Legion Commander, Lawrence Langley, Incoming Auxilary President Mrs. Kevin Dwyer.

LAWRENCE JOSEPH LANGLEY

Lawrence Langley was born in Cambridge, MA, in August 1918, one of thirteen children. He subsequently became a life-long resident of Scituate.

During World War II Lawrence was trained as a medic in New York and shipped out to England where he helped set up a 200 bed hospital on the coast in anticipation of the D-Day landings in Normandy.

In a journal, written in 1994 on the anniversary of D-Day, Larry wrote of his memories of that time:
"June 6, 1994 - Today is kinda cloudy and temp in 60's. This is the anniversary (50th) of Normandy invasion of allied forces onto French territory to start pushing back the German occupation of France in WWII. Lots of programs on TV showing the beach landings and the terrible slaughter of young men advancing to German positions. The Germans paid a tremendous price for occupation as all allied forces crushed all opposition.
"I was on the coast of England after our unit constructed a 200 bed hospital for just this occasion. The planes in the sky were from horizon to horizon just a blanket of all types of planes and on the ground tanks trucks and walking men tramped toward the boats awaiting to take them across the channel. It wasn't long before casualties came in and kept coming and coming. Being trained as a combat medic the sights were not pleasant to see at first but after a while it didn't take a second thought. We overflowed our beds in no time and we began set ups in the halls. We kept in high gear for months up into December when the breakthrough at Bastongne, Belgium by the German tanks and crack SS German troops. They hit hard at the front lines that were made up of fresh troops with not too much experience. We took a hell of a pounding with tank 88 guns and mortar fire from German forces.
"I came very close to being put into combat at this time as the German sharp shooters were killing off medics right and left. They would spot the red cross on our helmets and target in on them. I was put on alert twice but somehow was never called. We were so shorthanded that I'm sure this was what saved me. Besides I was a darn good medic and would have been very useful in a combat situation, but dead too."

After the war Larry returned to the United States aboard the Queen Mary. According to his daughter, Annette Langley Markward, "His dedication to his wounded and fallen comrades, and veterans of all wars was lifelong, including his role as Veterans of Foreign Wars Commander and Scituate Veterans Agent for many years . . . he also counseled veterans and their wives. As the organizer of many Memorial Day parades, the driving force in his life was keeping the spirit of America alive through honoring and revering those who sacrificed so much to preserve our freedom."

Lawrence Langley passed away in December 2003

November 21, 1944

Service Men's Committee;

I'd like to express my sincere appreciation for the very nice Christmas remembrance that I received from you.

The realization that the folks back home are thinking of us at this season brings the Christmas spirit of home much nearer.

I wish you all a very merry Christmas and hope that this time next year will find us all celebrating Christmas together again.

Sincerely

Pvt. Gene LaVange
U.S. Army

GENE LEVANGE

Gene LeVange, son of Benjamin and Margaret Duffy LeVange, left Scituate in February of 1943 for Fort Devens, where he performed troop train duty for six months.

Fort Devens, in Ayer, MA, was established in 1917. It covered 5000 acres of land. Twelve hundred wooden barracks were added to supply the demands of World War II.

At the end of the war it served as a demobilization center for returning servicepersons.

After spending some time at Camp Lee in Virginia, Gene was assigned to the 1780th Engineers at Fort Leonard Wood in Missouri. An Army Base 150 miles south east of Kansas City, it consists of 71,000 acres. Three hundred thousand troops trained there between 1941 and 1946. In 1991 Fort Leonard Wood was designated as a World War II Commemorative Community for the establishment of its museum, the only preserved and interpreted Company area in the United States Army. The buildings have been restored to 1943 conditions, the peak year of training at the Fort.

While he was in Missouri, Gene's brother passed away, and he went home on a short furlough. He was subsequently sent to the Pacific Theater of Operations in early 1944, where he remained until his discharge in 1946.

Engineering Divisions typically performed demolitions, obstacle emplacements, fortifications, and light bridge building. They also constructed and maintained Air Bases.

Gene is now eighty years old and reports that he is in fair health, living in Waynesville, North Carolina.

Ellsworth Litchfield

ELLSWORTH BLAIR LITCHFIELD

Ellsworth Litchfield, nick-named "Litch", son of Roy Ellsworth Litchfield and Nellie Edith Brown Litchfield, was born January 11, 1921. He entered the United States Army in the fall of 1942, and was stationed at Fort Adams in Newport, RI.

Fort Adams was constructed between 1824 and 1853 on the western side of Aquidneck Island, facing Narragansett Bay. Fort Adams was originally built for the purpose of coastal defense. Covering over 6 acres, it was the largest coastal fortification in the United States. Now designated a National Park, it is the home of the Newport Music Festivals, the site of Civil War reenactments, and social functions.

Litch left Newport and was transferred overseas, eventually serving in England as a Military Policeman.

After his discharge in late 1945, he returned to Scituate and helped to run Waterman's Flower Shop on First Parish Road. With the death of Mr.Waterman, Litch took over and ran the shop until his retirement in 1978.

Ellsworth married Marjorie Brown on April 28, 1946. They had three children and four grandchildren before he passed away on April 7, 1982.

12/31/42

Dear Friends,

This is written late to express my thanks for the present which I recieved from you. It came at a time when it was more appreciated than usual.

It has so happened that I have been on the supplementary pay roll the last two months and therefore was in need the day I recieved it. It was my day off and so you can see it arrived at exactly the right time.

Mrs. Ward was my favorite teacher when I was in grammer school. I looked forward to the Art classes each week eagerly.

Last Monday morning I recieved my Aircraft Mechanics diploma and was made an instructor but special order moved off men who had

been chosen to instruct to Chanute Field Illinois to attend the specialist school here.

Never think that soldiers are forgotten. If you could have seen our mail rooms it would have shown anyone in doubt that the folks at home remember us well. Also the people of towns near our bases treat us as kindly as they would the boys who have left there.

It certainly is a great feeling to know that we are so well remembered. I only know of one town who sent all their boys a card besides our although probably many have. I haven't heard of any other town that pitched in and worked to send us a gift as you folks did.

I wish that the New Year will be a victorious one for the allied nations and that the world will soon be at peace once more

Sincerely yours,
Francis W. Litchfield

FRANCIS M. LITCHFIELD

 Francis M. Litchfield comes from a long line of military men. He was born, as was his WWI veteran father, Ralph Litchfield, in the Driftway Road house that had been built by his civil war veteran grandfather on November 22, 1921.

A 1939 Scituate High School graduate, Franny attempted three times to enlist in the Army Air Force after the December 1941 attacks on Pearl Harbor. Being told he could not choose his branch of service or type of job, he decided to wait to be drafted. This happened on July 16, 1942 and Franny was off to Camp Devens and subsequently to Atlantic City, NJ for Basic Training.

For Christmas in 1942 Franny received his Scituate gift. His thank you note mentions that the gift arrived at a particularly fortuitous time as he had been put on supplementary pay status and was "therefore in need." He also remembered Mrs. Ward (the artist who designed the Christmas card) as one of his favorite grammar school teachers.

Franny's service took him to Lincoln Air Base, Nebraska, Chanute Field, IL, Las Vegas, NM, Buffalo, NY, Miami, FL, and ultimately to India where he worked in the electrical shop servicing C-87 aircraft flying the "hump". The "hump" refers to the Himalayan Mountains.

During WWII China was our ally, albeit an under-equipped and under trained one. In order to maintain the Chinese Army as a viable fighting force to keep the Japanese occupied in fighting a two front war, the United States undertook to supply them with much needed materiel. To reach its destination, equipment had to traverse long sea routes to India and airlift transshipment to China, over the dauntingly high Himalayas with their treacherous air currents. The servicemen who flew and those who supported the efforts served in the China-Burma-India Theater (CBI). Franny spent twenty-six months overseas and his base received a Presidential Citation in December of 1944 for shipping the most cargo over "the Hump".

Returning to Miami, FL in September 1945, Franny and Nancy Wade were married on November 7. Continuing the Litchfield family tradition, Franny and Nancy's children all have military connections. Steve became a 1st Lieutenant in the USN, Doug served in Viet Nam, Kenny flew helicopters in Panama and Karen married a USN Chief.

Franny's civilian life has been marked by always working for himself. He has done contracting and crane service for the harbormaster, served on the Conservation Commission and is an elected member of the Charter Review Commission.

Franny and Nancy still reside in Scituate.

WOODS HOLE SECTION BASE
NAVAL LOCAL DEFENSE FORCE
WOODS HOLE, MASS.

Office of the Engineering Officer.

1943
31st March

Dear Reggie:

I wish to express my sincere thanks
to you and the citizens of the town of Scituate for
the gift that was so thoughtfully sent me at Christmas
time. I have always been a most tardy correspondent
and hope that my apologies will be accepted in this
case. My time has been quite fully occupied and this
is really the first opportunity I have had to devote
any real time to correspondence.

I trust you are well and I know that the
town that we all love so well seems quite different
now with so many of the boys away.

Please give my best to everyone.

Sincerely yours,

C. B. Locklin,
Lieut., USNR

The Town of Scituate,
Mass.

Attention: Mr. Dennis Shea, Chairman,
The Board of Selectmen.

CBL/hes

CHESTER BOWMAN LOCKLIN

Chester Locklin was born in 1908 in Boston, MA. He joined the US Navy after being graduated from the Massachusetts Maritime Academy in 1942. Chester served as a Lt. Commander and Chief Engineering Officer of a 22,000 ton fleet auxiliary hospital ship in the South Pacific during World War II.

Upon retiring from the Navy, Chester owned and managed the Scituate Marine Service Company, where he sold, serviced, and installed all types of marine engines and equipment. He also repaired both sail and powerboats. He assisted other local boat yards with marine engine service.

Chester eventually sold the business and became General Manager and Mechanical Engineer for the concrete products and building materials division of Frederick V. Lawrence, Inc. in Falmouth, MA.

Chester married the former Lillian MacLeod of Hull, MA, and they had three children.

From 1950 until 1966 they lived in Fair Haven, NJ, where Chester was Vice-president and Chief Engineer of Marble Face Blocks, Inc. in Kenilworth, NJ, until his retirement in 1968. He then moved to Delray, Florida, where he pursued his hobbies of sailing and boatbuilding.

Chester Locklin passed away in 1989.

December 10, 1943

In regards to the Christmas Card you sent me with the money order enclosed. I think it was very thoughtful to think of the boys in the service. I am writing this letter to let you know that I appreciate it very much. It was a very nice card with a beautiful verse on it. This is just a few lines to let you know I appreciated it very much.

Yours Truly
Henry Madden.

HENRY MADDEN

Henry Madden was born on September 26, 1923 in Marshfield Hills. He graduated from Scituate High School in 1941. He enlisted in the United States Navy in November, 1942, and received his initial training at the Naval Training Station in Newport, RI. He also attended schools at Camp Bradford, Little Creek, Virginia; Solomon's Island, Maryland; Louisville, Kentucky, and Jeffersonville, Indiana.

In Panama City, Florida, Henry learned how to beach the LST 73, the vessel he sailed across the North Atlantic to Africa, Sicily, and Italy. He was transferred to the LST 61 for the invasion on D-Day, June 6, 1944, at Omaha Beach and later at Utah, Juno, and Sword beachheads. These were the code names assigned to the various landing sites in Normandy to preserve the secrecy involved in planning the massive operation.

The LST 61 was a 328-foot long vessel designed to carry equipment, cargo, and troops to the site of an amphibious landing. It beached itself directly onto the beachhead to deliver its battle participants. The LST 61 also carried two to six LCVP (Landing Craft Personnel) in order to enable troops and equipment to be landed further ashore in shallower water.

Henry was awarded the World War II Victory Medal, American Theater Medal, Good Conduct Medal, and the European African Middle Eastern Area Medal with one star.

After his discharge in January 1946, Henry ran the lumber mill at the Welch Company in Scituate Harbor for over thirty years. He married Elizabeth Knight in 1948, and they had 4 children, one daughter and three sons. They now have ten grandchildren. Henry is retired and still living in Scituate.

Henry's brother William also served during World War II. He was in the Army Air Corps and spent his service working with ground crews in Syracuse, NY. He had worked in construction with Allen Wheeler and Brad Weston both before and after his time in the Air Corps before going into business on his own. He married the former Evelyn Nichols and they had three children. William passed away in 1977 at the age of 57.

Dec. 25, '43

Richard L Mahoney F2/c

To all Concerned,

I received the card & money order from the town-people yesterday. I wish to express my thanks & let you all know how much it was appreciated.

Sincerely yours,

Richard L Mahoney F2/c
U.S.N.R.

Lawrence Mahoney on right with James Welch on left.

THE MAHONEY FAMILY

Lawrence, Richard, Paul and David Mahoney, all sons of Martin and Mary O'Donnell Mahoney, moved to Scituate from Manchester, New Hampshire in the 1930's. They all attended Scituate High School.

Lawrence was the eldest, he entered the United States Navy after high school graduation in 1942. He served aboard the battleship USS Iowa, the ship that carried President Roosevelt to Casablanca on his way to the Teheran Conference in November of 1943. This was the tenth major meeting of Churchill, Stalin and FDR held during World War II. Lawrence spent two years in the Pacific Theater before returning to the States for further training. He later served aboard the USS Quincy where he remained until 1946 when he was granted an emergency leave to return home due to his father's illness. After his discharge, Lawrence married the former Patricia Roulleau and they had seven children. Lawrence Mahoney passed away on February 14, 1991.

Lawrence   Richard
Mahoney   Mahoney

Richard also entered the United States Navy after his high school graduation. He became an electrician aboard the Destroyer Escort USS Charles R. Greer. He also served in the Pacific Theater. At one point, the USS Iowa and the USS Charles R. Greer passed each other and as the ships relayed signals back and forth, Richard and Lawrence were permitted to include personal messages to each other. Richard was also granted leave when his father became ill. He married the former Anne Jarvis in 1947 and they had eight children. Together with his brother Lawrence, he was the owner of Mahoney Electric Company.

Paul was drafted into the service from Scituate High School in 1944. He became an Army Glider Pilot and served in France. While in France, Paul volunteered for the Paratroopers. He became part of the 101st Airborne Division. He had the opportunity to view Adolf Hitler's mountain retreat, Berchtesgaden, in the German Alps. When he was discharged from the Army, Paul returned to Scituate High School, finished his education and went on to college. He became a State DPW Engineer. He married the former Mary McDonough and they had three children.

David enlisted in the United States Navy after his high school graduation. The war had ended and he was stationed in the Hawaiian Islands working as a decoder. After his discharge he became a mailman in Scituate. He reenlisted, this time in the Army in the 1950's and was sent to Germany as a communications specialist. He met his future wife there and they adopted a child. He remained in the Army for twenty years. David Mahoney passed away several years ago while living in North Carolina.

RALPH F. McCARTHY

November 20, 1944

Board of Selectmen
Town Hall,
Scituate, Massachusetts.

Sirs:

On Saturday, November 18th, at "Mail Call", I received
my Christmas Card and Money Order donation, sent to we men
in the service by the people of Scituate, through your
Service Men's Committee.

I cannot begin to tell you the feeling I had as I read
the verse on the Christmas Card. For a short fleeting moment, Scituate was in New Mexico. I could smell the salt
air, and hear the surf pound on the beaches. I could close
my eyes and see "The Pier", and all the "Oldtimers" I left
there three years ago. I know there are many more men from
Scituate who will receive their Christmas Cards in the very
near future, and I am sure that they too will experience
"a lump in their throat" as they read their cards.

It is a very warm feeling to be far from home, and know
that the people back there still remember you, and send their
Christmas Greetings, and with them, their own humble way of
saying "Thanks Soldier."

Congratulations to my old Art Instructor, Mrs. Ward,
for designing such a wonderful card, and my very sincere
thanks to the people of Scituate, and to you Selectmen, and
the Service Mens Committee.

Sincerely,

Ralph F. McCarthy

Ralph F. McCarthy
Technical Sergeant,
U.S. Army Air Forces.

RALPH F. McCARTHY

Tech. Sgt. Ralph McCarthy

Ralph McCarthy, the son of James and Mary Barry McCarthy, was born on June 24, 1913. After graduating from Scituate High School in 1931 he worked as a painter with his father. Ralph joined the US Army Air Corps in 1943. He attained the rank of Technical Sergeant and served mainly at Sandia Field, New Mexico. Formerly Albuquerque Army Air Field, Sandia was used as a training center for bombardiers, aviators, and mechanics. It was renamed Kirtland Air Force Base when the Army Air Corps became the United States Air Force in 1947.

In his letter written in November 1944, Ralph expressed his thoughts on receiving his gift: "For a short fleeting moment, Scituate was in New Mexico. I could smell the salt air, and hear the surf pound on the beaches. I could close my eyes and see 'The Pier', and all the 'Oldtimers' I left there three years ago."

On March 17, 1943 Ralph married Babe Schuyler, the sister of Red Cross Volunteer, Gretchen Schuyler and daughter of Colonel Philip Schuyler. Babe had a daughter, Gail and together she and Ralph had four sons: Tim, Terry, Sean and Patrick and a daughter, Colleen. After the war Ralph worked as a house painter and lobsterman, he served as shellfish warden and later, Harbormaster in 1964.

Ralph retired when he was in his seventies and passed away on June 30, 1980.

Edward Francis McCormack

EDWARD FRANCIS MCCORMACK

Edward McCormack was born in Weymouth, MA on February 27, 1919. His parents, John Francis and Ella Foley McCormack and brother Robert moved to Scituate in 1920. Edward was graduated from Scituate High School in 1939 where he played baseball, basketball, football, tennis and sang in the glee club. He went to work for Breen Construction as an equipment operator and married Virginia Ellen Thompson on November 28, 1940.

When the United States entered World War II, Edward and his friends Donnie Quinn, Bill Tobin and Bud Hollis volunteered to serve their country. Edward was activated in May of 1943 and his construction experience was put to good use in the SeaBees. This branch of the US Navy built docks, wharves, airfields and bases in all theatres of the war. Edward served in Midway, Manila, Leyte and the Marshall and Johnson Islands. He attained the rank of Chief Petty Officer. He also saw service in the Korean Conflict and the Viet Nam War. In the latter he was awarded a medal by the Vietnamese Government for constructing a bridge while under fire.

After World War II, Edward returned to Scituate where he and Virginia raised three sons and a daughter. He worked at the Quincy Shipyard and later for Anderson Fuel in North Scituate.

Edward retired in 1967 and now lives in Brownfield, Maine.

To the citizens of Scituate,

May I thank
you kindly for your Christmas gift.
It is swell to know that your friends
at home haven't forgotten you even tho
you may be miles away. I'm sure that
this little token of remembrance will
enhance and lighten the hearts of
many boys who are so away from home,
as it has me. Words fail to express
my true gratefulness. But it gives
me a great deal of pleasure to let
you know you are certainly doing your
part at home, by making such
pleasant gestures to those boys in
the Army. I hope I may do my
part as well and as successfully. Believe
me I am trying my very best.
                As I always hope to be,
                A resident of Scituate.
                S/Sgt R. McCormack

ROBERT MCCORMACK

Born on September 4, 1920, Robert McCormack moved with his family to Mann Lot Road in Scituate two years later. He attended Hatherly School and Scituate High School caddying at the Hatherly Country Club for six years during this period.

After high school graduation, Bob entered the Civilian Conservation Corps. The CCC, as it became known, was one of President Franklin D. Roosevelt's first "New Deal" programs, designed to provide employment for the thousands of eighteen to twenty-five year old men who were without jobs in the aftermath of the 1929 Stock Market Crash and the Great Depression. It was the most popular of Roosevelt's recovery programs. Men were assigned to camps around the country where they were provided with clothing, food, and shelter. They were paid thirty dollars per month with a mandatory allotment of twenty-five dollars to be sent home to their families. The program not only put over 505,000 men to work but also improved the overall economy by supplying money to purchase goods and services. The CCC planted over three billion trees across the nation, improved national parks with fire roads, fire towers, soil erosion protection and forest-fire fighting services. The men contributed to flood control in Indiana, Vermont and New York State and provided rescue services during the 1938 New England Hurricane.

After his CCC service, Bob went to work delivering milk for Whiting's Dairy and worked as an elevator operator in New York City, where he met Gene Krupa, Harry James and Marion Hutton, popular entertainers of those years. When Bob joined the Army in 1942, he was assigned to the Horse Cavalry at Fort Riley, Kansas. His was the last basic training group to leave for the border before the unit became mechanized. Bob was assigned to the Quartermaster Corps and trained in the Bakers and Cooks School. He eventually became an instructor in those subjects in Saint Louis, where he met his future wife, Glenna Mae Halley.

Assigned to the 421st Night Fighter Squadron, Bob was the Mess Sergeant of the unit, whose nickname for the mess tent was, "a particular place for particular people." While stationed on the Pacific Island of IeShima, Bob witnessed Japanese emissaries deplaning on their way to sign the surrender treaty. IeShima, a mere two miles from Okinawa, was the location where Ernie Pyle, the popular war journalist, was killed.

When Bob returned to the United States, he married Glenna Halley. They had two children and settled in Saint Louis, where Bob went to work in Human Resources for Monsanto, a provider of agricultural products including seeds and weed control substances. He was later transferred to Tucson, Arizona, where he lives now.

In 2001, Bob was inducted into the Scituate Sports Hall of Fame as the first four-letter athlete in the history of Scituate High School.

Merrill A. Merritt

MERRILL A. MERRITT

Merrill Merritt was born in Scituate on September 2, 1923, and was graduated from Scituate High School in 1941. He was inducted into the United States Army on March 17, 1943 and served in the 832nd Engineers, an Aviation Engineering Battalion, as a Construction Machine Operator. Merrill saw action in Normandy, Northern France, the Rhineland, Ardennes and Central Europe, building and repairing airstrips for the Army Air Corps.

Merrill was awarded the Good Conduct Medal, the Victory Medal and the European African Middle Eastern Theater Campaign Ribbon. The highlight of his Army life was when he met up with John Harrington, from Scituate, while they were both in England.

After his 1945 discharge, Merrill started his own plumbing business. On January 4, 1946 he married the former Anne Bailey, and they had two sons.

Merrill became Director of the Scituate Housing Authority in 1959, a post he held for thirty-six years.

Merrill A. Merritt passed away on November 8, 1995.

PFC Percival E. Merritt
New Zealand, 1944

PERCIVAL E. MERRITT, JR.

Percival E. Merritt, Jr., also known as "Cappy," the son of Percival E. Sr. and Harriet Curtis Merritt, was born in Scituate on October 11, 1919. He attended Scituate High School and then went to work for Merritt Building Movers, as had his father and grandfather.

In March of 1942, Cappy joined the United States Army, and after basic training, he was assigned as an anti-aircraft gunner. He operated a 37-MM gun, including its loading, sighting, and firing. He served overseas with Battery B, 950th Antiaircraft Automotive Weapons Battalion, from September 24, 1942, until March 21, 1945

Cappy's unit followed the First Marine Corps in its invasion of Guadalcanal in the Solomon Islands. This was the first large-scale operation against Japanese-held territory and became the turning point in the war in the Pacific. While on Guadalcanal, Cappy was stricken with malaria. In the hot, humid climate of the Pacific Islands, malaria affected thousands of American and Japanese troops. Caused by a parasite, the disease is spread by infected mosquitoes. It is a serious disease, which is sometimes fatal. In December of 1942 alone, 5,749 malaria cases were reported in the islands of the Pacific Theatre. This disease was the single greatest factor in reducing troop effectiveness. For every man who fell in combat, five fell to malaria. It causes the victim to suffer high fevers, shaking chills, headaches, and muscle aches. It can cause severe anemia and jaundice. Symptoms and complications may continue for years. As a result of contracting malaria, Cappy was eventually discharged as 100% disabled in 1945.

When he returned to Scituate, Cappy married Constance MacMillan on April 1, 1945. They had two children. He returned to work in the Building Moving Business.

Percival E. Merritt, Jr., passed away in 1976.

Tuesday 15 Jan

Dear Sirs —

    I'd like to express my appreciation
to you, the representatives of the people of the
town of Scituate, for their Christmas gift
to me. The kindly warmth of the gesture has,
I think, made all Scituate servicemen realize
more keenly the love and friendly spirit of the
people they left behind.
    We'll all be back at home some day
soon — until then

        Sincerely —

        Matt Miles

MATTHEW BAILEY MILES

Matthew Miles kneeling in front.

Matthew Miles, the son of Max and Margaret Bailey Miles, was born on November 3, 1926, in Kengtung, Burma, where his father was a medical missionary. Matt was graduated from Scituate High School in 1943, where he was joke editor of the <u>Chimes,</u> acted as class treasurer, and played football. His yearbook quote prophesizes: "Matt's the guy with all the knowledge. We bet that he can 'whiz' through college."

World War II intervened, however, and Matt joined the Army on April 12, 1945, the day of Franklin Roosevelt's death. While Matt was in basic training at Camp Gordon in Virginia, the war in Japan ended. He then studied Japanese in an ASTP (Army Specialized Training Program) at the University of Pennsylvania. Matt served as an interpreter for U.S. Forces in Japan from 1945 to 1946. After his discharge, he completed his undergraduate education at Antioch College, which was founded by the educational pioneer, Horace Mann, in Yellow Springs, Ohio. There he met and married the former Betty Baker in 1949. They had three children: Sarah, David, and Ellen, and three granddaughters

Matt furthered his education with M.A. and Ph.D. Degrees from Teachers' College at Columbia University. He pursued a career in education, becoming an educational theorist and innovator in group dynamics, organizational skills, school reform, and the social architecture of schools. He authored fifteen books, which included <u>Improving the Urban High School</u> and <u>Qualitative Data Analysis</u>. Matt also consulted with the U.S. Office of Education in Washington, the New York City school system, the World Bank, and the Carnegie and Ford Foundations. He was a consultant, as well, to national policy makers in Canada, the Netherlands, Sweden, Switzerland, Pakistan, New Zealand, and Australia.

Matthew Miles passed away on October 24, 1996, in Tappan, New York, at the age of 69.

"Fighting the War."

Outside barracks, Miami Beach.

Mr. and Mrs. Alden Mitchell, Hollywood, CA.

ALDEN MITCHELL

Alden "Dinker" Mitchell was born on March 28, 1923, in Scituate, Massachusetts. He was graduated from Scituate High School in 1941 and attended one year of school at the Brockton Business College in Brockton, MA. He then went to work for the Welch Lumber Company in Scituate Harbor.

With the encouragement of his family, Alden recently wrote a history of his World War II experiences. He felt it was important to chronicle the story of what he calls the "non-heroes" who served their country. In it Alden tells of becoming a "Volunteer Selectee" about a year after the war began. Along with his friends Monk Drew, Jamie Finnie and Dick Henderson, Alden took the Greenbush Train to the Boston Armory on February 16, 1943. The temperature that day was minus nine degrees, the coldest on record. He first went to Fort Devens in Ayer, MA, and then was sent to Miami Beach where the temperature was a balmy eighty-three degrees.

In Miami, Alden became a Drill Instructor for the Army Air Corps. He tells of taking part in a three-day bivouac at the Hialeah Race Track, where there was an obstacle course set up in the parking lot and flamingoes strutting around the racetrack infield.

In 1944 Alden returned to Scituate on furlough and married Connie Wade, who was working at the Hingham Shipyard. With his business school experience, Alden was put to work in the Commercial Transportation Office, where he was responsible for receiving hundreds of Air Force personnel, making train reservations for their furloughs home, and getting them and their luggage to the station.

The war truly began for Alden when he boarded the USS General Butner, a transport ship, and headed for the China-Burma-India Theater. This little-known, and less written about operation, performed the unenviable task of flying millions of tons of dry supplies and gasoline from bases in India over "The Hump" of the Himalayan Mountains to Kungming, China. The Assam Air Transport Command supplied our Chinese allies, under Chaing Kai-Shek, enabling them to continue to engage thousands of Japanese troops that would otherwise have been flung into the maw of the South Pacific campaign, thus prolonging the war. The Assam Valley bases were awarded a Presidential Citation.

Alden initially returned to his job at the Welch Company and went on to own and operate Scituate Cleansers in Harbor and North Scituate. Alden served on the Town Advisory Board for several years in the 1970's. He retired in 1988, raised tea roses, and enjoyed travelling in the United States and Europe. He is now pursuing genealogy. He and Connie had three children. They have seven grandchildren and five great grandchildren.

SECOND SIGNAL SERVICE BATTALION
Washington, D.C.

1/20/44

Mr. Dennis Shea,
Scituate, Mass.

My dear Mr. Shea,

I want to thank the Town Committee for their kind remembrance of me at Christmas. This note of appreciation is a little belated due to the fact that I moved from Baltimore to Washington just at the holidays and much of our mail was held up in the Pentagon Building. We are just now getting some of it.

I can understand now how it feels to be on the receiving end after having had the experience of collecting it formerly. It gives you a sense of security that people are thinking of you at home and so generously express it.

Army life is not easy especially when you have to subjugate your desires to those above you. However it is an experience which I would not have missed for anything. It makes a different person out of you. You meet people from all backgrounds and all parts of the country each with his own angle to present. It is surprising how we all blend and how beautifully we get along together.

The work I am doing is very vital to the war effort — the results of which cannot be told now but after the war when such things can be known will prove its worth.

Every one is very nice to service people here. I was at the Statler Hotel a few nights ago and sat at a table next to several congressmen. McInnes of Massachusetts was one of them who came over to talk to us.

Again please accept my thanks to the people of Scituate for their kindness.

Sincerely,
Mary Elizabeth Monahan,

MARY E. MONAHAN

 Mary E. Monahan, also known as Bessie May, was the daughter of George and Rose Cannon Monahan. She was born in Scituate on October 21, 1908. Bessie was graduated from Scituate High School in 1926, where she was a student in the Commercial Course. She went on to study at Bridgewater State Teachers' College and received her Bachelor of Science Degree in 1929. Miss Monahan taught at the Jenkins School, the Junior High School, and finally at Scituate High School where she taught history until 1961.

Taking a leave of absence from her teaching duties, Bessie enlisted in the Women's Army Auxiliary Corps (WAAC) on June 9, 1943. Separate and distinct from the Army and the Army Nurse Corps, the WAAC was such an unqualified success that, in 1943, Congress began hearings to authorize its conversion to the WAC (Women's Army Corps), making it part of the regular Army. This change entitled the women to rank, pay, and privileges equivalent to their male counterparts. All WAAC's were given a choice of joining the Army as a WAC or returning to civilian life. The majority decided to remain in service to their country, as did Bessie. She served as a Teletype operator and was awarded the American Service Medal, World War II Victory Medal, Good Conduct Medal, and the Meritorious Unit Service Plaque. She was discharged on February 28, 1946, at Fort Dix, New Jersey.

After returning to civilian life, Bessie taught again in the Scituate school system. Taking leaves, she taught the children of American service personnel in the Philippines and Korea. She adopted a son, Mark, during her time in Korea.

In 1964, while on the way to the Philippines for a visit, she suffered a heart attack and died aboard ship. Bessie May Monahan is buried in Arlington National Cemetery.

Mary Monahan, 4th from left.

WASHING CLOTHES: Pvts. Russell J. Wade, Lowell; Alfred J. Montanri, Scituate, and George L. Anderson, Waltham.

RECRUITS from the Greater Boston area are kept plenty busy at the U. S. Marines' corps training post at Parris Island, South Carolina.

ALFRED JAMES MONTANARI

Alfred "Zoom" Montanari was born November 21, 1924 in Kingston, Massachusetts, the 4th son of Primo and Theresa Montanari. The family moved to Jericho Road in the Sand Hills section of Scituate in 1927. He was graduated from Scituate High School in 1942

Alfred served in the 28th Regiment of the 5th Marine Division during World War II. The 5th Division was the spearhead of the invasion of Iwo Jima. They were awarded the Presidential Unit Citation for their bravery in combat.

Alfred was the recipient of the Purple Heart Medal for receiving wounds in action against the Japanese Imperial Marines on March 8, 1945.

Alfred received other awards, including the Asiatic-Pacific Campaign Medal, American Defense Medal, Japanese Occupation Medal, World War II Victory Medal, Good Conduct Medal, Marine Corps Medal, Iwo Jima Veterans Commemorative Medal, and the 50th Anniversary of Victory in the Pacific Medal.

On January 8, 1950, Alfred married Charlotte Ann Allen, and they had two daughters, Ann and Carla.

After the war, Alfred became a United States Postal Carrier for the Scituate Post Office.

One of Alfred's exceptional talents was designing, painting, and detailing. As a professional sign maker and artist, Alfred designed a flag that was adopted in May 1968 by the Scituate Board of Selectmen as the official town flag. This was the first time that the town had an official flag since its incorporation in 1636. The flag consists of Scituate's Town Seal in dark blue, centered on a field of white. Beneath the seal there is a gold banner scroll with "Town of Scituate" in dark blue. Today, thirty-five years later, the flag Alfred designed flies on municipal and business flagpoles throughout Scituate.

Alfred is now retired and living in Carver, Massachusetts.

TOWN FLAG ADOPTED — Scituate selectmen have selected a design incorporating the town seal for an official town flag. The design by Alfred Montanari was one of several dozen submitted by residents

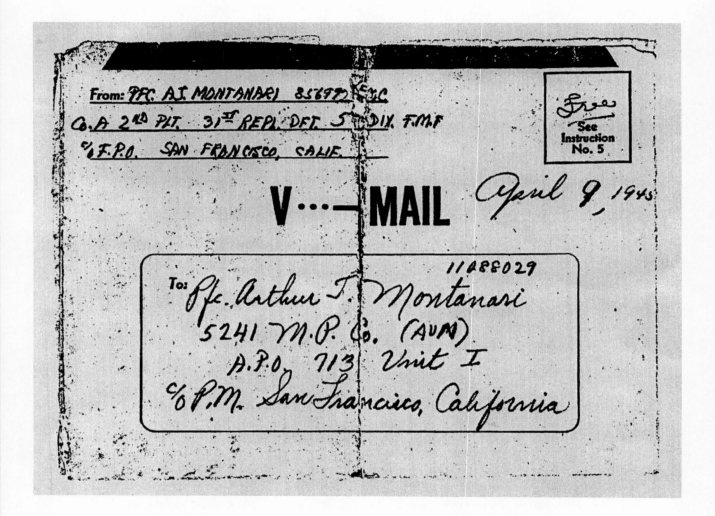

An example of the V-Mail used extensively during the war. It consisted of a single page on which the message was written, the page folded on itself and the address added to the outside. After a censor cleared the letter, it was transferred onto black & white camera film, which was shipped to a processing center where the letter was printed and delivered to the recipient. This process freed up overseas cargo space for vital war supplies and allowed the morale building mail to travel between servicepersons and their families.

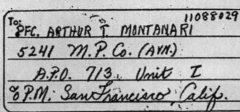

From: PFC. A.J. MONTANARI   MC
Co A.   -2ND PLT., 31ST REPL. DFT.
SN. 856992   5TH DIV. F.M.F.
℅ F.P.O.
SAN FRANCISCO, CALIF.

To: 11088029
PFC. ARTHUR T. MONTANARI
5241 M.P. Co. (AVN.)
A.P.O. 713, Unit I
℅ P.M. San Francisco, Calif.

P.H.H.
Naval Censor

[CENSOR'S STAMP]   See Instruction No. 2.   [Sender's complete address above]

Hello Toots;   IWO JIMA   MARCH, 3, 1945

How's the big brother comin' along? I hope that your making out OKAY. I've been here on Iwo Jima since D-DAY when we landed with the assault troops. Boy! I'm telling you this island is one hot son-ora-B-. I've had some PRETTY CLOSE CALL, BROTHER, let me tell you. I hope you never see combat. Now that I'm here and have SEEN,—NO ONE CAN TELL ME HOW WAR IS or how RUGGED THIS MARINE CORPS CAN BE.

I'm writing this in my FOX HOLE, this same hole I've been and JUST ABOUT LIVED A THOOSAND DEATHS, WONDERING IF THE NEXT SHELL OR MORTAR, HAD MY NAME ON IT.   I HAVE'NT BEEN HURT YET IN ANY WAY, BUT THERE ARE STILL DAYS AHEAD, BEFORE THIS ISLAND IS SECURE. THIS IS THE TOUGHEST ISLAND THE MARINES EVER ATTEMPTED, BUT DON'T WORRY. THE END ISN'T SO VERY FAR AWAY. I FEEL PRETTY GOOD. HAVE BEEN LIVING ON K RATION MOST OF THE TIME. I CAN SURE CALL MY SELF ONE LUCKY GUY AND A VERY FORTUNATE ONE AT THAT TO BE STILL ALIVE, THERE WERE TIMES WHEN I THOUGHT DIFFERENT. FIGHTING AN UNSEEN ENEMY IS REALLY HELL, WHEN YOU CAN'T SEE THEM OR FIGHT BACK. THERE ARE DEAD SAPS EVERY WHERE, AND THE MARINES REALLY FIELD STRIPPED THEM OF GOLD TEETH + SOUVERNIERS. AS YET I HAVEN'T BOTHERED WITH ANY, BUT I WILL TRY AND PICK SOME UP, BEFORE WE LEAVE. THE JAP TOKYO RADIO SAYS "THIS ISLAND IS ONE BIG BALL OF FIRE" AND FOR THAT I GIVE THEM CREDIT. THEY ARE RIGHT. THE TOKYO RADIO SAID THE JAP FLAG WAS FLYING ATOP THE SARUBACHI YAMA MT. BUT I KNOW DIFFERENT, I'M BUT A FEW YARDS AWAY FROM MT. SARUBACHI. AND IF THAT ISN'T THE OLD GLORY FLYING ATOP THAT MT. I'LL EAT IT. - LONG MAY IT WAVE. THE MARINE CORPS RIGHT BEHIND IT, AND ME WITH IT. THIS IS ABOUT ALL FOR NOW THAT SO TAKE CARE. I'LL PROBABLY BE WRITING TO YOU FROM ANOTHER PACIFIC ISLAND. I SURE MISS A HOT MEAL AND A GOOD BATH OR SHOWER, OR A SHAVE. I FEEL CORRODED AS HELL. SAY "HELLO" TO THE FOLKS AND MIKE + FLORA + SECUNDO FOR ME, WILL YOU? THANKS. DON'T FORGET TO GIVE MY "LOVE" TO BETTY WHEN YOU DO WRITE. SHE THINKS YOUR QUITE A CHARACTER. TELL THEM ALL NOT TO WORRY I'M OKAY. BE GOOD NOW, AND I'LL BE WAITING TO HEAR FROM YOU.
GOD BLESS YOU   AND HERE'S HOPING YOU DON'T GO THRU WHAT I HAD TOO.

                                                    YOUR
                                                    BROTHER
                                                    ALFRED

HAVE YOU FILLED IN COMPLETE      HAVE YOU FILLED IN COMPLETE
ADDRESS AT TOP?   REPLY BY V---MAIL   ADDRESS AT TOP?

12   10—28143-2 ☆ U. S. GOVERNMENT PRINTING OFFICE : 1943

United States Army
Air Forces

Dec. 18th 1943

Dear Sirs

I wish to express my most sincere thanks, and appreciation to the selectmen of the town, and to the good towns people of Scituate, who has worked so hard, and has really shown an interest in their work. for the very nice card, and money order. that I have just received. It is really wonderful the way the people of Scituate shows their appreciation towards the men & women in the service.

Thanks again for everything. and may you all have a Merry Xmas and a very Happy New Year.

Arthur Montanari

GUNTER FIELD
ALABAMA

Dec 1st 1943
Tuesday.

Gentlemen:

I received your unexpected gift to-day. and I really appreciate it very much I t really gives a soldier courage to do his daily duties when he knows the his parents and townspeople are doing there bit to see that the American Soldier is happy and counted for.

I really do hope other towns in the whole United States are doing as much for their local soldiers or should I say Men and women in the service as the Town of Scituate is doing for their Men and Women in the service.

I only wished I had joined up long before I did because I really like the branch that I'm in, and I do hope the other boys of Scituate like army life as as much as I do.

Give my best regards to the Men & women there in the offices of the town hall and I will Thank You again for you gift Wishing you all a Merry Xmas & a Happy New Year

and many more to come

I remain as
Ever
Arthur Montanari
898 Basic Flying Training Sqdn.
Gunter Field Ala.

P.S.
Thank Again.

Arthur Montanari

ARTHUR TUDOR MONTANARI

Arturo Tudor "Monty" Montanari was born in Gatteo, Italy, on October 1, 1913. He was the third of four sons born to Primo and Theresa Montanari.

Arthur enlisted in the Army in August 1942 and served in the MP (Military Police). On December 1, 1942, while at basic training in the 898th Basic Flying Squadron at Gunter Field, Alabama, Arthur wrote to the good residents of Scituate that "It really gives a soldier courage to do his daily duties when he knows that his parents and townspeople are doing their bit to see that the American soldier is happy and counted for." He later became a Corporal, Mechanic Specialist, in the 360th Air Service Group (Far Eastern Air Force) for over three years. For most of his military service, he was stationed in New Guinea and the Philippines, and he participated in three major battles: the Battle of Bismark Archipelago, the New Guinea Campaign, and the Battle for the Philippines. He was awarded the Asiatic Pacific Campaign Ribbon; the American Campaign Medal, the Philippine Liberation Medal, the Victory Medal World War II; the Good Conduct Medal; and three major battle stars.

While stationed in New Guinea, Monty assisted with the building of thatched huts that served as the military chapel and huts for the soldiers. He even grew tomatoes outside his hut to provide fresh vegetables for himself and his bunkmates. When the war ended, Arthur returned home to Scituate from New Guinea with one of his Scituate neighbors, Ernest Barbuto of North Scituate. In 1946, shortly after returning home from the war, Arthur went into business with Arthur Basler operating a local fruit and vegetable shop. The Fruit Spot was located on Front Street in Scituate Harbor and was a popular local market until it closed in 1963.

In November, 1947, Arthur married a local girl, Katherine (Kay) F. Scarsilloni. They had four children: James, William, Donna and Peter. For the next 20 years, Arthur was employed by the Town of Scituate as a bus driver and custodian for the Gates and Cushing schools in Scituate. "Monty" was much beloved by the elementary school students to whom he expressed his caring with good-natured teasing.

Custodian Arthur Montanari retired from the Cushing Elementary School after 20 years of service. Wishing him well were Mathew Morris, Meredith Allen, Joshua Weldon and Mathew Myers.
(Carol McCann photo)

As a member of Scituate Veterans of Foreign Wars, Satuit Post #169, Monty was a familiar figure in Scituate's Memorial Day Parade marching alongside other local veterans such as Ernest Kelly, John Daniels, John Brown, Thomas Patterson, and his brother, Alfred.

After his retirement in 1984, Monty moved to Carver, Massachusetts. He passed away in March, 1991, at the age of 78.

USS Fond du Lac

Stanley Murphy Storekeeper 2nd Class

STANLEY F. MURPHY

Stanley Murphy, son of Joseph N. and Isabel Harron Murphy, was born on July 25, 1914. He was graduated from Scituate High School and attended Springfield College before transferring to Boston University. After college, Stanley sold insurance for John Hancock and worked in his mother's Real Estate office in Minot. He married Alice Lantz on January 17, 1941 and they had one child before World War II. They later had two more children. Stanley's daughter, Elaine, taught at the Hatherly School for many years.

Stanley joined the US Navy on May 9, 1944. He received his training at the Sampson, New York, Naval Training Station, after which he was sent to Camp Pendleton Marine Base where he qualified as a sharpshooter. In Astoria, Washington, Stanley boarded the USS Fond du Lac, a newly commissioned ship where he served as a storekeeper second class. The ship and crew sailed to San Francisco, where LCVP's (Vehicle and Personnel Landing Craft) and LCM's (Mechanized Landing Craft) were loaded. After boarding combat troops, the ship proceeded to Espiritu Santo, New Hebrides. This was a major marshalling area for United States Army, Navy and Marine forces waging war in the Pacific.

From January to February 1945 the Fond du Lac was a Guadalcanal in the Solomon Islands. After participating in the assault on Okinawa on April first, the ship next transported casualties to Guam, Pearl Harbor and on the San Francisco. She then returned delivering fresh troops from the West Coast to the Philippines. Stanley was awarded the American Theater Medal, Asiatic-Pacific Medal and the Philippine Liberation Medal with one Bronze Star. This last was awarded for landing troops while under constant air attack.

After the war, Stanley resumed work in the insurance business. Alice passed away on September 4, 1967. In 1968 Stanley married the former Mary Chase Martin. He served the Town of Scituate for many years on the Board of Assessors where he was a longtime chairman.

Stanley Murphy passed away on April 5, 1993.

Scituate Ctr. Jan. 4, 1944

To whom it may concern:

I want you to know you have my heartiest thanks for the flowers which I received at Christmas in memory of my brother Edward.

They lessened a great deal the deep sadness which we had this year.

Sincerely yours,
Jeanette Hollis

GLIDER CRASH VICTIM — Lieut. Edward Nichols of Scituate, who was killed in a glider crash while en route from Missouri to Texas, was the only son of Richard A. Nichols and the late Eva B. Nichols. He entered the Royal Canadian Air Force in 1941, and a year later transferred to the ...

Edward Allen Nichols

EDWARD ALLEN NICHOLS

Edward Nichols, the only brother of seven female siblings, was born to Richard A. and Eva Allen Nichols on May 2, 1920. He was graduated from Scituate High School in 1938 and worked for a time as a carpenter with his father. However, like many young boys of that time, he was fascinated with the developing field of flying.

Because of his young age, Edward wasn't able to enlist in the United States Army Air Corps, so he traveled north and joined the Royal Canadian Air Force in 1940. When he became twenty-one, Edward transferred to the US Army Air Corps. As a trained glider pilot, he was commissioned a 2nd Lieutenant on September 15, 1941, in Arkansas.

Gliders were fragile, unarmed, engineless aircraft. They took off by being towed by a powered airplane and were meant to be flown only one-way - into battle, where their pilots became infantrymen once on the ground. The gliders were capable of carrying a fully loaded jeep or up to sixteen men. They provided the means to move troops and supplies into battle behind enemy lines.

While en route from Missouri to Texas on September 18, 1943, Edward's glider crashed in Tyler, Texas, and he was killed. Edward was twenty-three years old.

A letter from Edward's sister, Jeanette, was found among the servicemen's thank you letters. The town had sent a bouquet of flowers to her family at Christmastime in 1943 in memory of Edward, and she wrote expressing the family's heartfelt thanks.

Glider Pilot's Wings

McCloskey General Hospital
Temple, Texas

Dec. 27, 1943

Dear Sirs:
I want to thank you
and the people of
Scituate for your thoughtfulness of the fellas in
the service.
Thank you very
much for the five dollar
money order.
Yours truly
Walter O'Neil

McCLOSKEY GENERAL HOSPITAL
TEMPLE, TEXAS

Dear Sir,
I just thought I'd drop
you a short line for
the five dollar money
order I received from the
town. I want to thank
you very much. There
aren't many other guys
around that get presents
like that from these
towns & cities.
Walter O'Neil

O'NEIL FAMILY

Walter S. O'Neil

<u>Walter Stephen "Doc" O'Neil</u>, one of three sons of Christopher and Mary Webb O'Neil was born in Scituate on December 13, 1924. He attended Scituate schools graduating from Scituate High School in 1942, and began making his living lobstering.

On March 10, 1943 World War II interrupted Walter's life on the ocean and he joined the United States Army. He spent some time at McCloskey General Hospital in Temple, Texas. It was from Texas that he wrote two thank you letters to the Town for his annual Christmas gifts. Walter also served as a Military Policeman assigned to Headquarters, Special Troops Armed Forces in the Western Pacific. It was here as he told his friend, Sean McCarthy, that he was assigned to transport Japanese prisoners.

After his discharge in March of 1946, Walter returned to Scituate and the sea. He served the town as Shellfish Warden and assistant Harbor Master from 1948 until 1964. Along with his two brothers, George and Freddie, he was co-owner of Scituate Harbor Marina on Jericho Road. Walter loved hunting and fishing. Walter S. "Doc" O'Neil passed away suddenly on June 1, 1978 at the age of fifty-three.

<u>Freddie O'Neil</u> was Radioman 3rd class aboard the LST 506. He was graduated from Radio and Television School in Boston. He sold and repaired Motorola televisions. Besides being part owner of the Scituate Harbor Marina he also worked for Paul Young Motors. Freddie passed away in 1973.

<u>George O'Neil</u> served aboard the USS Manchester, a light cruiser built at the Fore River Shipyard in Quincy, MA. After his service he also participated in the management of the Scituate Harbor Marina and O'Neil's Fish Store situated on the west side of Jericho Road.

Walter O'Neil, June 1977
"Doc and Shasty".

Jan. 10, 1946

Dear Sirs:

I sincerely appreciate the gift which the people of Scituate sent me for Christmas, and wish to thank them for it. They were especially thoughtful, to have remembered us who are still away, now that the war is over. As I have been in New York harbor recently, the gift helped defray my expenses home over New Years.

Recently I was transferred from a submarine to this tender and now expect to spend the rest of the winter at Key West, Florida on this ship.

Thanking you again.

Yours Truly
Gordon Page

GORDON WELLS PAGE

Gordon Page was born on November 5, 1926, in Glen Ridge, New Jersey. He was the son of Eben and Dorothy Wells Page. Dorothy's father was the first person to cross the Brooklyn Bridge after its construction in 1883. Eben Page was a Scituate businessman who owned Front Street Transportation, which became Front Street Sales and Service. He sold and serviced Ford automobiles in the area that is now Harborside Shell. Gordon attended Scituate High School before transferring to Thayer Academy in Braintree.

After graduating from Thayer Academy, Gordon enlisted in the Navy V-12 program. Through this program he received officers' training at Williams College in Williamstown, MA, and went on to the Sampson, NY Naval Training Center. After further instruction he served primarily in the Pacific Theatre on the following submarines: USS Bluefish, USS Diablo, USS H.W. Gilmore, USS Bang, and the USS Gunnel. He took part in the siege of Tokyo Harbor.

Gordon was discharged in May of 1946. He was awarded the World War II Victory Medal, the American Theatre Medal, and the Asiatic-Pacific Theatre Medal.

Following his discharge, he married Doris Glasspool. They had 2 sons and 2 daughters. Gordon was graduated from Bowdoin College in Brunswick, Maine and began a career in banking and the manufacture of industrial machinery. He worked for the Fuller-Merriam Company in New Haven, Connecticut, where he eventually became part owner and president. Gordon later worked as a grinding systems analyst in the aerospace industry.

Gordon and Doris lived in Madison, Connecticut for thirty years. He passed away suddenly in December of 1993.

No. 37354

0-359455

(CENSOR'S STAMP) D.W. Parsons

To TOWN OF SCITUATE
TOWN HALL
SCITUATE
MASSACHUSETTS
U.S.A

From Major D.W. Parsons
(Sender's name)
69th Station Hospital
(Sender's address)
A.P.O. 3649° P.M.
N.Y.N.Y / 15
(Date)

Town of Scituate
Town Hall
Scituate Mass

No. Africa

Gentlemen,

Many thanks for your Christmas remembrance. It is certainly a pleasure to be thus thought of by the old Home Town when one is so far away from it.

I have been in this country nearly a year now, and the other day I accidentally ran into Eddie Dwyer. Eddie is a son Sara Hooper, and he has so far made two jumps in combat. I met him at our hospital where he was convalescing from an attack of malaria

He is the first Scituate boy I have seen over here, and it was good to see him.

The speed with which time war seems to be moving, leads me to believe that it wont be long before I feel the soil of Scituate under foot once more and you can bet that I wont be sorry when that day comes.

Sincerely,
R.W. Parsons

V····MAIL

DONALD WHITMAN PARSONS

Donald Whitman Parsons was born in Saugus, MA on August 19, 1914. He was graduated from Scituate High School in 1932. And after attending Harvard University and the University of North Carolina, he graduated from Harvard Dental School in 1938.

Donald did a residency in Dentistry at Pilgrim Hospital, Long Island, NY and then married Zilpha Rose on July 8, 1939, in Oneonta, NY.

Beginning as a 2nd Lieutenant in the Army Dental Corps, Donald eventually earned the rank of Lt. Colonel while serving in North Africa and France from 1940 until 1945.

The fighting in North Africa centered on the objective of keeping the Mediterranean Sea and the Suez Canal open as the British lifeline to their possessions in India and the Far East. President Franklin Delano Roosevelt agreed to aid the British by sending troops to North Africa in 1942 in exchange for British support of a major attack across the English Channel sometime in 1943 or 44.

According to his letter, Donald was assigned to the 69th Station Hospital. From March 28 until August 15, 1943 this unit was located in Casablanca, Morocco. In September the unit was moved to Assi Bou Nif, Algeria, about 8 miles south of Oran. Both are port cities on the northern coast of Africa.

After his discharge, Donald returned to Scituate and entered his father's dental practice. He served his patients until his retirement in 1983, at which time he moved to a farm in Newbury Vermont, spending winters in Estero, Florida. The dental practice continues to this day under the auspices of Donald's son, Bradford.

In 1953, Donald initiated the successful effort to fluoridate Scituate's water supply. The town was one of the first communities in the Commonwealth of Massachusetts to benefit from this most practical and safe means for controlling tooth decay in a community.

Donald passed away in February 2001 at the age of 86. He is survived by his three children and five grandchildren.

Camp Endicott
Friday 4,
1947

Scituate Social Community.
Scituate, Mass.

Dear Sir:

I wish to thank those people who made it possible the card and gift I received yesterday. If this gratuity pleases the rest of our boys as much as it has me I know that your aim will be accomplished, because then we know the people are still behind us and haven't forgotten us.

Before I close I want to wish everyone back home a very Merry Christmas and a Joyous New Year, and thanks again for my first Christmas gift.

Respectfully yours,
Frank W. Partsch U.S.N.R.

Frank W. Partsch, Jr.

FRANK W. PARTSCH, JR.

Frank W. Partsch, Jr. was born in Boston on April 3, 1924. His parents were Frank and Catherine Partsch of the Sand Hills Section of Scituate.

In 1942, the Scituate High School student quit school, lied about his age and enlisted in the United States Navy.

As a WT-2 (Water Tender, 2nd Class), he served at various locations in the South Pacific and was assigned to the 40th Naval Construction Battalion, better known as the "Sea Bee's." The international law banning civilians from resisting enemy military attacks prompted the creation of this Naval Construction Force. This group operated in all theaters of WWII. In the Pacific, they completed numerous projects including airstrips and support bases for US Army Air Corps fighter planes on Pacific Islands within striking distance of Japanese held territory. This enabled US forces to retake the islands that had been overrun immediately following the attack on Pearl Harbor.

Frank was awarded the World War II Victory Medal, American Area Ribbon, Good Conduct Medal, Asiatic-Pacific Ribbon and the Army Distinction Unit Citation.

Frank was reassigned stateside after contracting Malaria, a disease that afflicted thousands of our fighting men in the Pacific Theater.

Upon discharge in 1946 he returned to Scituate and opened Scituate Sheet Metal in North Scituate Village. Frank and his childhood friend, Agnes Bell married and had four children. Frank became Commander of the Satuit VFW Post #3169. In later life Frank owned a 27' Luhrs cabin cruiser which he named "Sea Bee".

On February 6, 2003 Frank Partsch died. His death was partially linked to his exposure to the coral dust produced by the crushing process used in constructing runways on islands in the South Pacific.

Charles P. Patterson, Mother Elizabeth (Stark) Patterson

Tom Patterson   Gilbert J. Patterson, Jr.
January 25, 1945

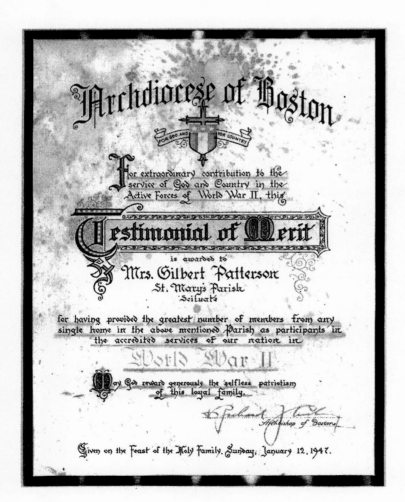

Mary Elizabeth Patterson

THE PATTERSON FAMILY

Gilbert J. and his wife Elizabeth (Stark) Patterson saw four of their seven children go off to serve in World War II. Mrs. Patterson attended daily Mass to pray for their safe return.

<u>Mary Elizabeth</u>, born in 1920, was graduated from Scituate High School in 1938. She then attended Carney Hospital School of Nursing. Mary enlisted in the Army Nurse Corps and served as a Lieutenant in London and Europe with the 162nd General Hospital. After the war, Mary married Thomas Killeen, who had been a patient of hers while in the service, and they had eight children. Mary passed away on April 6, 1996.

<u>Thomas A</u>. was born on January 1, 1924, and was named after his doctor. He was graduated from Scituate High School in 1941. Tom enlisted in the US Navy in 1942 and served aboard the USS Ranger, a light fleet aircraft carrier, in both the Atlantic and Pacific Theaters. He married the former Louise Riordan and raised three children. After the war, Tom became a Scituate Police Officer, retiring in 1978. He was also security officer for the Scituate Federal Savings Bank for ten years. Tom passed away on February 16, 2002.

<u>Gilbert</u> (also known as "Junie" and "Gibbie") was born on May 20, 1925. He served in the Navy aboard the USS Hyades, a refrigerated store ship that provisioned the fleet throughout the Pacific Theater. On October 12, 1949, he married the former Pat McDonald, and they had seven children. Gil was a Massachusetts State Capitol Police Officer before joining the Scituate Police Force after the war. He retired in 1978.

<u>Charles</u> was born on September 29, 1926. He was graduated from Scituate High School in 1945. Charles joined the US Navy Seabees and served in the Pacific Theater. After the war he married the former Elinor White, and they had six children. Charles was also a Scituate Police Officer. He served as Scituate's Harbormaster as well.

Alice   Charles Gilbert   Thomas   Evelyn   Olive   Mary

W B Pepper C.M.C. U.S.N.R
84 Batt Co A - 4
Fleet P.O. San Francisco
Cal

To the   Jan 19 1945
Servicemens Committee of Scituate

I wish to thank the members of the Servicemens
Committee + the people of Scituate for thinking
of the boys in the armed forces of the U.S.A., at
Christmas time.

For me, it is the second Christmas that I
have seen since I came overseas, + you
may be sure that it is with the greatest
of appreciation that I acknowledge your
thoughtfullness.

In some respects the time has passed quickly,
but at the same time it seems as though I
have been away from home for ages, and
it will be a most happy event for us all, when
we can come back to stay.

May Scituate always be proud of what she
has done for us.
                    Respectfully,
                    Walter B Pepper.

W B Pepper C M 1 C 5 2 8 9 R
84th Batt Co A - 4
Fleet P.O. San Francisco
Cal
Dec 8, 1943

The Board of Selectmen
Scituate Mass

Dear Sirs

It was with great pleasure that I received your
Christmas card and the money order for five dollars.
There is a lot of satisfaction in knowing that our friends back
home are thinking of us, + trying to do things to encourage
us. It is nearly seven months now since we left the states
and so far I have been fortunate to be in good health.
There are so many tropical ailments one can get here that
it will be a relief when we get away from here + get back
home. It is uncomfortably hot here now practically all the
time, but if what we are doing will only help to bring an end
to the war I guess one can not complain. We are receiving our
Christmas packages now from day to day + you may all be sure
that though we are far from our homes, we are all enjoying
the spirit of Christmas. Wishing you all a Merry Christmas + a
Happy New Year I remain one of the men from Scituate, Walter B Pepper

WALTER BROOKS PEPPER

Walter Pepper, son of Arthur and Elizabeth (Spencer) Pepper, was born in Scituate in 1904. After graduation from Scituate High School, he worked as a carpenter. His first love, however, was horses. Walter and his future brother-in-law, Matthew Peter Bubin, owned a racehorse together in the 1930's.

When World War II began, Walter was rejected by the United States Army during his physical. Despite that rejection, he was accepted into service by the United States Navy and became a member of the SeaBees, the naval construction units that provided extensive service in all theaters of the war. He was assigned to the South Pacific Theater and spent time in the Philippines and New Guinea.

According to the biographical information supplied by his family, Walter "had no use for those who would 'put down' the indigenous peoples. In particular, when some of the men were scorning the natives for not knowing how to use a hammer, he defended them asking the men if they could construct sophisticated structures without hammers, saws or nails, weaving grass and palm fronds together as the natives did. He tried to show them that it was a difference of culture not of intelligence."

In one of his two thank you letters, this one written in 1943, Walter mentions, "There are so many tropical ailments one can get here that it will be a relief when we get away from here and get back home." He did indeed contract a tropical infection and was shipped to a hospital in Australia to recover.

After the war ended, Walter pursued his love of horses by going to work as a groom at horse racing tracks, traveling the Atlantic seaboard from New Hampshire to Florida. In 1952, after a long courtship, he married Elizabeth (Dolan) Cole. They bought vacation rental cabins in Plymouth, New Hampshire, where they lived until his death in 1985.

Daniel J. Queeney

DANIEL J. QUEENEY

Daniel Queeney was born on February 19, 1921. He was graduated from Scituate High School in 1937. Daniel then went to work as a mechanic for the Perini Construction Company.

After enlisting in the Army Air Force on October 9, 1940, Daniel became a member of the 485th Base Unit. He received his training in Engine Mechanics at the Casey Jones Academy of Aeronautics (now the College of Aeronautics) in New Jersey. He later attended Gunnery School and was trained in Strategic Bombing in Orlando, Florida.

Daniel saw service in Tunisia, North Africa, in March of 1943; Sicily, Rome, Naples and Foggia, Italy, in December of 1943. He also saw air combat over the Balkans. He achieved the rank of Master Sergeant. Daniel received the Good Conduct Medal, American Defense Service Medal, and the European African Middle Eastern Theatre Campaign Ribbon with 6 Battle Stars. The Battle Stars indicate that Daniel was involved in six separate engagements within the European African Middle Eastern Theatre.

After the war, Daniel married Mary Horgan on October 27, 1951. They had two sons and a daughter. They now have two grandchildren. Daniel was a member of the Boston International Union of Operating Engineers for fifty-five years. He was a Eucharistic Minister, usher, and altar server at St. Mary of the Nativity Church in Scituate Harbor.

Daniel Queeney passed away on June 9, 2004.

John Queeney

JOHN "HART" QUEENEY

John Queeney was born on February 20, 1920. He attended Scituate schools and was graduated from Scituate High School in 1938. At Scituate High, Hart played football, basketball and baseball. He was in the Dramatics and Glee Clubs. He next attended Huntington Prep School, located in the YMCA building on Huntington Avenue in Boston. Following his graduation, Hart enrolled at Lowell Textile. This school was founded in 1895 to train technicians and managers for the textile industry. The school merged with Lowell State in 1975 to become the University of Lowell and in 1991 became a part of the UMASS system.

When John was in his junior year at Lowell, he enlisted in the United States Navy. He was sent to Officers' Candidate School and on to the Marine Air Corps. He saw service in Iwo Jima in the Pacific Theatre. He was discharged in February of 1946 and returned to Lowell Textile to finish his education. In 1947, he married Rosalie Kirby of Whitman. They had six children and now have fourteen grandchildren.

Hart worked as a textile designer in New York City for forty years before retiring as vice president of curtain and drapery design. After his retirement he played golf and sailed from his home in Stanford, Connecticut where he resides with Rosalie.

Donald Quinn first row bottom right.

Donald Quinn first row on left.

DONALD EDWARD QUINN

Donald E. Quinn, the son of Dennis and Margaret Sullivan Quinn, was born in Avon, MA on January 17, 1921. The family moved to Scituate when Donnie was about 2 years old. He attended Scituate schools and was graduated from Quincy Trade School, now known as Quincy Vocational-Technical School, in 1939. Donnie went to work for Bethlehem Steel in Quincy before joining the US Navy in 1943.

Assigned to the 123rd Naval Construction Battalion, Donnie began his service at the Newport, RI Naval Training Station. He was a Shipfitter, 2nd Class and saw service as a SeaBee in Guam and the Marshall Islands. He was awarded the World War II Victory Medal, American Area Medal, and the Asiatic-Pacific Ribbon.

On December 30, 1945 Donnie married the former Mildred Reardon in Brookline. They had four children and eventually five grandchildren. After his discharge Donnie became head custodian at Scituate High School. In 1954 he was appointed to the Scituate Fire Department and served until his retirement in 1980. He also lobstered aboard his boat, the Cathy Ann, out of Scituate Harbor. He was member of Scituate Veterans of Foreign Wars beginning in 1949 and was Commander and President of the Board of Directors at the time of his death on December 6, 1985.

According to his daughter, Marsha, Donnie and Mildred enjoyed vacationing at Lake Winnipesaukee in New Hampshire. Over the years they had a series of pets including "Pepe" and "Smokie" the dogs and "Midnight" the cat, that shared their lives for eighteen years.

Donald Quinn passed away on December 6, 1988.

1st Lt. Paul A. Reynolds

PAUL A. REYNOLDS

Paul Reynolds, the son of William and Margaret Farrell Reynolds was born in Dorchester on July 8, 1911. He spent summers in Scituate during his youth and in 1931, the family moved here permanently. Paul was graduated from Boston College in 1933 and entered the Merchant Marine. He sailed the Atlantic Ocean between New York and South America aboard ships carrying goods to and from numerous ports. Paul also spent time gathering Irish Moss for Fred Conroy off of First Cliff.

Following the Japanese attack on Pearl Harbor, Paul enlisted in the United States Navy. He initially served aboard a minesweeper patrolling the Caribbean Sea. He then attended Officer Candidate School at Princeton. He was assigned to the USS Shields following destroyer school at Norfolk, VA . The newly commissioned Shields performed escort and patrol duty in the Pacific Theater in and around Ulithi, Leyte, Eniwetok, Okinawa and Borneo. On June 26, 1945 she shelled Japanese shore installations at Miri, Borneo in support of Australian ground troops. This area was taken by the Japanese early in the war because of its oil fields. The Japanese war machine was starved for fuel and had made it a priority to capture territories that could provide this vital necessity. After their successful invasion, the Australians controlled the area for several years.

Paul was discharged after attaining the rank of 1st Lieutenant on November 30, 1945 and returned to Scituate.

After establishing a Real Estate business Paul married the former Pauline Thompson in 1958. She was an artist who taught art in the Scituate School System. Paul served on the Scituate Board of Assessors and as Town Treasurer from 1955 until 1968.

Paul A. Reynolds passed away on October 7, 1987 at the age of seventy-six.

Dec. 24/43

UNITED STATES NAVY

Dear Friends;

I wish to extend my thanks for your kind remembrance of me at Christmas time. The card and present arrived Dec. 20th and needless to say they were highly appreciated. I know my family will be deeply grateful for your thoughtfulness, even tho I may be on the other side of the world I was not forgotten. All the boys hope and pray that next Christmas will find us enjoying our loved ones at home.

Best Wishes for a happy and Prosperous New Year.

Edward M. Robschean.

Your thoughtfulness
and good wishes
are sincerely
appreciated.
Many Thanks!

Edward M. Robschean

Thanks
to all
of
You

EDWARD M. ROBISCHEAU

Edward M. Robischeau was born in Boston, Massachusetts, on February 11, 1903. After high school, he joined the United States Coast Guard and was assigned to shore patrols along the beaches of Scituate, thwarting rum-runners in violation of the Volstead Act (Prohibition).

A printer by trade, Edward worked for Rust Craft, a greeting card company in Boston. After his marriage to Martha Lockard Fuller, he moved to Scituate, where they settled and had two children.

When war was declared, Edward joined the United States Navy. He served aboard the USS Portunus, a ship named for the Roman god of the sea who had jurisdiction over ports and shores. Edward's ship serviced and repaired United States and Australian naval units operating along the New Guinea coast.

In 1943, Edward wrote in his thank you letter that he was grateful not to be forgotten "even though I may be on the other side of the world."

In February, 1945 the USS Portunus supported an assault on Panay in the Philippines and went on to establish a patrol base there after the successful mission.

In June of 1945 Edward was given an honorable discharge due to the serious illness of his wife. He returned to Scituate and went to work for the D. S. Kennedy Company, a radar equipment manufacturer in Cohasset.

Edward Robischeau passed away on May 15, 1965.

January 16, 1946

Chairmen of the
Board of Selectmen

Dear Sir,

I want to express my sincere
thanks for your thoughtful
remembrance at Christmas.
Many fellows in my detail
have remarked about this
splendid way in which the
townspeople have remembered
those in the service.

I'm really grateful for this
contribution and know that
all those who have benefited
by this gift feel the same
way.

Sincerely yours,
Robert H. Rouleau

ROBERT H. ROULEAU

 Robert H. Rouleau graduated from Scituate High School in June 1944. He spent a year at The College of the Holy Cross and then enlisted in the United States Navy.

Basic Training took place at the Sampson Naval Training Base in Geneva, NY on Seneca Lake, the deepest and widest of the Finger Lakes. Robert was then sent to Newport, RI for Fire Control School where Charlie Curran was an instructor. There has been a US Naval facility in Newport, RI since 1869. During WWII it was expanded to include training schools for Patrol Torpedo (PT) Boats, Anti-aircraft gunnery, the Naval War College and Fire Fighters School. It was also the homeport of the US Atlantic Fleet of over 100 ships.

Assigned to the still under construction aircraft carrier USS Kearsage, Robert went to Brooklyn, NY. The Brooklyn Navy Yard was one of the original federal shipyards. It was a major contruction/repair facility for cruisers and battleships during both world wars. The Kearsarge, the third US warship to be so named after the mountain in Carroll County, NH., measured 888 feet in length and at full complement carried 3448 crewmembers and 80 to 100 airplanes. Her keel was laid on March 1, 1944 and she was launched on May 5, 1945. Robert sailed on the ship's shakedown cruise to Panama.

Robert wrote in his thank you letter "many fellows in my detail have remarked about this splendid way in which the townspeople have remembered those in the service".

Robert was discharged in August 1946, after which he returned to college and entered the practice of law.

Robert married Ann Campell of Chelmsford and they had 3 daughters and a son. They both still reside in Scituate.

Lucien loading moss using his self-built equipment.

60 x 500 foot drying bed used for Irish moss. Beds could be flooded with salt water in the event of rain to prevent the dried moss from turning to gelatin as a result of exposure to fresh water.

Lucien and Lillian Rousseau "Citizen of the Year" 1982 awards banquet.

LUCIEN ROUSSEAU

Lucien Henri Maurice Rousseau was born in Chatillon, France on March 2, 1913. After his father was killed in World War I, his mother met and married Stephen Mahoney. The new family moved to Scituate in 1919 and settled on Tilden Road.

Lucien was graduated from Scituate High School in 1932. After graduation he returned to France where he was drafted into the French Army and was offered a commission as a colonel. Instead, he elected to return to the United States, taking advantage of his dual citizenship and in 1936 he was graduated from Wentworth Institute in Boston with a degree in Mechanical Engineering, Drafting and Blue Printing. On Valentine's Day, 1941, he married the former Lillian Adolfson of Braintree and began Irish Mossing in the waters around Scituate.

On June 16, 1942 Lucien was inducted into the US Army Air Force. He was qualified as a rifle marksman and assigned to the 342nd Base Headquarters at Greenville Army AirField in Greenville, SC.

After his 1943 discharge, Lucien returned to his family in Scituate and a son, Lucien Jr. was born in September, 1944. There were two more sons, Paul who was killed in a tragic house fire in 1950, and John as well as a daughter, Maila. Lucien worked as an electrician at General Dynamics in Quincy. He went on to purchase Fred Conroy's Irish Mossing business in Scituate, beginning a career that made him the successor to the title, "Irish Moss King." According to a 1982 Scituate Mariner article announcing his selection as "Man of the Year", "Over the years, Rousseau has employed hundreds of Scituate and Cohasset youth in his task of gathering moss . . many of these young people have helped finance their college educations with their earnings as moss farmers". Lucien improved the original mossing rake and designed and built hoisting equipment to ease the burden of lifting the heavy, wet moss from the dories to trucks.

Lucien served on the Scituate Waterways Commission, was an avid collector of rare stamps and coins and built eighteen-foot Nova Scotia dories from scratch. According to a biography written by his grandson, "Lucien could have gone on to (be) a millionaire but chose the harsh and simple life of the sea instead. He did what he loved to do."

Lucien Henri Maurice Rousseau passed away on May 22, 1983.

Lucien Rousseau in the French Army, back row, third from left.

John Salvador
Dijon, France April 1945.

JOHN A. SALVADOR

John Salvador the son of John S. and Catherine Berlo Salvador, was born in 1923 in Dorchester, MA. His mother's family had lived in Scituate since the 1890's. John and his family summered in Scituate until they moved here permanently in 1942.

John entered the Army Air Corps in 1943. After training at Fort Patrick Henry in Virginia, John was sent overseas aboard the Liberty Ship, SS Isaac Sharpless. When he arrived in Taranto, Italy he began his work as a driver and operator of a crash truck at Allied airfields. He later saw action in France and Germany. According to John, he and his crew would be the first to arrive at the site of airplane crashes on the field. They would be heading toward a crash when everyone else was running away. While the crash truck was at the site extinguishing fires, extracting survivors, and administering first aid, the ambulance crews and medics would be waiting at a safe distance until any unexploded bombs were detonated or safely removed. Crashes occurred during take offs as well as landings when as many as six B26 aircraft would lift off at once, followed seconds later by six more etc, all heading for bombing runs at distances that tested the limits of their fuel supplies.

When he was in Naples, Italy, John was checking the sign-in sheet at a Red Cross ice cream stand when he came across the name of Fred Dwyer, a fellow Scituate resident. Neither knew the other was in the area and they both enjoyed the reunion.

While John was stationed at Bari, Italy in 1944, the airfield was subjected to enemy air raids on March 8th and 12th. When he was on a ship in the Bay of Naples, he witnessed the volcanic eruption of Mt.Vesuvius. John was promoted to Corporal, then Sergeant while he was in Germany in 1945. He returned to Scituate in 1946, where he first took up Irish Mossing. He next started a business of hand carving seagulls that were sold through local gift shops.

On November 20, 1948, John married the former Barbara E. Gillen. They have six children. From June 1947 until April 1949 John worked as a member of the Capitol Police for the State of Massachusetts. In May 1949, the Scituate Police Department hired him, and he served the town until his retirement in October, 1978. In 1986 John went to work for the Scituate Federal Savings Bank where he is in charge of its records, archives and grounds, a position he still holds.

John and Barbara live in Scituate in their home close to Scituate Harbor where John continues woodcarving and enjoys lobstering.

Dec. 12, 1943

Town of Scituate
Serviceman's Committee
Gentlemen:

I just want to say a sincere "thank you" for the wonderful Christmas card and money order. It makes a person feel good to know that the folks back home are thinking of the boys and girls in service, and that they are trying to make Christmas as happy as possible for us.

I don't know exactly how I'll spend the money, but you may be sure it will be used for something very glamorous, something not covered by a Wac's tiny budget.

Thanks again, and I hope you have a very happy holiday season.

Sincerely,
Mary Schaffer

MARY SCHAFFER LYONS

Mary Schaffer was born in 1921 on Hollett Street in Scituate. She graduated from Scituate High School in 1937, worked for a few years and then enlisted in the WAAC in 1943.

The WAAC or Women's Army Auxiliary Corps was formed in 1942; its name was changed to WAC or Women's Army Corps in 1943. During WWI female civilians had served under Army contracts, although they had no official status and therefore had to provide their own food and lodgings. They received no medical care, disability benefits or pensions. Early in 1941, a Massachusetts woman, Edith Nourse Rogers proposed a bill to create a women's Army corps separate from the already existing Army Nurse Corps. As a result of her work, more than 150,000 women served during WWII. Their purpose was to support the war effort by performing noncombatant military jobs such as file clerks, typists, stenographers, motor pool drivers, weather forecasters and observers, aerial photograph analysts, radio operators, mechanics, electricians, boat dispatchers and classification specialists among other jobs. They freed up soldiers to take part in military operations, something that was extremely important to a country fighting a two-front war. Applicants had to be between 21 and 45 without dependents, be at least 5 feet tall and weigh over 100 pounds. The WACs served at home and overseas. Only the most qualified received overseas assignments. Oveta Culp Hobby was the first Director of the Women's Army Auxiliary Corps. Hobby observed, "WAAC's were to help the Army win the war, just as women had always helped men achieve success".

Mary Schaffer began her WAAC career as a baker at Maxwell Field in Alabama. She went overseas to Hollandia, New Guinea in 1945. Hollandia was a large base established as part of a two-pronged approach used by the Allies to keep Japanese forces divided as the Allies advanced toward the retaking of Wake Island and the Philippines. Mary later was sent to Manila arriving the night before V-J Day.

Mary's thank you letter mentions that she wasn't sure how her gift would be spent but "you may be sure it will be used for something glamorous, something not covered by a WAC's tiny budget".

After returning home, Mary worked for the Veterans' Administration where she met her husband, Joe Lyons. They were married in September 1956.

After Joe's death in 1962, Mary returned to work as a secretary and bookkeeper. She worked for various Town Boards in Scituate including the Planning Board and The Advisory Committee. She wrote in her biography, "The spirit which prompted the town in WWII to send all us service people a gift from the heart is still alive and makes me proud to say I love Scituate!"

Mary resides on Elm Street where she has lived since 1968.

PHILIP L. SCHUYLER
Chairman

W. J. LUMBERT
Vice Chairman and Chief Air Raid Warden

Safety Committee
ROY E. LITCHFIELD
M. F. STEWART
JAMES FINNIE
ELMER RAMSDELL

SCITUATE COMMITTEE ON PUBLIC SAFETY
36 COUNTRY WAY
GREENBUSH, MASSACHUSETTS

December 10, 1943.

Mr. Dennis H. Shea
Town Hall
Scituate, Mass.

My dear Reggie:

I thought you would be interested in a quotation which comes from a letter received recently from my daughter Gretchen who is, as you know, on duty in England.

"Yesterday I received from the Town of Scituate a money order for $5.00. I am amazed as I don't deserve that. Whose idea was that; who do I write to thank? I do appreciate the thought behind it. The little old town does remember all of us out here and, believe me, we remember the town too."

I have written her and I have no doubt that you will hear from her in the course of time.

Yours sincerely,

Philip L. Schuyler.

PLS:rmz

GRETCHEN SCHUYLER

Gretchen Schuyler, one of three sisters, was born on June 12, 1911 in Boston. According to her niece, Gretchen felt that her father (Colonel Philip Schuyler) always wanted a son and she often said that she tried her best to be one. The family moved to Scituate around 1918 and Gretchen was graduated from Scituate High School in 1928 where she was captain of the girls' basketball team and played shortstop for the girls' baseball team. She went on to study Physical Education at Sargent College (later part of Boston University) and earned a Master of Arts degree from Columbia University. After touring the world with the International Lacrosse Team for ten years she became head of the Physical Education Department at Cathedral School in Garden City, NY. She later taught the young Jackie Bouvier at the Chapin School Ltd. in New York City.

With the onset of World War II Gretchen wanted to help her country. Not wanting to be stuck behind a desk as a WAAC, she answered an advertisement for overseas service with the American Red Cross. She had an interview and was accepted as the head of Red Cross Clubmobile Group F. She served in England, France, Belgium, Germany and Holland with the Third Army under the command of General George Patton whom she referred to affectionately as "Uncle George". Gretchen's unit was responsible for delivering mail to front line soldiers earning her the title "Fetchin' Gretchen". On the eve of the Battle of the Bulge, fought  from December 16 to January 25, 1945, the mail trucks were needed to move troops and supplies. The Army planned to burn all the Christmas mail to prevent it falling into enemy hands. Gretchen volunteered to transport the mail to safety and drove 120 miles to preserve it. She then retrieved it and delivered it to the weary troops after the battle. She received a letter of commendation from Generals Omar Bradley, Troy Middleton and George Patton as well as a Bronze Star for her actions which "contributed to the maintenance of high morale" as cited by President Harry Truman.

After the war Gretchen returned to Boston University, where she taught for 28 years retiring in 1973. She was named to the BU Athletic Hall of Fame in 1974 as the first female honoree; the New England Women's Fund, honoring women in all sports in 1997; the New England Lacrosse Hall of Fame in 1999 and the Scituate High School Athletic Hall of Fame in 2000.

After her retirement she turned her talents to golf, shooting a hole-in-one in a Marshfield Golf Tournament. She later moved to Bradford, NH where she chopped her own wood, shoveled snow and continued to play golf until declining health forced her to move to an assisted living facility where she passed away on December 17, 2002 fifty-eight years after her heroic efforts to make Christmas a little brighter for battle-weary soldiers in Bastogne, Belgium.

Women's Army Corps

Wednesday
January 19, 1944

To whom it may concern:

I am taking this privilege to express my appreciation for the Christmas gift which I received from my own home town of Scituate.

It really makes one feel good when one gets a gift from the town and people which one loves. It makes one feel as though, that, no matter how far away you are, you're being thought of.

Again I say thank you, and I hope next Christmas Scituate will have all their boys and girls back, and then it really will feel like a Christmas again.

Sincerely,
Pvt. Elizabeth Seor
W.A.C.

WAC

Sunday
Jan. 1, 1945

Scituate Servicemens Committee:
Scituate, Mass.

Friends,

I am writing this letter in regards to your thoughtfulness to me at Christmas time.

It really makes you feel wonderful, to know how much everyone at home are thinking of you, when you are so far away from there.

Here's hoping next Christmas all the boys & girls from good old Scituate, will be back home with their loved ones. Instead of fighting for our peace in far off parts of the world.

I will thank you again for your kindness.

Sincerely,
'Bette Seor'

ELIZABETH SECOR

Elizabeth Secor, daughter of George and Helen (McIntire) Secor, was born in Scituate on July 21, 1923. She was graduated from Scituate High School in 1941. After high school she went to work as a cashier at the First National Store, a grocery store in Scituate Harbor.

Elizabeth enlisted in the WAC on November 16, 1943. She spent her service as a supply clerk at Camp Crowder in Neosho, Missouri, where 47,000 US troops were stationed during the course of the war. The camp also served as home to German and Italian prisoners of war and was the basis for the popular comic strip "Beetle Bailey," in which it was renamed "Camp Swampy".

Elizabeth was married to Joseph Bogusz and left the service in January of 1946, when she was pregnant with the first of her two sons. She and Joseph later adopted a third son. After the war Elizabeth was a homemaker, returning to the workforce after the death of her husband. She worked at the Gilchrist Department Store, in the Scituate School system as a cafeteria worker, and, for many years, at Ronnie Shone's Variety Store in Scituate.

A long time devout Red Sox fan, Elizabeth Secor Bogusz passed away on July 7, 1991. Her son, Steve, would like to think that she was looking down happily on the Sox during their 2004 winning season.

A Portrait of an Artist

HEADQUARTERS
528th BASIC TRAINING FLYING SQUADRON
LEMOORE ARMY FLYING SCHOOL
Lemoore, California

December 3, 1942

Dear John,

The Christmas card and gift that enclosed, was very pleasantly received this afternoon, and, as it was in your name, and, as the card stated that it was from the citizens of Scituate, I'm afraid that you will have to express my thanks to these good citizens for the time being. In a few weeks I hope be on my way to old Satuit, and I'll try to thank them in person.

The nearest native son of Scituate is located about two hundred and fifty odd miles from my post, and it might interest you to know that it is none other than, S/Sgt. William (Shilalah) Curran, a popular Third Cliffter. In all probability he also received a similar gift, and maybe he will use his little gift to venture up this way for a short visit. I said maybe.

The only odd thing that has occurred since I've been here is that I found an edition of the, Scituate Herald, at the Post Library, a couple of months ago. I imagine that it has been in odder places than this by now, since the Local Draft Board has been in action.

Since I've been away from home I've heard some weird stories about the gentlemen that have been called to the colors, one item heard was that a popular young Harbor Socialite, has or rather is a meat inspector in a Southern Army Camp. When this little tiff with the Axis has been settled up, such men as Ed Merritt and George Otis, had better watch out. I'm referring to Mr. or Pvt. Robert Hall, formerly of Brook St.

Well John, I'll have to close now, and let me thank you again, and I hope to see you soon.

Sincerely yours,

Sgt. William A. Sexton
528th B. F. T. S. (Sp)
Lemoore Army Flying School,
Lemoore, California

WILLIAM ALBERT SEXTON

Bill Sexton, son of William E. and Katherine Mowery Sexton, was born in Scituate, MA, on June 21, 1918. The *1989 Scituate Town Report* noted, "When Bill Sexton arrived into the world in Greenbush on June 21, 1918, his first act was to sketch the doctor looking down at him…." Bill's artistic talent was honed during his grammar school years and continued through high school, where he captured the essences of his school friends and teachers. His work appears in the *1938 Scituate Chimes High School Yearbook*.

Self-portrait

Bill enlisted in the United States Army in 1940, and was assigned to the 538th Basic Training Flying School in Lemoore, California. He served fifteen months in the Pacific Theater as a member of the 7th Air Force, working his way up to Sergeant and performing duties as a Draftsman.

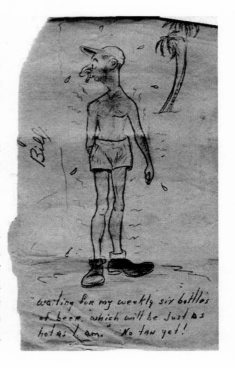

In appreciation for the town's gift of $5.00, Bill sent back a thank-you cartoon, depicting a soldier dreaming of his favorite Scituate places: the Old Oaken Bucket, the Lighthouse at Cedar Point, and the Lawson Tower.

After his discharge in November of 1945, it was said that Bill received a job offer from a major motion picture studio to put his artistic talent to work in their animation department. Bill turned down the offer and returned to the town he loved, going to work for the Town of Scituate Division of Public Works. He worked his way up to Foreman of the Sign Department.

In the ensuing years, Bill's artistic talent grew and he bestowed his sense of humor on local citizens, politicians, and other town workers by immortalizing them in caricature. It was considered a high honor to have your life depicted and preserved forever in a "Sexton Sketch". Some of the honored recipients include Police Chief James O'Connor, Robert "Punk" Clapp, Walter "Brother" Allen, Robert "Brother" Tilden, Nathaniel "Nat" Tilden, Ed McCann, William "Teek" Sherman, Earnest A.P. "Kell" Kelley, Police Chief Gilbert "Gibby" Patterson, Carl (Chub) Chessia, Attorney Michael "the L" Loring, and Fire Chief Charles "Grunt" Curran.

On February 26, 1962, Bill married the former Margaret Fallon in Plymouth. In the late 1970's, when the *Scituate Mariner*, a local newspaper, was launched, Bill created cartoons for the weekly publication, which drew attention to local political issues.

Bill retired from his job with the Town of Scituate in 1980 after 30 years of dedicated service. Margaret had passed away in August of 1979. William A. Sexton died on March 28, 1992, at the age of 73.

Branch Hydrographic Office
San Juan, Puerto Rico

December 10, 1942

Scituate Service Committee
North Scituate
Massachusetts

Gentlemen:

The other day I was very surprised and
particularly pleased to get your Christmas card.
Of course the gift was welcome as it will be everywhere, and I thank you for your generosity.

It means a lot to know that the towns
people would go to considerable trouble to remember
the men in the service so suitably. I have been very
proud of the many fine comments and compliments to
the town from those who have seen your card.

I am sending you a pair of bookends made
locally of Santo Domingan mahogany. Please put these
in the library, town offices, or wherever they will
be most useful.

Please allow me to remain anonymous in this.
Rather consider that they are from all of us who are
away from home, since we are so scattered that we can
not unite to express our appreciation.

Very truly yours,

Leslie F. Simmons

**Sextant used by Leslie Simmons during his Naval
Career, on display at the Scituate Historical Society's
Maritime & Irish Mossing Museum.**

LESLIE FARRAR SIMMONS

Leslie Simmons

Leslie Simmons was born on February 23, 1911, in Norwell, Massachusetts. He was descended from John Alden, a Mayflower passenger, and Robert Cornet Stetson, who arrived in Scituate in 1634. Leslie attended a one-room schoolhouse in Hingham, Massachusetts, and was graduated from Hingham High School. His family moved to Scituate in the 1930's. He was also graduated from Tufts University in Medford, Massachusetts, which he attended on a full scholarship. Leslie worked for Lever Brothers, a manufacturer of soaps and detergents, before entering the United States Navy in February of 1942.

Commissioned a Lieutenant Junior Grade, Leslie was assigned as officer-in-charge of the Branch Hydrographic Office in San Juan, Puerto Rico. Duty aboard the USS Salinas, a tanker operating in the North Atlantic, followed his promotion to full Lieutenant.

In October of 1943, Leslie married the former Geraldine Heres, and together they traveled to Stockton, California, where he reported aboard the USS Hydrographer, a surveying ship. After repairs to the ship were completed, Leslie began his duties as Deck Officer and later was promoted to Executive Officer. During his two-year tour of duty in the Central Pacific, Leslie was again promoted, this time to Lieutenant Commander.

The USS Hydrographer performed duties that fulfilled the need for detailed charts in the Pacific Theater of Operations. These waters were poorly mapped and therefore extremely dangerous to Naval Operations. There was a need for the rapid survey of these areas of strategic and tactical interest. Operating fathometers and wire-dragging anchors, the sailors examined invasion beaches prior to Marine and Army landings. They reported tide information, blasted through coral reef formations, and printed and distributed charts, all while being subjected to Japanese bombing raids and kamikaze attacks.

In December of 1945, Leslie returned to civilian life and was briefly employed as a chemist in New York City. He and Geraldine had three sons and settled in Williamsville, New York, a suburb of Buffalo. The family returned to Scituate every summer to visit the family home on Rebecca Road.

Leslie Farrar Simmons passed away at age eighty-nine in November of 2000. His sons continue to visit Lighthouse Point over Labor Day each year with their families.

Clark University
Worcester, 3, Mass.
January 3, 1944

Dear Sirs,

I wish to thank you for your Christmas present. It was a gift that every service man can use. To a lot of fellows a check like that ment the difference between a Happy Christmas and a day no different from any other day.

Out of over two hundred towns represented in this unit there was very few towns that remembered their service men like Scituate did. I know that the other fellows that recieved this gift from Scituate feel the same way I do.

Sincerely Yours
Pvt. Everett E. Southerd

EVERETT EUGENE SOUTHARD

Everett Eugene Southard was born in Winterport, Maine, on July 24, 1924. He was graduated from Hingham High School in 1942, and went to live with his parents on Country Way across from the Egypt Garage in Scituate. He worked at the Bethlehem Hingham Shipyard as a Second Class Handyman Electrician from September 28, 1942, until April 13, 1943, when he was drafted.

Everett received his basic training at Camp Blanding in Florida, after which he was sent to Clark University in Worcester, Massachusetts, for specialized training. It was from here in 1944 that Everett wrote his letter thanking the Town for its Christmas Gift, stating, "To a lot of fellows a check like that meant the difference between a Happy Christmas and a day no different from any other day. Out of over two hundred towns represented in this unit there were very few towns that remembered their servicemen like Scituate did."

He next participated in an exercise called "The Middle Tennessee Maneuvers." According to a 1992 article in **The Tennessee Magazine,** 600,000 U.S. Second Army troops were trained in rural Tennessee. Chosen because its terrain was comparable to that of 1940's Europe, much of the terrain was given new names like Normandy, Bastogne, and the Rhine. War maneuvers were carried out as a dress rehearsal for the grim and dirty business of the real thing.

In August of 1944, Everett took part in the Battle of the Bulge. As a member of the 101st Infantry, Everett was awarded a Bronze Star in January of 1945 and a Bronze Star with Oak Leaf Cluster in February of 1945 for service in France and Luxembourg. In separate instances, working under heavy and constant barrage, Private First Class Southard worked tirelessly and without let up to restore broken communication lines. To quote his

citation, "Stunned by a nearby explosion while in Luxembourg, he persisted in his mission and succeeded in repairing the break in the line. His heroic action enabled the Battalion to reestablish communications with the company on the right flank at a critical moment in the coordinated effort to repulse the enemy counterattack."

Tent City in Germany

After his discharge, Everett worked for the family business, then as a plant manager of a toy factory, a brewery and a soft drink production company. In 1950 he married the former Shirley Litchfield of Scituate, and they had two daughters. He was a Commander of the Marshfield Veterans of Foreign Wars. He retired in 1950.

In retirement, Everett has become an avid golfer, with six "holes-in-one" to his credit. He and Shirley now have four grandchildren and two great granddaughters.

U. S. NAVAL TRAINING UNIT
TUFTS COLLEGE
MEDFORD, MASS.

Tufts College
Dec. 14, 1943

Service Men's Committee.
Dear Sirs:

I received your lovely card and the enclosed money order Friday. I appreciate the gift very much and extend my sincerest thanks to you. Money is really the only thing that a service man really needs, and it is appreciated much more than other gifts. Thank you again.

appreciatively,
Walter F. Spear

Nov. 25
1942

Situate Service Committee
Scituate, Mass.

Dear Sir,

I am writing this note to try and convey in a few words, my sincere appreciation for the Christmas card and money order which I received from your committee last week. It gives a fellow a swell feeling to get something like that which says "We, the people of Scituate, are all behind you."

For nearly a year now I have been in a jungle outpost with a few natives, monkeys, and parrots for company. Have been back to the main post only about four times. Days follow one another endlessly each one the same as the preceding one. It does get a bit monotonous. But the news is becoming more cheerful every day and maybe we'll soon be back in good old Scituate There is no other place quite like it. Heard "the Old Oaken Bucket" over the radio the other night — memories.

With only sincere wishes for the best of everything to the citizens of Scituate this Christmastide and thru the years to come.

Very sincerely,
Sgt. Arthur L. Spear

THE SPEAR BROTHERS

Arthur, Walter and Robert

Arthur, Walter and Robert Spear, all sons of Chester F. and Bertha Cushman Spear, were born in Scituate, MA. Bertha Cushman was descended from Robert Cushman who was one of the chief managers of the Mayflower voyage. After trying to cross the Atlantic on the aborted voyage of the Speedwell, he finally arrived on the Fortune in 1621. Bertha, born in 1899, grew up at the Scituate Lighthouse, where her father John Cushman was the keeper of the light. Bertha would row herself across the harbor to attend the Jenkins School.

Arthur Livingston Spear was born on January 8, 1914. He was graduated from Scituate High School in 1931 where his yearbook quote states " Arthur Spear has brains they say, he'll knock the world agog someday." While attending Colby College, Arthur enrolled in Officer Candidate School and subsequently served in the Army Signal Corps first in Florida, then in Panama, and finally in England, France and Germany. After his discharge in 1945, Arthur continued his education at Bentley College and became a purchasing agent for United Engineering in Boston. He married the former Erma Nichols and they had one son and one daughter. Erma passed away in 1967. Arthur was very active in the Masonic Organization, holding numerous offices. He was also an avid golfer. He married the former Betty Vogel in 1969. Arthur Spear passed away on February 12, 2003 at age 88. He is buried in Union Cemetery, Scituate.

Walter Franklin Spear was born on January 12, 1922. After graduating from Scituate High School where he played football, he went to work for General Electric. Walter served in the United States Coast Guard beginning in 1943. After the war, he was graduated from Brown University. He married the former Jean "Penny" Pentz and they had two daughters. Walter was a professional engineer in Connecticut, Massachusetts and New Hampshire. He worked for United Technologies for many years, retiring in 1989. He was also active in the Masons. Walter Spear died on July 27, 1997 at age 75 in Bloomfield, CT.

Robert Ellsworth Spear was born on March 11, 1924. He was graduated from Scituate High School in 1941 where he was the publicity director for the Senior Class Play. Robert entered the Army on March 10, 1943. He served in the 150th Engineer Combat Battalion as a construction foreman in Normandy, Northern France, the Rhineland and the Ardennes. This was a Battalion consisting of men from New England. Their mission was to enable the Allied armies to cross European rivers whose bridges had been destroyed by the retreating German Armies. They constructed prefabricated "Bailey Bridges", often under fire from German batteries. The 150th was awarded a Presidential Unit Citation for their accomplishments. After the war, Robert became an engineer for Bethlehem Steel. He married the former Joan Beale of Hingham and they had two sons and a daughter. Robert now lives in Alabama.

4 Dec 44.

Dear Mr. Ahen.

Just a few lines to let you
know that today I received a most
welcome gift from the Service Men Committee.
I certainly appreciate the gift and the thought
that prompts you people to remember all
the Scituate boys at this time of year. The
card and expressed sentiment were really
great.

Best Regards
Ed. Stewart.

EDWARD L. STEWART

Born July 15, 1909, Edward Stewart moved to Scituate in 1926. After graduating from Boston College, he began his teaching career at Scituate High School. In 1932, Edward, married Scituate native, Glea Cole.

His service to the Scituate School System was interrupted in 1944 by his commissioning as a Lieutenant Junior Grade in the United States Navy. He served as a line officer performing convoy duty in the North Atlantic. This service consisted of providing protection from German U-boats (submarines) for United States Ships sailing to Europe from ports on the East Coast of the United States. In 1944 these ships were carrying troops and supplies to support the DDay Invasion of France and the ensuing battles for control of Europe. During the month of December 1944 alone, the Allies employed four hundred and twenty-six escort vessels and four hundred and twenty RAF (Royal Air Force) Coastal Command Aircraft to patrol the North Atlantic.

Upon his discharge from active duty in 1946, Edward returned to Scituate to resume his duties as teacher, coach, Athletic Director, Assistant Principal, and Superintendent of Schools. He remained in the Naval Reserve, however, retiring as a Commander. He retired in 1971 from the school system.

Edward and Glea had five children: three boys and two girls. All three sons served in the Viet Nam war.

Edward L. Stewart passed away on February 24, 1998.

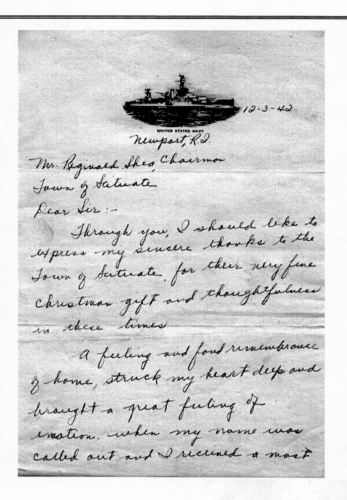

UNITED STATES NAVY

12-3-42

Newport, R.I.

Mr. Reginald Shea, Chairman
Town of Scituate

Dear Sir:—

Through you, I should like to express my sincere thanks to the Town of Scituate, for their very fine Christmas gift and thoughtfulness in these times.

A feeling and fond remembrance of home, struck my heart deep and brought a great feeling of emotion, when my name was called out and I received a most attractive envelope, marked "Christmas Mail." No one could have designed a more appropriate card than our own Doris Ward. The star and nurse, brought back memories of the happy holidays at home and the Carol singing. The Virgin Mary and Jesus, of the true Christmas spirit. I will be frank, my eyes were filled with tears of happiness and my day was perfect.

Say hello to all the folks at home. Tell them I am happy at Newport, in the routine of "boot" training and that they will be proud of me. I am proud to be in the Navy. Best wishes and a happy holiday. Many thanks again

Sincerely,
John P. Stone

December 20, 1943

Town of Scituate

To The People of Scituate, Mass:

Again you are keeping Christmas for the boys away from home and it means so very much to all of us. Your Christmas gift was certainly appreciated and the beautiful card, with a message of sincerity and encouragement, was "swell". Scituate always keeps Christmas for her boys in her own unique way.

This has been a very busy Christmas Season for me at Fleet Post Office in New York, and one I shall never forget. The mail for servicemen abroad has been tremendous and to look at it early in November, one would think it would never be sent out but we, through every good Grace bestowed upon us completed our work before our official date. Many days or I should say weeks on end, we worked almost 14 and 16 hours a day and the least was 12, to complete the gigantic task set before us, the job of seeing that mail shipped out. No time off for two months but just continual plugging. I can readily say and with all true faith, that there was no complaining. You may doubt this but I spent many hours working with boys and men of all types and they were happy in their work, knowing that there buddies would get some package or some little thing for Christmas.

We realize we are fortunate in working here in New York, of being in this grand old country of ours, but then again it is a job that must be done—a very important one too. You must agree to that. Mail plays a front line job for our servicemen and it is my every thought, to give my utmost devotion.

Now to the citizens of Scituate I say thanks again for keeping the faith. When we know the ones we have always known at home, are rooting for us, when we think of the old familiar landmarks of Scituate, it gives everyone courage to keep on going—that familiar glow of happiness. We walk proudly with heads high, where ever we are. Scituate is certainly a "GEM", not of just the South Shore, but of the whole world. To the MOTHERS of Scituate, the ones who they say are really fighting the war, I repeat this little prayer, which I recently read in a small paper at the Y.M.C.A.

"God, Father of Freedom, look after that boy of mine, wherever he might be. Walk in upon him. Talk with him during the silent watches of the night, and spur him to bravery when he faces the cruel foe. Transfer my prayer to his heart.

Keep my boy inspired by the never dying faith in his God. Throughout all the long days of hopeful victory, wherever his duties take him, keep his spirit high and his purpose unwavering. Make him a loyal friend. Nourish him with the love that I gave him at birth, and satisfy the hunger of his soul with knowledge of my daily prayer.

He is my choicest treasure. Take care of him, God. Keep him in health and sustain him under every possible circumstance. I once warned him under my heart. You knew him anew in his shelter under the stars. Touch him with my smile of cheer and comfort, and my full confidence in his every brave pursuit.

Fail him not—and may he not fail YOU, his country, not the mother who bore him."

After a beautiful prayer there isn't much else one can say, so I will close with every Good Wish for everyone in Scituate and a Grand Christmas. Keep faith with us and we will for you. Many thanks again for everything.

Sincerely yours,

Jack Stone, Y (2) /c
Jack Stone
U.S.N.R.

5 West 63rd. Street
Y.M.C.A.
New York, N.Y.

JOHN S. STONE

John S. Stone, nicknamed "Jackie," son of Chester and Jane (Taylor) Stone, was born on November 30, 1917. He was graduated from Scituate High School in 1935. After graduation he went to work as a clerk at the Scituate Post Office.

Jackie enlisted in the United States Navy in November, 1942. He received his basic training at Newport, RI. It was from here that he wrote his thank you letter at Christmas in 1942, stating, "No one could have designed a more appropriate card than our Doris Ward. The star and verse brought back memories of the happy holidays at home."

Because of his work experience, he was assigned as a Mail Clerk and stationed first at the Fleet Post Office in New York, processing mail to service people in the European Theater of the war. Here he toiled fourteen to sixteen hours a day during the Holidays to assure delivery of mail and packages from home. According to his 1943 thank-you letter, "I can readily say and with all true faith, that there was no complaining. [We] were happy in [our] work, knowing that [our] buddies would get some package or some little thing for Christmas."

From New York, Jackie was sent to Honolulu, Hawaii, and spent the rest of the war processing mail going to the Pacific Theater. He was awarded the World War II Victory, American Theatre, Asiatic-Pacific Theatre, and Good Conduct Medals.

After his Navy service ended, Jackie returned to Scituate and his job at the Post Office. He retired in 1972 after thirty-two years of service.

John S. "Jackie" Stone passed away on January 2, 2003.

Dec. 6, 1944
Fort Belvoir Va.

Dear Mr. Shea;
       I wish to take this opportunity
to let you know that I received
the Christmas gift from the
town of Scituate, and I wish to
express my deep appreciation
for the wonderful gift.

                    Sincerely
                    Pvt. William B. Stone

WILLIAM BISHOP STONE

 William (Bill) "Stoney" Stone was born on July 5, 1918, to Walter and Mary (Bishop) Stone and was graduated from Scituate High School in 1936.

He married Dorothy Whittaker on November 11, 1940, at St. Mary of the Nativity Church in Scituate. They had three children: William, born in 1942; Thomas, born in 1944; and Patricia, born in 1954.

Bill was drafted into the Army in 1944, where he served in the Army Corps of Engineers building Bailey bridges in Germany and Czechoslovakia. A common military tactic utilized by both the Allied and Axis armies was to blow up a bridge after crossing a river to prevent their enemies from following them. It was an effective deterrent that prevented men and supplies from being delivered to key battle areas. Comprised of prefabricated components, Bailey bridges were used to temporarily span rivers until permanent bridges could be built. Thus, soldiers, supplies, food and traffic could be deployed to both the soldiers and the civilians.

Bill was in Czechoslovakia when the United States and Russian armies joined forces to stop the advancement of the German Army. A friend of Bill's, another soldier, spoke Russian and helped interpret for the Allies.

In 1946, Bill received an honorable discharge as a Sergeant, and he returned to Scituate to take up his life again. He worked as a carpenter for Gene Blanchard before going into the contracting business himself.

Bill's extensive knowledge of construction and building codes eventually led to his appointment as Building Commissioner and Zoning Enforcement Officer for the Town of Scituate. He served the town and its residents in that role from 1968 until his retirement in 1982.

Never a man to stay idle, Bill began making wooden toys after his retirement. In his workshop, Bill made wooden cars, trucks and trains, which became popular items with local children.

Bill passed away in February, 1991 at the age of 72.

George Story

GEORGE EDWARD STORY

George Story, the son of George W. Story, Jr., and the former Josephine Petrick, was born in Fairfax, Iowa, on July 11, 1916. He grew up in Cedar Rapids, Iowa, and joined the United States Navy in 1934. He served as a Gunner's Mate aboard the USS Saratoga; originally a battle cruiser, the ship was converted to the first fast carrier in the US Navy. He was discharged on November 12, 1938. While in California after his discharge, George met Ruth Dwyer from Scituate through mutual friends. They married on October 11, 1939, and moved to Scituate.

On October 15, 1943, George again enlisted in the United States Navy. He was a Gunner's Mate 3rd Class aboard the USS Wisconsin, a battleship assigned to Admiral Halsey's Third Fleet in the Pacific Theater. George was awarded the Good Conduct Medal, American Campaign Medal, Asiatic-Pacific Campaign Medal, WWII Victory Medal, Navy Occupation Service Medal, Philippine Liberation Medal, Philippine Republic Presidential Unit Citation, and three Bronze Stars.

After his second Navy discharge, George and Ruth lived in Scituate and had two children, Carol and George. There are now six grandchildren and nine great grandchildren. George worked for Tom Dwyer processing Irish Moss on the Proving Grounds property. He also worked at the First National Store in Scituate Harbor and the City Bank and Trust in Boston. He retired in the 1980's and enjoyed golfing.

George Story passed away on March 22, 1993, at the age of seventy-six.

A.P.O. #873
June 5, 1943.

Dear Citizens of Scituate:

To each & every one of you people back home I wish to express my sincere thanks for the lovely card & gift of money. The good will behind it sure made me feel good & I might add that Scituate would look pretty good to me just now although the English people have been toke to us over here. I sincerely hope that the day will soon arrive when I will be with all my friends in good old Scituate.

Sincerely Yours,
Sgt. Erving L. Studley Jr.

Return only to A.G.O.
Please

Clerk in Charge, APO 653
Hq, 12th Port T.C.
15 December, 1943

Dear Citezens of Scituate:

About a year ago I received a money order for five dollars from the people of Scituate which, at the time, afforded me a great deal of pleasure. Having again received this year a similar token of the kindness and generosity of you people, I am again placed greatly in your debt. It's grand to think that after being away from home, or for that matter overseas, for more than a year and a half, that you haven't forgotten me or the rest of the gang.

I really can't thank all of you enough, but I do want to say that I'm very, very grateful to all of you, and that I hope sincerely that all of you have a very merry Christmas and that the New Year will see all of us together again in good old Scituate.

Sincerly,

Erving L. Studley Jr.
Erving I. Studley, Jr.

EIS/jk

ERVING LINCOLN STUDLEY, JR.

Erving Studley, Jr., son of Erving L., a firefighter, and Katherine Gillis Studley, was born in Scituate on July 25, 1917. He was graduated from Scituate High School in 1935, where he sang in the Glee Club and played football and basketball. He spent time racing Model "A" and "T" Fords up and down the steep hills between Country Way and the railroad bed with his friends, including Joe Clapp. The family lived in the "James House" on the Driftway in what is now the Scituate Mossing Museum.

After high School, "Red" worked as a truck driver until he enlisted in the United States Army on September 18, 1940, along with his friends George Flaherty, Joe Barry, Bill Curran, and Ray Gillis.

Red was assigned to the 240th Field Artillery Battalion as a Postal Clerk and Combat Infantryman. Serving in the European Theater, he fought in the Rhineland and received the Good Conduct Medal, American Defense Service Medal, and the European-African-Middle Eastern Theater Campaign Ribbon. He attained the rank of Sergeant.

After the war, Red returned to Scituate, he was joined in a short time by his English bride, Shirley Fields. They had a son, Timothy. Red worked as a truck driver, laborer, and carpenter before joining the Scituate Fire Department in 1949.

Red passed away on January 27, 1984, and is buried in the Massachusetts National Cemetery in Bourne.

5 Scituate men enlisted on the same day.

**Front Row: George Flaherty, Joe Barry Second Row: Red Studley, Bill Curran
Back Row: Ray Gillis.**

Robert M. Sylvester

December 7, 1944
Ormac Bay - Philippine Islands
U.S.S - L.S.M. - 318
Struck & sunk
by KAMI KAZE PLANE

ROBERT M. SYLVESTER

Robert "Sully" Sylvester was born on December 24, 1925, to F. Lester and Esther (Merritt) Sylvester. He was graduated from Scituate High School in 1942 and was a lifelong resident of Scituate.

Sully enlisted in the Navy in November, 1943, and he spent 14 weeks in electrical school in Newport, Rhode Island, and in amphibious training at Little Creek, Virginia. He was then sent to Chicago, Illinois, to board the USS LSM-318 (Landing Ship Medium), an amphibious ship with standard armament that included one 40 mm cannon twin mount and four 20 mm cannons. The crew consisted of four officers and 54 enlisted men.

On December 7, 1944, three years to the day after Pearl Harbor, Sully was aboard the LSM-318 during the invasion of Ormoc Bay in the Philippines, when his ship was sunk by a Japanese kamikaze (suicide) plane. On that same day on the eastern shore of Ormoc Bay, the destroyer *USS Mahan*, and the high-speed transport *USS Ward* were both damaged by suicide planes and subsequently sunk by United States forces after being abandoned by their crews. Other U.S. vessels damaged that day were the destroyer *USS Lamson* , the high speed transport *USS Liddle,* and the tank landing ships *USS LST* 737, *USS LSM*-18, and the *USS LSM*-19. As the ship blazed, Sully escaped over the starboard side of his ship, in his words, "without touching a single d*** rung." After the battle, Sully returned to Scituate for 30 days survivor's leave; then he was stationed in California, Washington, and Oregon until he was reassigned to the AKA-70 (Tate), an Attack Cargo Ship.

After receiving an honorable discharge in June 1946, Sully returned to Scituate, where he went to work building houses with his father. In 1949, he married Lillian S. (Baker), and in the years to follow they had two sons, Robert, Jr., and James B. Sylvester.

In 1952, Sully joined the Scituate Fire Department. He was promoted to the rank of Captain in 1965 and held that rank until his retirement in 1987. He was a familiar figure as he drove around Scituate in the fire alarm truck repairing and maintaining the fire alarm boxes that could be found in every neighborhood until they ceased being used in the 1990's.

Sully's hobbies included ham radio operation, and helping local fisherman with the repairs of their navigational and electronic equipment. He was a founding member of the Southeastern Signalmen's Association; the National LSM Association, Northeast Chapter and the National Chapter; and a member of the Scituate Veterans of Foreign War.

Sully passed away on December 28, 1999, at the age of 74.

Wednesday, P.M.
Jan-24-1945
Island X.

My Dear Mr Shea:
    Received your gift from the people of
the town of Scituate. And want to take
this time to thank them thru you for
it. It was a fine present.
    And wish I could send a little of our
heat here back to you folks to repay
you for it. From my letters from home
I know you would like a little of it.
    Think of you folks back there often,
and wish many times a day that I
were there. So thanking the people of
the town and you again. I remain.

                    Sincerly Yours
                    William E. Tobin SF 3/c
                    76th N.C. Batt A-3

U. S. NAVAL CONSTRUCTION TRAINING CENTER
CAMP PEARY
WILLIAMSBURG, VIRGINIA   Dec 16, 1943

To the Board of Selectmen
Mr Shea, Chairman.
Dear Sirs.
    I want to thank you. For the nice present. It
sure will come in handy. At this time. Hope that
you. And the people of the town. Have a nice Xmas
and New Years. Best of luck to you all. I remain.
                    Sincerly yours.
                    W. E. Tobin

WILLIAM E. TOBIN

NAVAL RESERVE, 'SEA BEE' CLASS 6, 1957-58
SPECIAL TRAINING CO. WEAPONS BN.   M.C.R.D., PARRIS ISLAND, S.CAR.
ANNUAL FIELD TRAINING, 2 MAR - 16 MAR. 1958
INSTRUCTORS
SGT. J.H.GRABOWSKI   SGT. J.A. JONES

William Tobin, 2nd row, first on right.

William Tobin was born in Wellfleet, MA, on March 7, 1907. He lived most of his adult life in Scituate and was a Scituate High School graduate. Bill married Barbara Brown in 1930. They had one daughter, Jean.

During World War II, Bill enlisted in the Navy and became a SeaBee, the Naval Construction Units whose mottos include "We Build, We Fight" and "Can Do." Eighty per cent of the Naval Construction Force was concentrated in the Pacific Theater, where they built one hundred and eleven major airstrips, four hundred and forty-one piers, two thousand, five hundred and fifty-eight ammunition magazines, seven hundred blocks of warehouses, hospitals for seventy thousand patients, and housing for one million, five hundred thousand men.

Bill spent some of his service on Guam, an island in the Mariannas Chain in the South Pacific. Early in the war, Guam was fortified with a mere seven hundred US Marines. The Japanese easily overran it in December 1941. On July 24, 1944 US Marines conducted amphibious landings, and by August first were once more in possession of the island. The SeaBees reconstructed the airfields that had been damaged, and US B 29's went on to use the islands as a base for bombing the Japanese Homeland.

Bill remained in the SeaBee Reserves after his discharge from active duty. He returned to his job with the Boston Police department and married Evelyn Logan. They had one son. Bill was well known as owner and operater of the Smith Fish Market on Front Street in Scituate Harbor and in its second location in North Scituate. He retired in 1962.

William Tobin passed away in November 1985.

U.S.S. Trenton
December 6, 1942

Scituate Service Committee
Town Hall
Scituate, Massachusetts

Members of the Service Committee:

I wish to inform you that I have received your very generous gift and greetings for the Season.

I thank you, and want you to know that I appreciate your thoughtfulness.

Hoping that you all have a very pleasant Holiday and a prosperous and happy New Year, I remain,

Sincerely yours,

Harold C. P. Toomey

H.C.P. Toomey M.M. 1/c

HAROLD C.P. TOOMEY

Harold Toomey was born on Beacon Street in Boston, Massachusetts, in 1916. His family moved to Scituate, and Harold was graduated from Scituate High School in 1935. He joined the Navy after high school and was required to remain in the service at the outbreak of World War II. He eventually served a total of twenty-seven and a half years, eight and a half of which he was aboard the light cruiser USS Trenton. Light Cruisers were approximately eight thousand tons and five hundred and fifty feet long. They carried a crew of four hundred and fifty-eight and were armed with twelve six-inch guns, four three-inch guns and ten twenty-one inch torpedo tubes. They were named for United States cities and fulfilled a need for a speedy type of cruiser capable of better heavy weather seagoing performance than a destroyer. They were used as scouts and as leaders for screening forces. The USS Trenton was launched in 1923.

Machinist Mate First Class Harold Toomey wrote to thank the Town of Scituate for his Christmas gift from aboard the USS Trenton on December 6, 1942.

Harold married Roberta Harper on August 1, 1944. They would eventually have four daughters, eleven grandchildren, and ten great grandchildren.

Harold saw action during World War II in the invasion of Okinawa beginning on April 1, 1945. It was to be the last amphibious landing of the war. However, at the time servicemen expected to then prepare for the coming invasion of the Japanese Home Islands.

After his discharge from the Navy, Harold farmed in Milford, New Hampshire, for ten years. He then reenlisted in the Navy and served as a recruiter working in Worcester, MA, for an additional ten years. He was retired off the USS Constitution in 1972 as a Chief Petty Officer.

Harold Toomey passed away on August 31, 1995.

U. S. Naval Training Station
Sampson, New York

Saturday
Jan 1, 1944

Dear Mr. Shea:

I received a money order from the Town of Scituate for $5.00 today. I want to thank you very much as this will come in very handy. When a man is in the service and away from home it it certainly comforting to know that someone is thinking of him at home. I have only been in the service 2 weeks but I certainly miss the good old Town of Scituate which has been my home since birth. Again I want to thank you for that wonderful gift.

Sincerely yours
Alden S. Torrey

7 December 1944
Charleston, S.C.

Dear Mr. Shea:

I received the Christmas present from the Town of Scituate and wish to thank them through you for the thoughtful rememberance. The present will come in very handy and I sure will make good use of it.

We are all hoping and praying that by next Christmas we will all be back in good old Scituate the Town we love where we can live in peace and security.

Again I wish to thank you for the fine gift.

Yours sincerely
Alden S. Torrey

ALDEN SPEAR TORREY

Alden Torrey, a ninth generation Mayflower Descendant, was born in Scituate in October 1913. His father, Archie Torrey was a Scituate firefighter who was the Fire Chief in 1935.

A graduate of Scituate High School, Northeastern University and The American Institute of Banking at Williams College, Alden was employed by The Rockland Trust Company for 42 years.

In 1943, Alden joined the US Navy where, because of his banking experience, he was assigned to be the ship's storekeeper (SK/3c) aboard the USS Todd, an attack cargo ship that carried troops and supplies to the Philippines, Okinawa, New Guinea and Yokohama, Japan. Alden is quoted by his son, Alden Junior, as often stating that because of his role as storekeeper, "the only person who ate better aboard ship was the captain". Alden and his ship were present in Tokyo Bay when the Japanese surrender was signed on September 2, 1945.

In 1944 when Alden received his gift from the Town of Scituate, he wrote back to thank everyone for their remembrance and prayed that"we will all be back in good old Scituate, the town we love, where we can live in peace and security".

Alden married the former Alice Southard and had two sons: James B. and Alden S.

After the war, Alden returned to The Rockland Trust Co.where he worked until his retirement in 1977. He served as Treasurer for the Scituate and Cohasset Branches of the Salvation Army and The March of Dimes for 40 years, he was Treasurer of the Scituate Masonic Lodge, President of Groveland Cemetery Association, member of the Scituate and Cohasset Rotary Clubs and the Scituate American Legion. The Legion, which was founded after WWI, is the world's largest Veteran's organization. It was instrumental in the creation of the Veteran's Administration and is recognized as the originator of the GI Bill of Rights. After WWII, it assisted families in accomplishing the return of the remains of their loved ones who had perished and had initially been interred overseas.

Alden Spear Torrey died November 22, 1990 and is buried in Groveland Cemetery, Scituate, MA.

FORT GEORGE G. MEADE
MARYLAND

Mr. Dennis Shea   Jan. 20, 1943
Chairman Board of Selectmen
Scituate Mass.

Dear Mr. Shea,

I would like to thank the citizens of the town of Scituate through you for the very beautiful card and the money order which I received for Christmas.

It certainly was appreciated and made me feel very happy that the people of Scituate were thinking of us in the service.

No matter where I go I will always be proud to say that I am a resident of the town of Scituate.

Sincerely yours
P. F. C. Benjamin V. Turner

BENJAMIN T. TURNER

Benjamin Turner was born in Baltimore, Maryland, on May 24, 1913. His parents died when he was a child, and he went to live with his grandmother and sister on Otis Place in Scituate Harbor. Benjamin was descended from Humphrey Turner, one of the original "Men of Kent" who settled the Town of Scituate in 1628.

Benjamin was drafted into the Army in February of 1941. He and his sweetheart, Bernadette Lavoine, married in June of that year.

Benjamin received his basic training at Camp Edwards on Cape Cod and went on to train new recruits at Camp Campbell, GA, Camp A.P. Hill, VA, Fort Jackson, KY, and Camp Meade, MD. He was sent to France in August of 1944 with the 101st Infantry Division (known as the Yankee Division from its service in the Civil War). In December of 1944 he fought in the Battle of Bastogne in Belgium where German Panzer (tank) Divisions surrounded American troops. In a newspaper interview he gave when he was eighty-five years old Benjamin recalled, "It was the worst battle I was ever in. The snow was five feet deep and at night you would be lying down in it trying to get warm and the Germans would throw mortar and artillery at us." Sgt. Turner fell into a foxhole one night, injuring his leg and he was sent to a hospital outside of Paris to recover.

Benjamin Turner was awarded The American Theater, Good Conduct and European Theater Medals, as well as The World War II Victory Ribbon. He was also eligible for the Bronze Star, which wasn't given to him until Veterans' Agent Edward P. Horn

discovered that he had earned it in 1988. The medal was presented at a special Memorial Day ceremony held on Lawson Common.

After the war, Benjamin worked for the Welch Company in Scituate Harbor, which at that time was primarily a building supply business.

Benjamin Thomas Turner passed away on May 24, 1999, exactly eighty-six years from the day he was born.

Henry L. Vinal

Frank Vinal

HENRY AND FRANK VINAL

Henry and Frank Vinal were the sons of Edward and Elsa Adolfson Vinal. Both brothers served in the US Armed Forces during World War II.

Frank Vinal was born on May 25, 1914 in Scituate. Educated in Scituate schools, he married the former Mary Anne Mahoney in 1940. Mary Anne worked at the Hingham Shipyard during the war. Shortly before he shipped out to Germany, Mary Anne was able to join her husband in California after an arduous train trip across country. Frank served as a Tank Commander with the Third Armored Division in Normandy, Northern France, the Ardennes, and the Rhineland. It was during the Battle of the Bulge between December 16, 1944 and January 28, 1945 that Frank was taken prisoner and held at Stalag 3B in Furstenberg, Germany. Mary Anne received many letters from ham radio operators telling her that Captain "Binal" from Scituate had been captured. According to Angelo Spinelli's book "Life Behind Barbed Wire", the camp held 3,500 Americans, 12,000 Russians, 8,000 Frenchmen and 1,000 Serbians. The prisoners slept on wooden benches and depended on a system of bribery and trading to obtain enough food to survive. With approach of the Russian Army in January of 1945, the entire camp was forced to march day and night for a week to reach Stalag 3A. They remained there until the camp was liberated on April 22, 1945. Frank was discharged on September 8, 1946. He received the Purple Heart. Frank and Mary Anne had a son, Stephen, and a daughter, Marie. Frank Vinal passed away on July 16, 1962.

Henry Vinal was born on August 27, 1921. He was a career soldier. He served from December 19, 1939 until July 24, 1945 in Tunisia and Central Europe. According to his niece, Henry was also a Prisoner of War in Germany during World War II. He was awarded a Bronze Star. Henry went on to serve his country in Korea. He married the former Minnie Wilson and had one son and three daughters. Henry Vinal passed away at the age of 49 in 1970 at Fort Hood Hospital in Texas, where he had been stationed.

From
Lt. W.C. Vines USNR
Navy 93
% Fleet P.O. N.YC
12/21/43

Dear Reggie :—

Will you kindly extend my sincere appreciation to the Scituate Service Men's Assn for sending me that $5.00 M.O. for Christmas. I have told everybody over here on our Station about it and all agree that it is one of the finest gestures they have ever heard of. You can't beat the good old home town of Scituate no matter where you travel and believe me I'm prepared to make such a statement and will back it up to the limit.

Ma & Dad have told me how nice you have been to them and don't forget that I really appreciate that also.

We are as happy as can be for being away from home and loved ones this Christmas but before the next one rolls around, we are quite sure the hobgoblins Hitler & Hirohito will be safely "socked" away, and we can then go about our normal American way of life.

Again many thanks, and I'm proud to say "I come from Scituate".

Sincerely,
Wes Vines

WESLEY VINES

 Wesley Vines was born in South Portland, Maine, in 1906 and moved to Scituate, Massachusetts, in 1917. He was a graduate of Northeastern University in Boston, MA. Wesley's father, Daniel Vines, was plant manager for Boston Sand & Gravel, a large concrete supplier.

In 1929 he married Dorothy Loebig. They had two children, Daniel and Patricia.

Wes had been in the Coast Guard as a young man, and because of his experience, he enlisted in the Navy in 1942 at the age of thirty-six and was commissioned a Lieutenant Junior Grade. His service took him to the Charleston Navy Yard in Charleston, South Carolina, where he oversaw the construction of numerous LST (Landing Ship Tank) vessels from April of 1942 until February of 1943. He later had the opportunity to bear witness to their well-built construction when he was Commander of a Small Boat Flotilla during the assault-boat landings on Sicily and Anzio in Italy.

Wes was awarded the Legion of Merit for his "exceptionally meritorious conduct in the performance of outstanding service as Commander of Small Boat Flotillas during the amphibious assault on the Island of Sicily." He also received the Silver Star for "conspicuous gallantry and intrepidity in action as dispatching officer for the assault boat waves in the Gulf of Salerno during landing operations in the amphibious assault 8-9 September, 1943. Lieutenant Vines took his post in an exposed position on the top deck of the USS PC 559 and skillfully directed the assembling and launching of successive waves of assault craft. For a period of eight hours, despite continuous fire from enemy shore batteries, he calmly and efficiently, with complete disregard for his personal safety, gave directions to the craft under his charge."

In 1943, between the Sicilian and Anzio landings, Wes wrote to thank the Town of Scituate for his Christmas gift. He stated "I'm proud to say I come from Scituate."

In 1944, Wes suffered a heart attack and was sent to the Charleston Naval Hospital to recuperate for six weeks. He was then sent to the Hingham Shipyard until the end of the war. When he was discharged from the service, he returned to the Bucyrus Erie Company, manufacturer of mining machinery, where his pre-war position had been held for him while he served his country. The family later moved to Ocala, Florida, where Wes raised racehorses after his retirement. He and Dorothy had five grandchildren and eleven great grandchildren.

Wesley Vines passed away in 1992.

December 19, 1944
Somewhere in
Germany.

Dear Sir,

I was very Pleased to received a Christmas card from you all, and wished i could do the same, but i am sorry i am not able to do so. The day will come and we will be able to repay, but till then, i hope you all have, a, Merry Christmas and a Happy New Year. from Pvt. Wagner.

George Richard Wagner

GEORGE RICHARD WAGNER

George Richard Wagner, son of George R. and Emma (Ellis) Wagner, was born August 30, 1925, in Cohasset, Massachusetts. The family moved to Scituate in 1938. George left school in the eighth grade and began a welding apprenticeship in Quincy, Massachusetts.

This pursuit was interrupted by the draft on November 8, 1943.

"Rich" served in the United States Army in the 746th Tank Battalion, seeing action in Northern France, The Rhineland, Ardennes, and Central Europe. He earned the Good Conduct Medal, Victory Medal, and the European African Middle Eastern Theater Campaign Ribbon. He was discharged in February of 1946.

Proud of his service to his country, Rich became a member of the Veterans of Foreign Wars Satuit Post and later of the Old Colony Post in Rockland, Massachusetts.

George Richard Wagner married his longtime sweetheart, Florence (Jackman) in 1949 at St. Mary of the Nativity Church in Scituate Harbor. They built a house on First Parish Road and started the family that would grow to include three children and four grandchildren. In 1963 the family moved to Rockland, and he continued his work as an equipment operator.

George Richard Wagner passed away on September 15, 1983.

JOHN D. WEBB

To you who answered the call of your country and served in its Merchant Marine to bring about the total defeat of the enemy, I extend the heartfelt thanks of the Nation. You undertook a most severe task—one which called for courage and fortitude. Because you demonstrated the resourcefulness and calm judgment necessary to carry out that task, we now look to you for leadership and example in further serving our country in peace.

Harry Truman

THE WHITE HOUSE
September 27, 1946

JOHN DUNBAR WEBB

John Dunbar Webb, the son of Henry and Mary Winifred LaRue Webb, was born in Scituate, Massachusetts, in July of 1904. He attended Scituate schools and was graduated from Scituate High School. John came from a long line of seafarers, including Captain Seth Webb and Captain Jesse Dunbar, who were both mariners and merchants based in Scituate and involved in coastal trading in the nineteenth century. They each had substantial mansions at opposite ends of Front Street. Captain Webb's is now the rectory of St. Mary of the Nativity Church. Captain Dunbar's was demolished in the 1930's and is now the parking lot for T. K. O'Malley's Restaurant. The restaurant is located on the site of Dunbar's private wharf. John continued the family tradition by joining the United States Merchant Marine in 1941. Specializing in ship communications, he rose from Mate to Captain by the end of World War II.

John served aboard the SS Winchester Victory, SS Levi Woodbury, and the SS Thorstein Veblen, all unarmed ships operating in war zones. The Thorstein Veblen was involved in the invasion of southern France from August 15, 1944, through September 25, 1944, landing troops and munitions while under fire and earning a Battle Star for the operation.

Married to the former Gladys Powers in 1927, John had six children and sixteen grandchildren. After the war, he worked on a barge for the Perini Corporation.

At the time of his death, in May of 1962 John was working as a tugboat captain for Boston Sand and Gravel. He was stricken ill and died in Norwich, Connecticut.

U. S. ARMY AIR FORCES

January 12, 1943

Scituate Service Committee:
　　Dear Committee,

　　　　I wish to thank the Scituate Service Committee for their kind rememberance at Christmas time.

　　　　It makes one feel that the Home Town and Old Friends are really much nearer, and in these trying times the more one hears from his home the more one realizes how important and necessary this war really is in order to maintain the freedom of living that we all hold dear.
　　　　　　Sincerely Yours.
　　　　　Richard W. Wunderoth

RICHARD W. WENDEROTH

Richard Wenderoth was born in Newport, Kentucky. When his father took the position of Treasurer for *The Boston Herald*, the family moved to Brookline, Massachusetts. They summered in Scituate and in 1937 became year round residents.

Richard developed a love of sailing and as a young member of the Scituate Yacht Club became an avid sailor. He attended the University of Vermont and traveled around the world as part of the University Cruise Program. After his college graduation, Richard published his own local magazine, *The South Shore Light*, copies of which are held by the Scituate Historical Society.

During World War II, Richard enlisted in the Army Air Corps. He was stationed in Charleston, South Carolina, Langely Field, Virginia, and the Aleutian Islands, off the coast of Alaska. The Aleutians were significant during World War II in that they are located within striking distance of the Japanese Home Islands. In 1942 the Japanese attacked the islands on which a small American detachment maintained a weather station, an Army Base, and a naval facility. The maneuver was thought to be a diversionary tactic to take focus away from the main attack on Midway in the Central Pacific. By the summer of 1943, the entire Aleutian Island chain was again in American control.

During the war Richard married the former Edith Duthie. When he returned from the service, Richard and Edith returned to Boston, and Richard entered the field of sales and advertising and eventually worked in the newspaper industry.

Once they had children, Richard and Edith decided to return to Scituate, and they purchased his parents' home. Richard was active in Scituate's youth programs, as well as the Cub Scouts and Boy Scouts for many years. He was also an active member of the Old Colony Power Squadron.

Richard Wenderoth died in August of 1975.

Dec. 9, 1944
Saturday

Gentlemen

Just a few lines
to thank you for the
christmas card, and
the present.
I think it is a fine
thing for the town to
take the trouble to
send a gift to the
boys in the service. I
am sure that every-
one of us appreciate it.
I only hope that
next christmas the
the war will be over
and all the boys will
be home again. So until
then.

Sincerly yours
Frank Westerhoff

FRANK WESTERHOFF, JR.

Frank Westerhoff, son of Frank and Florence Perkins Westerhoff was born in Scituate on October 31, 1925. He lived in the harbor section of the town, and his most vivid childhood memory is of the "pier sitters," a group that would gather at the Town Pier and tell stories of 19th century Scituate as they saw and lived them. Today, he reflects that those stories were an invaluable part of his education and a means of making history come alive.

In 1943 Frank enlisted in the United States Navy. After Basic Training at Sampson, New York, he was assigned to an LSM (Landing Ship Medium). He took part in the Pacific Campaign and saw action in the Philippines, Saipan, and Guam. Frank participated in the invasion of Okinawa and was preparing for the invasion of Japan when the war ended. He also served in China after hostilities were over.

After his discharge, Frank returned to Scituate. He married the former Loretta Ballou and eventually had two boys and two girls. The family moved to Cape Cod, and he started the Westerhoff Construction Company. After twenty years, Frank retired and moved to Freedom, New Hampshire, to spend his days fly fishing and skiing. He and Loretta now have five grandchildren; as of 2004 Frank no longer skis, but he is now the Chairman of the Board of Freedom Press Association, a book publisher.

Frank occasionally returns to Scituate but feels that the Town has moved on to the next generation, as, in his words, it should, and hopefully the old "pier sitters" have been replaced by tellers of 20th century stories told by people who saw and lived them.

From

Cpl. H. P. WHITE

2nd Signal Service Bn

Washington, D.C.

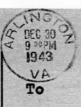

ARLINGTON
DEC 30
9 30 PM
1943
VA.

FREE

To

The Town Hall

SCITUATE

MASSACHUSETTS

UNITED STATES
★ ARMY ★

12-30-43

Dear Sirs:

I greatly appreciated your thinking of me this Christmas by sending me
the money order for five dollars. So far
as I know, I was the only person here to
have received such a gift and I thank
you very kindly.

Sincerely

Hayward P. White

Hayward Peirce White

HAYWARD PEIRCE WHITE

Hayward Peirce White was born in Brookline, Massachusetts, on May 19, 1913. He was graduated from Harvard University in 1936, where he was a starting pitcher for the baseball team. He worked as a stock trader in Boston after his graduation.

Hayward's family had summered in Scituate since the 1920's. The family can trace its roots to Captain Michael Peirse, who fought and died in King Phillip's War.

In 1943 Hayward returned to Harvard and enrolled in an intensive seven-month course in the Japanese language.

Because of a childhood eye injury, Hayward was rejected for combat service in World War II. He served instead in the 2nd Signal Service Battalion. He performed confidential duties as a translator, processing military documents and radio intercepts. His unit was given a commendation from Brigadier General W. Preston Corderman stating, "the accomplishments of the Signal Security Agency have been materially instrumental in bringing Allied Victory. . . . The war time performance of this agency has established exceedingly high standards that will require the most diligent application of those associated with it during peace time."

After the war, Hayward married the former Ann Mitchell from Hingham, MA. He went to work as an analyst for the National Security Agency at Fort Meade, Maryland. The Whites had two sons and, eventually, two grandchildren.

Hayward ended his government service in 1972. He passed away in February of 1981, and his funeral service was held in the First Congregational Church, Scituate, MA.

Robert John Whittaker

ROBERT JOHN WHITTAKER

Robert Whittaker was born in Scituate on August 9, 1923 to Edgar and Katherine Lacey Whittaker. He was graduated from Scituate High School in 1941 and enlisted in the United States Marine Corps in March 1942.

Bob served aboard the battleship USS Massachusetts, nicknamed "Big Mamie." The ship was built and launched from the Fore River Shipyard in Quincy, MA, in 1942. She is now berthed and is open to the public at Battleship Cove in Fall River, MA. During World War II, the USS Massachusetts fired the first salvo from her 16-inch guns to open Operation Torch in North Africa. She also fired the last shots at the Japanese Home Islands at the end of the war. The ship and crew survived thirty-five engagements and earned eleven battle stars. No crewmembers were lost in combat.

Robert served as anti-aircraft machine gun crewman. He participated in operations in Casablanca, North Africa; New Guinea, The Gilbert Islands, Marshall Islands, Western Caroline Islands, Leyte, Luzon, Okinawa, Iwo Jima, in the Pacific Theater and the Occupation of Japan.

Bob married Pauline Sylvester from North Scituate, MA, in April 1947 and they had five daughters. The family moved to Florida in 1950, and Bob passed away in 1984.

Camp Maxey,
TEXAS   22 Dec.

Town of Scituate:
    Service mens Christmas Committee:
c/o Selectman, D.H. Shea.

        Your very nice Christmas
greeting and Gift have been received
and enjoyed by me.
        Please accept my sincere
thanks; and best wishes for the
coming new year.

                    Greatfully
        Pvt. Malcolm E Welder

MALCOLM EVERETT WILDER

Malcolm "Huck" Wilder was born March 7, 1912 to Russell J. and Vera Lazelle White Wilder. He was graduated from Scituate High School in 1930. Until his entry into the United States Army in 1943, Malcolm worked for Wilder Brothers, a tire sales and repair shop in North Scituate. He was married to Ina Bailey Litchfield on June 29, 1939. She passed away in 1977.

After entering the United States Army, he was initially sent to Fort Devens in Ayer, MA for ten months, then, eventually, to Fort Bragg. Located just west of Fayetteville, North Carolina, the fort was home to 159,000 troops during the war years. Utilizing the skills learned in the family business back home; he preformed automotive work for the Army with the 125th Infantry Division.

Malcolm returned to Scituate after his discharge in 1945, again working at Wilder Brothers. He eventually took over and ran the business until his retirement in 1974. In 1996 he married Marjorie Brown Litchfield. They live in the neighboring town of Norwell, Massachusetts.

Raymond Zucker

Ray Zucker on right.

RAYMOND V. ZUCKER

Ray Zucker was born on December 24, 1917 in Springfield, MA to Louis and Hazel Hanifan Zucker. He was graduated from Scituate High School in 1934.

In September 1940, before the United States' involvement in World War II, Ray enlisted in the Army Air Corps. He was trained as a rear tail gunner, flying on B24 Liberators. These were primarily heavy bombers but were also very effective fighter aircraft. They carried a crew of seven: pilot, navigator, radio operator, bombardier and three aft gunners.

Staff Sergeant Raymond Zucker operated a 50 caliber Browning machine gun, performing over fifty missions from Italy to Casablanca.

Ray Zucker was awarded the Good Conduct Medal, American Defense Medal, North African Invasion Ribbon, Tunisia, Sicily, and Italy Combat Ribbons with three Bronze and Silver Stars, Air Force Medal with five Bronze and one Silver Oak Leaf Cluster, and a Purple Heart for shrapnel wound to his left leg.

After his military service, Ray returned to Scituate, where he opened Zucker's Garage and Service Station in North Scituate. He married Rose O'Neil, and they had four children.

In August of 1953, at the age of thirty-six, Ray was tragically killed in an automobile crash. His friend, John Sieminski, took over running his business until Ray's sons were old enough to take over. The station was owned and operated by the Zucker family until 1999 when it was sold and became the recently expanded McBrien's Diagnostic Repair.

Ray's siblings were also in the service during World War II. His older brother, Richard was in Company C of the 501st Parachute Infantry. He served in the European-African-Mideastern Theatre of Operations and was awarded the Good Conduct Medal, Distinguished Unit Badge, American Defense Service Medal with Clasp, European African Middle Eastern Theater Campaign Ribbon and the Purple Heart.

Ray's sister, Ruth served as member of the WAAC.